# John Gould

# MAINE LINGO

## Boiled Owls, Billdads, & Wazzats

Down East Books

Camden, Maine

Published by Down East Books

An imprint of The Rowman & Littlefield Publishing Group, Inc.

4501 Forbes Boulevard, Suite 200, Lanham, Maryland 20706

www.rowman.com

Unit A, Whitacre Mews, 26-34 Stannary Street, London SE11 4AB, United Kingdom

Distributed by NATIONAL BOOK NETWORK

Book design by Guy Fleming

British Library Cataloguing in Publication Information Available

**Library of Congress Cataloging-in-Publication Data**

Gould, John, 1908-

   Maine lingo : boiled owls, billdads & wazzats / John Gould, written in collaboration with Lillian Ross and the editors of Down East magazine.

     pages cm

   I. English language—Dialects—Maine—Glossaries, vocabularies, etc. II. English language—Maine—Glossaries, vocabularies, etc. III. Americanisms—Maine—Dictionaries. IV. Maine—Languages—Dictionaries. V. Title

   PE3101.M3 G6

   427/.9/741

73084185

ISBN: 978-1-60893-566-6 (pbk : alk. paper)

ISBN: 978-1-60893-567-3 (electronic)

*With Love to Karyn Ellen*

"I THINK THIS THING IS
HOTTER'N A SKUNK!"

— *Peter Partout*

# MAINE LINGO

*Boiled Owls, Billdads,*

*& Wazzats*

# AUTHOR'S SUBTLE
# COMMENT

---

ONE DAY *a summer lady came into Ivernia Wallace's little store in Friendship and said something which Ivernia didn't* catch. *The lady had an apple, and she was inquiring if Ivernia had a fountain where she might find* whoater *where she could* wowsh *her apple before eating it. When communication had been established and Ivernia had directed the lady to the sink over behind the sody cabinet, Ivernia said: "You don't want to mind the way* you *talk; I go around all the time sayin'* bo't *when I ought to say* boat!"

---

# OVERTURE

❧ / IT BURNED DOWN AFTERWARDS, BUT AROUND THE TURN of the century the Tontine House at Brunswick was considered Maine's finest inn by those who had every right to know—the traveling salesmen, or *drummers*. The Tontine was operated by Colonel Brewster, whose southern fried title and affectations were spurious, but who could have been the artist's model for the whiskey-label Colonel Sanders who appeared nearly a century later to sell chickens. Colonel Brewster had never been farther south than Cape Elizabeth.

The "warm, southern hospitality" of the Tontine was rounded out by a bar under the lobby, and as Maine was then legally drier than a two-hour August sermon, the existence of this bar was a well-kept secret known to every merchandising artist between Baffin Land and Timbuktu. A shot of good whiskey sold for twenty cents, three for a half-dollar. Colonel Brewster himself tended bar.

When a drummer came to Brunswick and took his usual room at the Tontine, he liked to bring in the local tradesman he was working on and *shout* him to a whiskey. Colonel Brewster would open the little door to the downstairs, and the three would go below. Colonel Brewster would sidle behind the bar, set out three glasses, and fill them to the brim with excellent good whiskey which he caused to be smugg...imported from Portsmouth, New Hampshire, by sloop, via South Harpswell. This done, he would replace the cork in the bottle, pick up the third glass, and, before draining it in one gulp, would say in hearty plantation tones, "Well, Gentlemen, Many Happy Days!"

Then he would add, "That'll be fifty cents."

As Colonel Brewster went through life permitting his hotel guests to pay for his own liquor, he became a legend in his own time. If two salesmen chanced to tipple in a Chicago barroom, and one of them lifted his glass to say in Dixieland tones, "Well, Many Happy Days!" the other one would reply, "Oh, so you've stopped at the Tontine!"

This antique anecdote is meant to be specific about the general purpose of this book. There is something of Maine about everywhere, and it is usually recognized as such. The esoteric passes, grips, and words have created a down east freemasonry that few localized regions of the world can duplicate. It is a fact that two strangers sat side by side on a Fifth Avenue bus in New York City, and when one of them inquired about his destination the other one, instead of answering, asked, "What part of Maine are you from?"

"Derr'um. You?"

"Vigh-enny."

(Probably they celebrated this chance meeting by descending to exchange "Many Happy Days!")

There has been some scholarly presumption that Maine people retain their character, their attitudes, and their speech through the geographical isolation of being perched on the nation's edge; that Mainers have remained aloof, bound down and hemmed in, while everybody else has forged along. In this way older habits persist, and archaic speech remains. The absurdity of this hypothesis is evident if anybody cares to consider the history of Maine. No state in the Union has been more worldly and cosmopolitan. The remarkable thing is that with all the state's exposure to the four corners of the Earth, the people have retained their own lingo as they have —and it is sufficient to fill a volume.

History, as she is taught, does Maine many an injustice. Consider, as a starter, Christopher Columbus, who is the discoverer of America. The standard biography of Columbus has one revealing sentence which is always ignored by schoolmarms and never remembered by schoolchildren. It says that as a boy Columbus made a voyage to the British Isles. It was what we, in Maine, call a *Hannah Cook* voyage. Inasmuch as the ancient Phoenicians sailed to Cornwall for tin, there is nothing wonderful in that, except that the significance of it is missed. Fishing vessels from the British Isles had been coming to the Grand Bank for a long time, even though Columbus was then a small boy and hadn't yet discovered America. Let us suppose that young Columbus fell in, on that occasion, with some Irish fishermen in Belfast who had just returned from the usual rendezvous harbor at Damariscove Island with a *highline* load of salt cod. It could have happened, and probably did.

In the conversation in a waterfront pub, the bright little boy from the Mediterranean expounds his remarkable idea. He says he can sail westerly until he comes under the belly of the earth and arrives at the riches of the East Indies. At this point in all well-conducted history lessons, the teacher always says that people laughed at Columbus, because they all knew the Earth was flat. It is true, but not for that reason, that the Irishmen laughed at his contention. They choked on their beer in hilarity. O'Cassidy, skipper of a *banker*, recovers his voice and says, "Ye can't do it, me bye!"

"Why not?"

"Because they's a whole big continent out there in the way."

"How do you know?"

"Because I been there. We've all been there. We just came back."

Thus was America discovered, not because of the vast treasures of the Far East, but because codfish brought a good penny. But what every Irish fisherman knew was unknown back home, and Columbus conned Queen Isabella as per the history books. Take, again, the Pilgrims. The company of English gentlemen who had a charter to New England from James I had sent Captain George Waymouth in his vessel *Archangel* in 1605 to scout a likely place in Maine for the first English settlement. It was not spices and gold and precious gems that motivated them, but fish. With Waymouth was one James Rosier, a scribe, and Maine's first director of publicity. Rosier described "The Maine" in glowing terms, but he called it the main because offshore fishermen had been calling it the main for two centuries. When Rosier and Waymouth rendered a report, the Popham colonists were sent over in 1607.

Now, an exciting fact our school teachers almost always downplay is that the French king had already given a charter to New France to the Sieur de Monts. New France and New England were essentially the same region, and when the Popham colonists arrived, the French already had successful fisheries and peltries established in Penobscot Bay, in Frenchman's Bay, and at Ste. Croix Island, as well as at Port Royal across in Nova Scotia. In 1613, British warships sacked these French communities, establishing English supremacy in that part of Acadia which is now the State of Maine. It was the intention, or hope, of the Pilgrims to settle in "The Maine." But the landholding company turned them down on the grounds that their dissenting disposition might prove incompatible with the work-a-day purposes otherwise established. This explains why the Pilgrims were told to find some place south of the Piscataqua River. We could have had the Pilgrims in Maine, but we didn't want them.

When the *Mayflower* crossed the ocean, she followed the course of the fishing boats, and thus her first landfall was Monhegan Island. Plymouth (Massachusetts) records tell us that there was a pause off Monhegan while some cods were taken. This conjures a pleasant tableau concerning a fisherman's wife at Port Clyde, who looked off one morning and saw the *Mayflower* hove to for some handlining. She calls to her husband, "Who do you suppose that is?"

He shields his eyes to look, seems puzzled for a moment, and then recollects. "That's got to be the Pilgrims," he says. "They've come at last!"

The parent company had, indeed, alerted its Maine people to the intended arrival of the Pilgrims. The company journals in Plymouth (England) show this. Orders were sent that if any favors might be accorded the Pilgrims, they should be offered "in the name of the Company," and this explains an entry in Governor Winslow's diary. When he came in the Pilgrim shallop in 1622 to cadge needed food from the fat fishermen at Damariscove, he noted how the food was willingly donated, and adds that the Maine fishermen " . . . would not render any bill for the same." They couldn't; they were being charitable on orders from England.

Squanto, who astonished the Pilgrims when they arrived by stepping from the puckerbrush to greet them in English, is variously mistreated by History. He was a sachem of the Pemaquids, and his bilingualism is probably an understatement. He undoubtedly spoke French as well. He had been kidnapped in 1605 by Waymouth, along with four other Pemaquids, and carried to England in the *Archangel*. He thus learned English in London, and there is nothing astonishing about that. Some teachers, regarding the kidnapping of these Indians, miss the point. They were not taken to England to become slaves, or to be exhibited as curiosities. The intent was to permit the gentlemen adventurers to question them, and thus learn about America. Sir Ferdinand Gorges, one of the investors and Maine's patron saint in some ways, says as much. In his memoirs he wrote that the capture of these Indians "must be acknowledged the means under God of putting on foot and giving life to all our plantations." Squanto was entertained while in England by John Popham, Lord Chief Justice, and that's a Blue Book listing. He came back to Maine in 1606, and was accordingly on hand to greet the Popham colonists in 1607, and he had already greeted a number of arrivals before the Pilgrims.

We can assume that every time Squanto heard that a boat had come from England, he mused, "Hmm, wonder if it's anybody I know?" as he strode from his Pemaquid wigwam to go greet them and find out.

As to his speaking French, contemplation teases us. As early as 1532 the Indians of Maine were acquainted with that language. André Thevet, a French schoolmaster, had come to America and written the inevitable book about his voyage, and he told how he had sailed up the Penobscot to a place "where the French formerly had a fort" (somewhere near present Rockland), and how the Indians rushed down to trade in such numbers that it reminded him of flocks of starlings. There was no language problem—Maine Indians spoke French. Suppose, then, that trilingual Squanto had got himself fouled up in the courtship of Miles Standish?

Poet Longfellow says that Miles was a man of war and bumbling in speech so he couldn't whisper sweet nothings in the shell-like ear of beautiful Priscilla, which is why he asked John Alden to woo her in his cause. Bosh. Priscilla Mullein was a French Huguenot, and didn't speak English. John Alden could speak French. The thing came off badly, because Priscilla married the go-between instead. So, suppose that in this romantic exchange, Miles had happened to ask Squanto instead of John, and Squanto had sired a brood whose descendants now belong to the Mayflower Society? It would have put Maine in an enviable position.

There's no reason why Squanto shouldn't have known what a Huguenot was. The Sieur de Monts had been one, and the first Christmas services in the New World had been at Ste. Croix Island with both Catholic and Protestant clerics collaborating, a broad-mindedness that didn't prevail otherwise for a long time to come. That was in 1602.

So, early Mainers were aware of many things. Later, in the days of sail, Mainers went the world around and had their *gams* in Bombay, Liverpool, Rio. They sailed *in company* over the oceans. *Hen frigates* took so many wives and children to sea that Maine passed a milestone education law that paid a mother teacher's wages when she taught her own youngsters away from home.

There was a family Down East whose sons were named after the ports where they were born—Montevideo, Calcutta, Marseilles, Sydney, and San Francisco. That is, Monty, Cal, Marse, Syd, and Fran. Andy Scholfield, late of Brunswick, had the middle name of Islands. His full handle was Andaman Islands Scholfield. Mainers have never led secluded lives.

In the Civil War, Maine contributed a greater proportion of sons than any other Northern state, albeit the war was *some* unpopular here because it ruined our seafaring prosperity. After that war, Maine was further drained as young men moved to the prairie lands and beyond. Almost every Maine family had somebody *out West*. Today's television shows that depict a Montana cowpoke of the 1880s talking with a Montana accent are abusing the facts. The Montana cowpoke of the 1880s was probably off a Mattawamkeag farm, saying *ayeh* and *daow* and hankering for a feed of creamed codfish. And then, soon after that war, Maine was discovered by the *summer complaints*, and the place has never been the same since. They have contributed to the Mainers an awareness that surpasses understanding.

Something else that should be recalled is the migration of Maine men into the timberlands of the North Country and the Pacific Coast. They took their *peaveys*, their *kennebeckers*, their clanking *Lombards*, and their woods lingo to *let daylight into those swamps*. There was some corner of each distant cutting that was forever Maine. With the exception of two words, lumberjack and timberjack, almost all the lumbering terms of the western forests originated in the pine and spruce history of Down East.

All in all, there's no reason for Maine to have an isolated and distinct lingo. Every fact of history suggests converse with other peoples and other places. Philologists tend to look at words one at a time, and their scrutiny usually overlooks the fluidity that is mighty important in the way Mainers put words together. Maine speech is essentially a conversation of poetic images in which similes and metaphors are derived and applied. Classical poets, striving in their towers for simple beauty of expression, hardly do more than any Maine lobsterman does when he *guesses* the weather. Maine language is a picture language, in which the man in his cups reminds of the filled sails on a schooner; facing up pretty apples in a barrel reminds of the proper *deacon* sitting in church; growing old is *getting over in your book;* and a blabbermouth who can't keep a secret leaks like a *basket.*

It was not the Kentuckian affectations of Colonel Brewster that made him memorable and brought him fame in far places. It was because he offered something out of his personality, his remarks, his hospitality, and his Maine-isms that rendered him special. His three drinks for fifty cents gave his drummers something to carry home in their minds; something to tell people about in Hartford, Springfield, Boston, Providence. Moreover, he was a man whose native Maine turn of phrase offered improbable similarities in upturned situations, until his simplest remarks shone like a polished star in the firmament of dull diction as spoken by others. Each nugget was carried away as treasure by his fawning *drummers*, to be repeated until Colonel Brewster was the most quoted man alive.

This continues. Back in Philadelphia, somebody has just said, "When we were in Maine this summer, we had a guide, and he said . . . " Or a lady just back from Squanto's Pemaquid will report, "There was this fisherman, and one day . . . " For the most part, the great Maine secret of saying memorable things is exposed in this volume. Mercenary motives are not entirely the cause of this publication. There is a sly feeling that if more people learn to talk like Mainers, the world's conversations will be notably improved.

# B

**❧ / B, BEGIN WITH**   In early Maine days, amongst deep
water sailors rather than fishermen, there was superstition
about naming a vessel anything which commenced with an
A. Tales were told of the dire mishaps that befell the *Are-
thusa* and the *Alice*. Indeed, one of the last *bankers* out of
Maine was the *Aberrance* of South Freeport, whose owner
defied the tradition in spite of warnings from old salts on
the waterfront. She lost men at sea, grounded out several
times, figured in weird collisions, and finally caught fire.
The *Aberrance* was a *Jonah*, a hard-luck vessel. So, "Begin
with B!" has its meaning in Maine, almost a pleading. (The
A's in this compendium will be found betwixt the B's and
the C's.)

**❧ / BACK AND FILL**   To handle sails so they repeatedly
catch and then spill the wind, a maneuver to tack or work
a vessel to windward in a narrow channel with a favoring
tide. Thus, to *back and fill* is to *fuddy-dud* about without
great accomplishment, to vacillate. A politician who won't
state his position, but talks around it, is *backing and filling*.
The term is used by farmers for turning a cart in a small
area, by repeatedly backing and going ahead in short takes,
but a farmer might also call this hackin' and hammerin',
deriving from short, ineffective strokes with a tool. For conversational backing and filling, the term is hemmin' and
hawin'.

❦ / BACK HALL   In the sporting and vacation camp with the central dining room for guests, the back hall is the eating place for the help—guides, waitresses, *choreboy*, etc. There is a coziness to the *en famille* situation which *sports* and guests never get to know about, and in the evening when a squeeze-box and harmonica are turned loose, or when the guides get to yarnin', there can be fun no paying customer can buy.

❦ / BACK IN   A change of wind from, usually, northeast to north to northwest. Most of Maine's bad weather comes from the northeast, and if a northeast storm clears by *backing in* it will usually bring one fair day, which is a *breeder*, and then it will likely storm again. But if the northeast storm clears by *hauling around* through the south into the northwest, there should be a spell of good weather. (See *veer*.)

❦ / BACKHOUSE RAT   The ultimate in utter stupidity, used only in the Maine simile, "Crazier than a backhouse rat."

❦ / BACKWATER   To reverse oars or engine so the craft backs. Hence, to change direction, and one's mind: "He agreed to trade cows, but then he *backwatered*." As a noun, a *logan* or eddy in fresh water, or water backed up in a pond by a dam. Pulpwood which gets stranded in *backwater* must be *picked* and thrown back in the current. *Atlantic Advocate*, magazine for the Maritime Provinces, recently said, "Maine is the economic *backwater* of the U.S.A."

❦ / BAGGIN' THE BOWLINE   Not unlike *makin' a granny*; tying a knot the wrong way; botching the job. All useful seafaring knots had a double function—to hold fast as desired, but to come undone quickly and easily when required. The reef, or square knot, can be mis-tied into a *granny*, and the bowline can be *bagged*. Neither comes apart smoothly if improperly made. Another explanation of this phrase is that the bowline holding the weather edge of a sail must be rightly set or the sail will bag, making for sloppy sailing. Thus, a man who doesn't know what he's talking about, or tries to do something he can't, is *baggin' his bowlines*. The expression can be a way of calling somebody a liar.

❧ / BAISTER Possibly *baster*. Indicating large size and used somewhat like *rauncher*. Often with the adjective "old": "He hooked an old *baister* of a togue." (See *lunker*.) The word is apt for a storm: "An old *baister* blew up." A high swell which jolts a lobster boat may be described as an old *baister*. The word comes from a big rooster or roast which requires much basting in the oven.

❧ / BAIT The constant importance of bait in the Maine fisheries is reflected in many allusions and expressions. (See *get your bait back*.) To grind your own *bait* is to do your own work. To *fish or cut bait* is a choice, but you must do one or the other, or go ashore. *Bait* to a lobsterman is usually *brim*, and trucks that deliver it are *bait* trucks. *Bait* bags, *bait* tubs, *bait* irons, *bait* barrels, *bait* houses—all such terms explain themselves. Mainers also use the word as elsewhere to cajole, entice, torment, etc. *Bait* is also the Maine term for the fulcrum in leverage, meaning a block of wood or a rock placed under a crowbar or pole in lifting: "Give me a little more *bait* and we'll h'ist this sill into place."

❧ / BAIT IRON The needle-like tool used by lobstermen to insert bait in their traps. It is not unlike a chef's larding needle; a steel rod with a sharpened point and an eye, and a wooden handle. The imagery has come ashore: "He jumped's though somebody *bait-ironed* him!"

❧ / BAKER A reflector oven, used at outdoor fires. Now mostly for camping out, they were once important on river drives, where Cook would have them in a circle around a fire baking pies, cookies, bread. The word is also used for a range that has good baking qualities; some ranges are better *bakers* than others. In Aroostook, a potato that bakes well. The Burbank is a *baker*.

❦ / BALLED UP   In soft and wet snow, a horse's steel shoes will gather snowballs until he can hardly walk, let alone pull his load. Teamsters watch for this and knock them off. To be *all balled up* is to be in no condition to respond: "I got so *balled up* I forgot what I was going to say!" Ruder etymology sometimes brings this out as bollixed up, but the image of the snowballed horse is right.

❦ / BALM O' GILEAD   The North American poplar which yields an oleoresin much admired in former times as a home remedy. Possibly because of Biblical connotation (see Jerimiah 8:22), Mainers liked the *Balm o' Gilead* as a lawn shade tree, and some may still be seen before older farm homes. In the spring, the sticky buds were put in alcohol—some say rum—to make an antiseptic lotion. On a cut finger, the alcohol was antiseptic anyway, and for internal use the rum was all right. Drops on a lump of sugar were good for a cold or cough, and evils from phthisic to catarrh were averted by wearing a pad soaked in *Balm o' Gilead* around the neck. (This didn't stink in schoolrooms so much as the equally efficacious camphor bags!) Medicinally, *Balm o' Gilead* had a pleasing aroma, and its connotations in Maine memories are happy.

❦ / BANGOR RULE   See *log rule*.

❦ / BANKER   A fishing vessel that went to the Grand or Georges Bank, or a crewman aboard. Cappy Dixon once said, "He tol' me he was a *banker*, but he had a necktie on, and I says, 'Just what kind of a *banker* be ye?'"

❦ / BANNOCK   An old Scots word without lefthanded connotation in the British Isles, but in Maine it means a coarse meal cake intended for a dog—before patent dog foods. It is a rough johnnycake made from stock meal. If somebody says, "She fed me *bannock!*" it means the food wasn't that good.

❧ / BARK   On a tree (apart from being a vessel). Mainers use the word in a variety of contexts. To be "close as the *bark* to a tree" is to be stingy, *near*. A *bark* canoe is a birchbark canoe. Peeled pulpwood is said to be *barked*. Pulpwood which has lost some or all of its *bark* during a drive is said to be river-*barked* or river-peeled. A mill or machine which takes *bark* off logs, whether for pulp or lumber, is a *barker*, and so is the man who *barks* or operates a machine. Hemlock *bark* was a good penny in the old days for tanning hides, and towns with tanneries appointed *bark* inspectors (see *fence viewer*). A child who scuffs a knee in a fall is said to *bark* himself. Henry Plaisted, who was a *barker* at the Lyndale Sawmill, had the conversational flux, and one time under "Occupation" on a government form he wrote in: "Master excoriationist of arboreal raw products in the supply division of the construction industry."

❧ / BARM   By no means originally Maine-ish, the yeasty fermentation of the brewers was the basis of early yeast bread and rolls, and welcome in a diet that ran regularly to sal'ratus biscuits. The barm was carefully kept alive and was handed mother to daughter at weddings. Mainers never used the word *sourdough* too much, although they knew what it was, but their *barm-bread* was essentially the sourdough of the western prospectors. Although some think *barmy* (not just right in the head) derives from this *barm*, more likely the term is balmy, to become soft. Mainers, however, pronounce *barm* and balm alike.

❧ / BARSTARD   Spoken usually in Maine as *bahstid*, the word is seldom applied to illegitimates. Instead, it is often no more than a synonym for fellow or chap: "He's an odd *bahstid*; he eats eels!" The word can even be friendly and complimentary: "Why, you old *bahstid*, you—never thought to see YOU in church!" If the word intends deprecatory shading, it is usually preceded by "dirty": "He's a dirty *bahstid*" means he'll bear watching in a cow trade. Ritch-bahstid (see *ritchbitch*) carries full disrespect for some summer people. This word should not be attempted in the Maine way by strangers without special study and considerable practice in private.

❦ / BARN DOOR  A barn door will take a load of hay, so anything *as big as a barn door* will be sizeable. A juror in York County who believed in the innocence of a man the county attorney wanted to indict once shouted, "Give me a NO ballot the size of a *barn door!*"

❦ / BARN SHOVEL  Used to clean out manure behind stabled animals, the *barn shovel* was extra wide in the blade. The tool figures in the expression to describe poor marksmanship: "He couldn't hit a bull's arse with a *barn shovel!*"

❦ / BARNEY'S BRIG  Whoever Barney was, he was not a shipshape sailor. The complete expression is: ". . . like *Barney's brig*, both main tacks over the foreyard." It means such complete disorder as to be ridiculous.

❦ / BARREL OF FLOUR  Even though barrels of household flour are a thing of the past, the memory lingers. Instead of saying, "The stork brought you," Maine mothers would say, "You came in a *barrel of flour*." One old-timer adds that since a barrel of flour lasted about so long, there was usually a new one being moved under the pantry shelf about the time Mother was ready.

❦ / BARROOM  The bunkhouse of a lumber camp, although the place was as often called the bedroom. In either instance, it was not a taproom. The *deacon seat* was in the *barroom*. Since the cookshack, or dining-room, could not be used for conversations, the traditional cook's reproof ran, "Dis room is for h'eat, you wanna talk, you go on de *bar-ROOM!*"

❦ / BARSE-ACKWARDS Euphenism throughout Maine for what it is when it isn't.

❦ / BARVEL The leather apron (leathern ap'n) worn by the man on a fishing vessel who salted down the catch. Other men in the crew had to provide (or find) their own gear, but the skipper provided *barvel* and boots to the one on salt duty. Today, occasional reference to "barvel and boots" means a little frosting on the cake; a special consideration.

❦ / BASKET Pronounced bah-skit. A leaky boat, or a kettle with a hole in it; hence, a person who can't keep a secret. "Tell it to that *bahskit* and it's all over town!" Otherwise, the word is heard in such Maine expressions as, "He can't carry a tune in a *basket*," and, "He went to Hell in a *handbasket*—drink, you know!" In Aroostook County a certain Indian-made *basket* for field-gathering potatoes is standard harvest equipment. It has no particular size but is small for children and large for grown-ups. Its shape is distinctive. Occasionally Mainers call, "Fetch the *basket!*" to indicate a task is finished—from the undertaker's *basket*. For the same meaning, they also say, "The child is born!"

❦ / BATEAU This French word for a boat, in general, is used in the Maine woods for the long, rakish, double-ender that became the workboat of the river drives. Possibly an effort by French-Canadians to make the war canoe of the Indians more practical, it was ideal in the white water of the spring freshets. Poled more than rowed, and often paddled, it was mostly a downstream boat; it would be carted back upstream after the drive. In good hands it was almost unswampable and not difficult to manage. The *bateau* figures in the 1775 expedition of Colonel Arnold to Quebec, and the trouble he had with them may have stemmed more from unfamiliarity with them than from their alleged poor quality. Certainly they were well used later without the problems he experienced. They were sizeable; at Kennebago Lake in 1958 one with seventeen men and all their *plunder* aboard got drawn down at the stern by an outboard motor until the boat swamped. The men waded to shore, and the boss chided them for not saving their axes and peaveys. In older Maine writings, the plural is usually Englished to *bateaus*.

❧ / BATTEN DOWN   To make weather-tight. Hatches over a ship's cargo holds were fitted in place and covered with canvas. Sawn strips of wood called *battens* were then nailed to secure the edges of the canvas. To *batten down* the hatches easily evolved into *batten down* for making almost anything secure and tight. A house *battened down* for winter would have the storm sash in place, banking about the foundation, and the cellar full of goodies. A person *battened down* is ready for come-as-may. (See *mud pattens*.)

❧ / BAULKIN'   The process and method of bringing long ship timbers from the forest to the shipyard. One early journal tells of a mast being drawn "by about two and thirty oxen before, and about four yokes by the side of the mast between the fore and hinder wheels." (See *town team*.) *Baulkin'* a "mahst" called for precise maneuvering around corners.

❧ / BAY   *Over the bay* means one has had more than enough to drink and is temporarily out of contact. Compare the general expression, "*half seas over*."

❧ / BE   The subjunctive mood survives in certain Maine remarks, and grammarians will find it usually parses correctly. "What time *be* it?" "How *be* you?" And the recurring refrain still written into deeds: "*Be* it the same *be* it more or less."

❧ / BEACH   A sandy shore, but in Maine coastal talk the word has special contexts. Any floating object, including a boat, will *beach out* by washing or drifting ashore; accordingly, an unemployed seaman is *on the beach*. To *beach out* a boat is to ground her by bringing her in over the shore so she is left by the outgoing tide; this is usually done for repairs. *Beach* can mean a rocky shore if a boat *beaches up* by accident on rocks. *Beaching* a boat is not the same as *beaching out*, as when picnickers *beach* on an island, i.e., go ashore. *Beaching* is not used for the *hauling* of a boat, which means she is brought ashore above tidewater, either for storage or for longer than one-tide repairs.

❧ / BEAMY   Wide. The width of a vessel is her beam, and a *beamy* boat is traditionally a comfortable one with *room for name and hail* (which see). *Beamy* is a favorite Maine adjective for a lady with steatopygous accumulation.

❧ / BEANS   "He don't know *beans*!" suggests unnatural ignorance. The first reference to beans in Maine history is in the records of Ste. Croix Island, 1603, and beans have been staple in Maine ever since. Reference is, of course, to the baked bean, which served well in feeding ships' crews and the lumbering crews. "Please pass the *beans*!" is a jocular cry traditionally made as a person comes within hailing distance of a table. Aboard ship and in the home the earthenware beanpot was, and is, standard, but in lumber camps, and particularly on drives, Cook liked a cast-iron pot for his *bean*-hole. Baking *beans* in a *bean*-hole uses the retained heat principle of the *clambake*. Recipes for baked *beans* vary from Maine-home to Maine-home, but all call for a *junk* of pork, molasses, ginger, etc., and slow baking. Although Mainers use and like the smaller "pea" beans, the yellow-eyes, soldiers, kidneys, and Jacob's cattle have good play. The Jacob's cattle is a native Maine bean whose spots remind of the Bible story (Genesis 30:39); and the soldier bean seems to have a grenadier at attention. The yellow-eye, from its spot, gives us the expression for faulty illumination: "That lamp don't give as much light as a *yellow-eye bean!*" (See *snapper*.)

❧ / BEAR DOWN   To approach another vessel from windward. This is a nautical position of advantage. Thus, Mainers *bear down* on an opportunity, such as persisting in an argument. Parents who *bear down* on their children are strict, severe. A person approaching purposefully, often agitated, is *bearing down*: "She *bore down* on Susie's teacher and gave her what-for!"

❧ / BEAUTY   Used to denote excellence, but not always prettiness. A fine buck deer may elicit the cry, "Ain't he a *beauty!*" Sometimes, just *beaut*.

❧ / BEAVER BOG   The flowback from a beaver dam will be surrounded by considerable mushy terrain. The term is applied to anything suggesting a morass: "In the spring of the year our road is just a *beaver bog!*" The beaver bog gives us the expression "*to bog down*," which is used literally for being stuck in the mud, and also for less physical predicaments: "The meeting got all *bogged down* over technicalities."

❧ / BECKETS   Rope handles on sea chests. When rightly fashioned, one has no knot. Somehow the word came to mean a man's pockets: "He was amblin' along with his hands in his *beckets*." Cap'n Mert Scholfield once had his *beckets* picked at Topsham Fair!

❧ / BEEHIVE   Maine word for what Washington Irving called "The Yankee Farmer's shingle palace." A foursquare home with hip roof and central chimney. Real estate agents now like to call them "desirable old Colonials" and this puts the price up somewhat.

❦ / BELLS   Time aboard ship was divided into *watches*, and the ship's bell was struck by hand every half-hour. Purists smile at summer tourists who like to "find" old ship clocks that strike the *bells*. The authentic Maine ship clock will be a wall clock, either round or octagonal, without pendulum, and it will not strike the bells. That kind came later. Aboard ship, nobody took chances on automatic striking. If the bells didn't sound, all hands turned out to see what had happened to the man on watch. (See *rope*.)

❦ / BELLY   The amount of curve in the body of a sail; the center portion of a trawl net; the mid-section of a vessel. (See *poke*.) The "*belly*-flopper" taken in the ol' swimmin' hole often comes out in Maine as *belly*-thumper and *belly*-whacker. Similarly, the *belly*-bumper that means a face-down flop onto a child's sled is often, in Maine, a *belly*-bunt or a *belly*-tunk.

❦ / BELLY SIGN   The only certain portent for successful trout fishing. Expert fly-casters of the purist type have always amused Maine guides with their ideas about the best time to take trouts. The guide's answer is, "The best time is when the sign is in their bellies." That is, when they're feeding.

❦ / BELLYACHE   Traditional Maine pleasantry for any home-town weekly newspaper. The Ellsworth American— The Ellsworth *Bellyache*. "Anything in the *Bellyache* this week?"

❦ / BEN   As in Franklin, and "How ya ben?" Maine is one place the rhyme really rhymes:

> Of all sad words of tongue or pen,
> The saddest are these—it might have ben.

●

❧ / BEND   To fasten or secure a line, in which sense it is the nautical word for tie. Sails were *bent* on the yards; a line was *bent* to the anchor. In shipbuilding, strakes, planks, and wales attached to the outside of the hull are *bends*. To *bend* a necktie is to get all rigged out sartorially. The word is used in un-nautical contexts: "*Bend* the hasp on the shed door when you come by." Fasten.

❧ / BEST   Used with noun understood: "That's the *best* I ever see!" or, "That's the *best* ever!"

❧ / BETWEEN THE FACE AND EYES   Along the Maine coast nobody is ever struck in the face—always *between the face and eyes*. It can involve a physical blow with a fist, or some startling news that leaves you stunned.

❧ / BILGE   The rounded lower part of a ship's hull, inside near the keelson. Stagnant *bilge* water collects there and, when excessive, is pumped overside. Hence, a bad cup of coffee, over-watered rum, or any distasteful liquid  or food. Also, silly speech: "Never heard such a spout of *bilge!*" When somebody is putting you on: "Don't give me that *bilge!*"

❧ / BILL   Maine word for a divorce action started by the wife: "Myra's sending Harry her *bill.*"

❧ / BILLDAD   One of the mythical animals of the Maine woods, said to secure its food by standing on a bank and slapping trout with its tail. The noise, very like a beaver's warning slap, is a "wazzat," from the *sport's* usual query, "What's-at?" The *billdad* is small, about ankle high (see Job 8:1). Anybody scouting *billdads* is looking for a drink; if he finds one, he's had one.

❧ / BIRD WATCHER   Without reference to the Audubon buffs, this is what Mainers call the throngs who come spring and fall to see the Canada geese, usually *damnbird-watchers*. They proliferate in the Merrymeeting Bay area, but there is one place at Farmingdale on the Kennebec River where geese put down, and Route 201 gets jammed with *bird watchers*. *State workers* (which see) use this as an excuse for showing up late: "I couldn't get through the *damn-birdwatchers!*"

❧ / BISCUIT    Maine usage limits this to the cream-tartar and sal'ratus hot bread; raised *biscuits* made of yeast dough are called rolls. Except for the old sea *biscuits* and dog *biscuits*, the word is unfamiliar in Maine for a cracker. What Mainers call *biscuit* dough is ALWAYS the basis of shortcakes; a sweetened shortcake may have its pleasant side, but Maine cooks stick to the "bakin'-powd-duh" kind (although for shortcakes they add extry shortening). The biscuit has always been mighty important to people eating at farm, lumber camp, and shipboard tables where yeast wasn't always easy to come by, and most Maine people know how to bake a decent *biscuit*.

❧ / BISCUIT MAKER    See *baker*, as to a cookstove. The best biscuit maker was a double-ender Kineo model made by the Wood & Bishop Foundry in Bangor. It had an oven door on each side, and while this was so the stove could be put against either wall as desired, the legend grew that the two doors were part of the efficiency: "You just pahss 'em through, and they come out light's a feather!" Knowing Maine's reliance on hot biscuits, salesmen used to claim their competitive ranges were better *biscuit makers*, but the Kineo was hard to beat.

❧ / BISCUIT WOOD    See *edgings*. Often dry alder, used to brown off the bake after other wood had done the work.

❧ / BITTER    Not just in Maine, the *bitter end* of a rope is that last streak of hemp that high-tails through the pulley when by accident or ill luck a line gets away. Thus, to "come to a *bitter* end" means an untoward happening. In the plural, bitters has a more localized Maine meaning. In the old days several bottlers of tonics operated in Maine, making the flavored alcoholic pseudo-medicinal beverages that were good for a sour stomach, etc., and which, because of the taste, were known as *bitters*. A citizenry sponsoring political prohibition was adept at make-do. *Bitters* came to be a term for a drink, and to *pay* (for) *the bitters* was a gentleman's duty when his turn came: "This one's on me, I'll pay the *bitters*."

❦ / BLACKJACK   Gingerbread. West Indian trading made Mainers a Barbados or dark molasses people, so their gingerbread was more black than golden. Johnnycake, always made in Maine from yellow meal, was *yellowjack*. (See Jack [2] .)

❦ / BLASTOW BUTTONS   A toggle-type clothes fastening, homemade from short pieces of small alders. Two-three inches long, they were grooved midway for sewing and tying, and would thrust through an opposite hole or loop. First devised at Blastow's Cove on Little Deer Isle, where *boughten* buttons were hard to come by, they may now be found world-wide on stylish sports jackets.

❦ / BLAT   Perhaps blaat, and even blaht. Any loud cry or noise. It derives from the bawling cow whose desire for gentleman company has gone unnoticed. Parents give a *blat* to bring the children to supper; a foghorn *blats* all night. Also, to blurt out or blab; to *blat* a secret.

❦ / BLAZE   An ax mark (now more likely to be a squirt from a spray-can of paint) on a tree to show the direction of a woods trail or a lot or town line. A *blazed* trail has the marks so they may be seen by one coming along; a spotted trail has the marks so they are abreast the shoulder of one passing. The difference is to prevent confusion when two trails intersect.

❧ / BLIND   A roll-up window shade, but also the outside shutters for a window. Mainers liked outside shutters green, so *blind* green became a color of paint to ask for at the store. A *blind* is also a concealment for duck hunting.

❧ / BLISTER PLASTER   A mustard plaster; a remedy for aches and pains in the bygone. Their efficacy was presumed to lie in the "heat" of the mustard, and when a child got one applied for the croup it could blister. There was always great cry when Mother peeled one off.

❧ / BLOATER   A smoked herring or alewife, and sometimes a mackerel. (See *Kennebec turkey*.) A freshly smoked alewife is also called a *smoker*.

❧ / BLOODLESS WAR   The Aroostook War of 1836–1839. The dispute between the United States and England over Maine's northern boundary never came to gunfire, and was settled by the Webster-Ashburton Treaty. The only casualty was a soldier named Hiram Smith, whose demise is variously attributed. Some say he died of pneumonia; some, he drowned; some, he was run over by a wagon. His grave is by the side of the *Military Road* (which see) and his unfortunate fate gave Mainers another simile: "to have the luck of Hiram Smith" is to be one out of many, and the one to get it in the neck.

❧ / BLOW   A good wind. Often, a windy period, as in three day *blow*, when a steady northwest wind will continue for some time. Coming on to *blow* means a wind is making up. *Blow* high or *blow* low means to let come what may. To *blow* over is to pass, as a storm, or to let a quarrel be forgotten: "Jim and Hank had words, but the fuss *blew* over." A *blow*-hard is a loud-mouth. To be *blown* over is to be astonished, much like "bowled over."

❧ / Blow-down   A forest tree that has been uprooted by the wind, or an area where many trees have toppled. The crisscrossed logs make it difficult to pass, so woodsmen may say, "I'd-a got here sooner, but I had to go around a *blow-down*." A single *blow-down*, with dirt still hanging to its upturned roots, makes a fine shelter for a *wickie-up* (which see).

❧ / Blowin' fit to make a rabbit cry   A harsh, cold wind that brings tears to the eyes. Rabbits (erroneously) were supposed to have no tear ducts.

❧ / Blowin' out endways   A gale that whips the family laundry on the line to the horizontal. Marty Buker claims in such a wind he once spit from Port Clyde clearn to M'n-higg'n!

❧ / Bluebacks   Certain fish have blue back markings and are called bluefish and *bluebacks*; hence, old sea charts with blue paper backing.

❧ / Bluenose   A nickname not always appreciated by Nova Scotians, whose noses are supposed to reflect the rigors of their climate. As Nova Scotians were competitive on the fishing grounds, Mainers used the term deprecatingly, and even contemptuously, for both the people and their boats. Philologists say, however, that *Bluenose* comes not from weather-colored noses, but from the bluish potatoes favored in the Province. For lumbercamp equivalents of the coastal *Bluenose* and *Herring-choker* (New Brunswicker) see *Pea-Eye*.

❧ / Blue paint   Most fishermen consider blue an unlucky color for a boat, good "only for wheelbarrows and tipcarts." Farmers, on the other hand, have always preferred blue for tipcarts, so *tipcart-blue* joined *barn-red* and *blind-green* as colors to ask for at the store.

❧ / BLUE WATER MAN   Or, *blue water* sailor. A mariner licensed for or experienced in sailing all the oceans of the world. Also known as a deep water man. (See *apple-tree-er*.)

❧ / BOARD AROUND   In early Maine school districts see *deestrick*) teachers lived with different families during a school year. Thus *boarding around* became a term for having no home, and it is still heard in such a sentence as, "No, Mother sold the old place after Dad went, and now she's *boarding 'round*. She comes to be with us next month."

❧ / BOHEA   When still heard today, this means tea. Originally it was a strong, inexpensive, black tea from the Bohea hills in Fukien, China, and was one of the many exotic products seafaring made commonplace in Maine. Tea is more popular than coffee in some parts of Maine, and one can still hear, "Nothing like a mug of *Bohea* for what ails you!" Maine lumbercamps are great places for tea, where it is served in huge pitchers, but the inland Mainers didn't have the Chiny Trade lore of the coast, and *Bohea* remains wholly tidewater.

❧ / BOIL A FEW WALLOPS   To bring to a hard, rolling boil for a short time, as water for a pot of tea.

❧ / BOILED OWL   A presumptive, last ditch meal than which, in Maine cookery, there is nothing tougher: "I'm hungry enough to eat a *boiled owl!*"

❧ / BOILER   Uncomplimentary term for a woods cook whose talents are limited to boiled foods. Life in camp is bad enough without having a cussid boiler in the cookshack.

❦ / BOILING SPRING   Non-Mainers who hear this term sometimes think it means a hot spring. The eastern shed of the White Mountains gives Maine a great many clear, bubbling springs of water where the issuance suggests boiling. Famous Poland Spring, for instance.

❦ / BOLD   Forward; said of a child who is unmannerly and a nuisance: "She's far too *bold*—comes right into the house 'thout knockin'!"

❦ / BOLD SHORE   A high, rocky coastline with deep water close in. In this sense, *bold* means both deep and safe for navigation; *bold water* is deep water, not only close to shore but in a harbor with good depth.

❦ / BOLT   Seemingly a Maine original for a four-foot length of log cut for a turning mill. Pulpwood as well as cordwood for fires is also handled in four-foot lengths, but the sticks are not called *bolts*. A *bolt*-mill is a sawmill specializing in *square-bars* and *shook*, and a *bolter* is a man or machine sawing *bolts*. Birch, ash, maple, and some oak are likely lumber for *bolting*. Shorter pieces of pine and cedar for shingles are called shingle-*bolts*. Proper Maine pronunciation of *bolt* is difficult to indicate; try *boult*.

❦ / BOND   A noun; a Canadian workman in Maine under a special immigration permit. Used for *choppers* in the woods, and also for farm help in the Aroostook potato harvest. The employer has to post a *bond* for each person thus hired. When the term originated, the procedure was somewhat complicated, but long experience has rendered it simpler. "Halfway to The Fort I picked up a couple of *bonds* and gave 'em a ride to town."

❦ / BOOK, THE   The full penalty of the Maine law: "He pleaded guilty, and the judge threw *the book* at him!"

❧ / Boom   A word with several very different Maine meanings, first of which is the well-known spar that extends the bottom edge of a sail and must be ducked when it swings. A vessel taking full advantage of the wind is said to *boom* along; accordingly a person making haste is *boom-in'*. Inland, a logging *boom* is a linking of tree-length timbers to guide floating logs during a drive, or to impound them in a lake. When brought to a full circle for towing, the *boom* and its impounded logs form a raft (see *alligator*). *Boom* piers were constructed for anchoring, and some may be seen (amongst other places) in the Kennebec River between Gardiner and Augusta. Logging on the Penobscot led to the establishing of a Maine state official known as Commissioner of the Penobscot *Boom*, whose function was to regulate lumbering navigation, and naturally Bangor was the first *boom* town. The activity of river driving thus gave us the term *boom* times.

❧ / Boomjumper   A specially designed fresh-water boat used in river driving for navigating waters clogged with floating logs. The name derives from the function; they can tool along in open water, jump a *boom*, and continue through the timber. Heavily powered and heavily built, they have under-structure to fend off damage to the propeller. As river driving dwindles, the *boomjumper* is becoming a museum piece. In 1971 the Great Northern Paper Company offered to sell a number of *boomjumpers* it no longer needed, but boat buffs showed little interest; there isn't much you can do with a *boomjumper* except jump *booms*. A *boomjumper* is not to be confused with a tow boat as used in lumbering. (See *alligator*.)

❧ / Boondocks   Heard somewhat in Maine today, and perhaps introduced by outsiders fairly recently; as used for the back country, Mainers would more likely say *pucker-brush*.

❧ / Booot-cher   Acceptable Maine way to say butcher. The extended *ooo* sound is heard in butcher shop, butcher's twine, butcherin' a hog, and for the brand-name Butcher's Wax, made by Mr. Butcher. To *bootcher* anything is to do it badly: "That joker sure *boootchered* my woodlot!" If you get a poor haircut, you've been *boootchered*. *Canucks* are accused of *boootchering* English.

❧ / Border patrol   The enforcement arm of the U.S. Immigrations Service, which has a unique situation along the northwest border of Maine, facing Québec. Here, Canadians come to work in the Maine woods, and the activity is quite unlike anything along the rest of the U.S.-Canadian line. Working out of Jackman, the Maine unit of the *Border Patrol* covers the vast wilderness area from Coburn Gore to Estcourt, and to Canadians improperly present in Maine the B.P. is a forest bogeyman.

❧ / Bored or punched   A measurement of ignorance. Not to know if a hole is *bored or punched* is to be uninformed.

❧ / Boston   To quite an extent *Boston* means Massachusetts, and sometimes anything in that general direction. A "trip to *Boston*" may mean Springfield, or in extreme generalizations even Philadelphia. In Nova Scotia, the United States of America are the *Boston* states, and Maine shares something of this down-eastism; no doubt it is a holdover from the coasting days when *Boston* really had a maritime importance to the region.

❧ / Boston eggs   Brown eggs. In the days of the family farms Maine crated and shipped eggs, but kept the browns and whites apart. White eggs went to New York.

❧ / Bo't   Only coastal Mainers manage this rendition of boat. There is no phonetic sign for it. True Maine tongues are supposed to be able to say, "Well, I guess I'll put on my co't and go down the ro'd and see the *bo't* come in." Some fancy this mannerism with "o-at" words is a lingering from very old Anglo-Saxon, when there was almost a two-syllable tingle to go-at, bo-at, co-at, etc.

❧ / BOTTLE   Mainers seldom buy a *bottle* of liquor; they "go for a *jug*." However, the word *bottle* became the Maine word for the 100-pound steel cylinders of propane gas, common outside rural homes. There is a story that Mr. Anderson, who pioneered the L.P. (bottled) gas business in Maine, tried to borrow money at a Portland bank by offering his *bottles* as collateral. The banker thought in terms of glass bottles and a contretemps ensued. Mr. Anderson's *bottles*, of course, were worth a great deal of money.

❧ / BOUGHT YOUR LUCK   Almost every seaport had an "auntie" with supposedly magic charms. Buying some trinket from her before a voyage was a good thing to do, and this was *buying your luck*. Tossing a coin overboard as the vessel left the dock did the same thing.

❧ / BOUGHTEN   Store bought, as distinguished from something made at home. A woman who puts *boughten* bread on the table ought to be ashamed. A young lady in a *boughten* dress has something pretty fine.

❧ / BOXBERRY   Maine term for the checkerberry, a common pasture and sourland plant. The pulpy red berries would elsewhere be called checkerberries, but a boy brought up on a Maine farm will call them *boxberry* plums.

❧ / BRAD   The sharp steel point on a wooden ox goad. *Brad* and *gad* (which see) are somewhat interchangeable in Maine speech for bringing somebody to attention: "He'll go along with us if we *brad* him enough." *Brad* is used in the sense of driving, teasing, cajoling, needling, and plaguing (see *plague*). The *brad* was often a heavy sewing needle set into the end of a wooden wand. In its various transferred usages, *brad* is an exceptionally vivid word to anybody who has seen oxen driven.

❦ / BRANCH    Used in Maine as elsewhere for that portion of a river before a confluence; the East *Branch* and the West *Branch* of the Penobscot River. But in Maine there is local meaning for a region drained, in terms of logging off. Loggers speak of the "West *Branch*" as an area as well as a stream. The term *branch*-water as a highball ingredient is seldom used by true Mainers; a man in the West *Branch* would more likely ask for a "small slop of *sluice* juice." Try that after a couple of martinis!

❦ / BREACH    A rupture, a hernia. A whale's bursting above the surface. A lobster trap, being hauled, *breaches* the water at the side of the boat. A cow that jumps fences is *breachy*.

❦ / BREAKER    A heavy wave that breaks on shore. The small keg of water carried in lifeboats is a *breaker*; accordingly, a touch of liquid refreshment just at the right time. On the original one-lunger marine engines, such as the Smith & Langmaid and the Hartford, the firing of the cylinder was done by a *breaker*. Mechanically these were known as *make and break* engines. *Breaker* trouble was routine, and *breaker*-language was the profanity heard on shore as a lobsterman struggled with his crankpin.

❦ / BREEDER    General throughout Maine and the Maritimes, deriving from the weather patterns of the region. A *breeder* is a salubrious day that is making up a storm. It has been said that Washington County never has a good day—just storms and *breeders*.

❦ / BREEZEN    Usually with up. A breeze is good sailing weather, and so is a fresh breeze and a stiff breeze. But if it then *breezens* up, it is too much of a good thing. A person with a short temper may be said to *breezen* up unduly.

❧ / BRIDESMEN   Still heard from older folks for the ushers at a wedding. It was customary in earlier times for the bridesmaids and *bridesmen* to march together in the procession.

❧ / BRIDLE CHAIN   Lumbering and farm term for a chain wrapped around a sled runner to serve as a brake on a downhill skid, to keep the load from running ahead on the animals. To "put the *bridle chain*" to somebody is to restrain him from some foolish activity.

❧ / BRIM   Salted bait used by lobstermen. The words *bream* and *brim*, as varieties of non-Maine fish, are probably not the root of this term. But somehow *brim* became a Maine term for trash fish. Specifically, *brim* is the head and skeleton of the ocean perch or redfish, after edible fillets have been cut and packed for market. The fish-packing plants sell the residue and bait-trucks deliver it to the lobster ports. Recently, to the amusement of Maine people, a nationwide company named a new brand of coffee *Brim*.

❧ / BRINDLE   A certain brownish-yellow color not considered attractive by discerning Mainers. If we may euphemize, the full term is fecal-*brindle*; otherwise, calf-turd yellow.

❧ / BROAD SIDE OF A BARN   See *barn shovel* and *barn door*. The *broad side of a barn* is a large target where marksmanship is considered: "Boy! Is my bowling off tonight! I can't hit the *broad side of a barn*!"

❧ / BROTHER   This seems to be a localism among Maine lawyers, who use it for a fellow attorney. It amuses lawyers from out-of-state. A lawyer summing his case may say, "My learned *brother* errs in his contention, etc."

B / 23

❧ / Brow   A place where logs are piled to await further disposition. It may be a sidehill in the woods, or the bank of a river. It is also the rollway at a sawmill where logs are unloaded. (See *yard* and *tier*.)

❧ / Browsing   See *brush*.

❧ / Brush   Maine uses this word in several ways not found in the dictionaries. (See *puckerbrush*.) Softwood limbs and tops left in the woods, also called *slash*, are *brush*. Evergreen boughs used for banking a home for winter are *brush*. A *brush*-fire is a woods fire, but one that burns through lesser growth. To *brush* out has no connection with a bristle brush or broom, but means to cut bushes; each summer the town highway crew *brushes* out along the rural roads. Summer cottagers may hire a man to trim away small growth so they can see their ocean, and the man who does this will tell you he is *brushing* out. The term is similar in meaning to *swamping*, but swamping suggests a bigger job. *Brushing* is also the gathering of evergreen tips for making Christmas wreaths. These upland meanings have no connection with several coastal meanings; the latter derive from the *brushin'* or *dustin'* that a vessel gets from an unexpected quick wind: "We took a *brushin'* and heeled over *some*." The nautical *brushin'* often comes out as *browsin'*, to rhyme with *dousin'*: "The flu went right through 'em; I never knew a fambly to take such a *browsin'!*"

❧ / Bubble and squeak   Numerous Maine cookbooks treat this as endemic, and most recipes have no similarity to the English dish of the same name. In Maine it's a left-over contrivance: cold cooked beef, cold smashed potatoes, cold cabbage, shredded onion, etc., browned in pork fat and served with vinegar. It's hearty, and cleans out the refrigerator.

❧ / Bubblegum machine   From the light globe on the top, a Maine State Police cruising car on the highway.

❦ / BUCK  To cut a felled tree into pulpwood and cordwood of four-foot lengths. (See *Polack fiddle*.) Lately, pulpwood is being transported to paper mill yards by trucks in tree lengths. In the mill yard the former *bucking* is done by power saws and is now called slashing. The tool used for *bucking* is the bucksaw.

❦ / BUCKET, KICK THE  To die, often with the implication of giving up. Some say there was a shipboard superstition about tipping over a bucket; the origin is undoubtedly nautical since nobody ever kicked the pail. There were no pails aboard ship; only buckets.

❦ / BUCKO  A ship's officer of any rank who used fists or weapons to enforce orders.

❦ / BUFFALO COAT  Although not all of them were made of buffalo hide and fur, this was the general term for the heavy winter protection for the Maine teamster. It was a sort of badge of the office. Being stable oriented, they became tangy, and having a teamster step into your kitchen to get warm left an impression. Any kind of a fur lap-piece to cover people riding in a sleigh was similarly dubbed a *buffalo* robe. There are some sniggering and not altogether genteel references in Maine speech to both the coats and the robes, as you may surmise.

❦ / BUGGER  With hardly any impolite and negative connotation, this word is used in Maine as a synonym for chap, fellow, jeezer, joker, etc.: "He's a comical *bugger!*"

❦ / BUILD  First used in speaking of a boat that had good construction, the thought was easily extended to the human figure. A woman who is well *built* will have pleasing proportions; a man of sturdy stature will be *built* like a stevedore. Depending on her appearance, a lady may be *built* like the back end of a barn, or she may be *built* like a clipper. The common and perhaps most popular Maine usage of this simile is to describe a woman as "*built* like a brick backhouse." This suggests that a certain ampleness is not unattractive.

❧ / BULL   To push a project by main force and stubbornness. The word suggests lack of know-how, but eventual success. "He won't get no prizes for finesse, but if you want things *bulled* right along, he's your man."

❧ / BULLBEEF   Maine dairy beef offered for table consumption to a local clientele. *Cow beef (vive la différence!)* wasn't that different, but tended to be less chewy. When Maine law forbade serving game in lumber and sporting camps, *bullbeef* was a term for the occasional venison, caribou, and moose that appeared and fooled nobody. Venison, however, was sometimes announced as *lamb*.

❧ / BULLCOOK   A lumbercamp *choreboy* or handyman. The one thing he never did was cook. While the word *choreboy* is used, the *bullcook* was usually a mature man with, 'twas said, a strong back and a weak head. If somebody is compared to a *bullcook*, it suggests *gorm*.

❧ / BULLDOZED ROAD   A wilderness and usually private road made ready for logging except for a gravel surface. It always opens new hunting country, and sportsmen can and do negotiate it with four-wheel drive. After gravel is applied and the logging starts, most such roads are open only to company vehicles. The term has another meaning: after a logging operation is finished, the company will send a bulldozer to throw up barriers of earth so the road is closed off. Hunters like to think this is done to spite them, but the reason is quite otherwise. The barriers keep rainstorms and spring run-offs from washing  gravel away, so the road will be fairly good in another fifteen years or so when needed again. A bulldozer can quickly level the barriers when the time comes.

🌺 / BULLHEAD   Maine word for our only fresh water catfish, the hornpout. Sometimes "bullpout." Their barbels give them an ugly look, but they are good panfish—although not esteemed by trout-loving Mainers.

🌺 / BULL PINE   A pasture pine; i.e., one that grows in open country and thus doesn't shoot up straight and tall like a forest tree. A *bull pine* has big limbs close to the ground and won't make good boards. It will go for pulp.

🌺 / BUMP   Maine term for what the Massachusetts Highway Authority calls a frost heave. When winter creates a *yes-marm*, the highway crew puts up a warning sign that says "*Bump.*" Another use of *bump* in Maine speech has to do with a "*bump* on a log." Somebody who sits by and doesn't take part, who shirks and perhaps even sulks, is compared to a *bump* on a log.

🌺 / BUMPER   Not the traditional cup filled to the brim for a toast, but in Maine a flat-bottomed tin cup with handle meant for drinking at the spring, well, and sink. It holds about a pint.

🌺 / BUNCH   A Maine-ism for what a surgeon might call a growth, mass, cyst: "This *bunch* came on my arm, and I went right to the doctor."

🌺 / BUNG   The plug in a barrel; but in Maine boat-building it means a wooden stopper that covers metal fasteners. The screws or nails are countersunk, and the *bung* driven in to protect the metal from the weather. Home-workshop buffs make them with a tool called a *plug-cutter*, and call them *plugs*. A bung is made cross-grain, so when it is in place its grain runs with the grain of the boat's planking and deck; a dowel runs lengthwise of the grain, and will not suit in boat construction. To be all *bunged* up does not seem to derive from this kind of *bung*, but probably is a way of saying all banged up; used, bruised, beaten, spent.

❧ / BUNGDOWN   Like *bunged* up, this probably comes from "bang." It means battered, used up, belabored: a *bungdown* truck, a *bungdown* hat, the same old *bungdown* reasons for sobriety.

❧ / BUNGS UP   Rolling badly in a heavy sea, a vessel is *bungs up*, i.e., careening so the *bungs* in her planking are visible. Accordingly, a gentleman *feeling no pain* might be *bungs up* on his way home.

❧ / BUNGS UP AND BILGE FREE   This term derives from the bung in a barrel. Casks in the hold had to be stowed *bungs up*, so bilge water couldn't intrude. It is a term for being shipshape, and anybody who is *bungs up and bilge free* is behaving properly, perhaps a mite sanctimoniously.

❧ / BUNK   That part of logging sleds on which the loaded logs rested. Each bunk was fitted with *sled stakes* to keep logs from rolling off. With a load on, the teamster would sit atop the logs, but returning with empty sleds he would ride the *bunk*. Hence, to ride a *bunk* is to be lightly occupied, perhaps between jobs, and even taking things easy.

❧ / BUREAU   Never heard amongst Mainers for any kind of an office until bureaucracy; a bureau is an article of furniture in the bedroom. You keep your shirts in the *bureau* drawer.

❧ / BURGOO   Once oatmeal porridge or gruel, the word now means any of several stews, usually thick. Thus the word makes a happy substitute for the overworked pea-soup fog: "It fogged in thick as *burgoo!*"

❦ / BURN   Forestry term for a place that has had a fire. Even if the fire was long ago and trees have regrown, the area may be called the *burn*. A *burn* is also the method of fire-pruning Maine wild blueberry lands; sometimes done by controlled *brush* fires, and in recent years done by a machine that passes back and forth with a flame-throwing device. In the old days, when early settlers cleared land, the unwanted trees were piled up and a *burn* would be made just after frost left the ground; each spring's *burn* meant a new field to plant.

❦ / BURN OFF   An early morning fog or land mist that dissipates in sunshine is said to *burn off*.

❦ / BURNT HOLES IN A BLANKET   A description of morning-after eyes. "His eyes were like two *burnt holes in a blanket*." Sometimes, much less delicately, "two cane-holes in a cow flap."

❦ / BURYIN'   A funeral. Incidentally, along the Maine coast a *buryin'* ground is often called a *buryin'* point.

❦ / BUSHES   A well-used Maine term for the locale of philandering. To take a girl into the *bushes* means what it means, but the sense has been generalized. It may be the bushes but it doesn't have to be. (See *chips*. The chip pile has a similar nuance of dalliance.)

❦ / BUTT   A cask, and specifically a cask of drinking water aboard ship. As crewmen met at the *butt* they would exchange remarks, and this gave us "scuttlebutt" for gossip and loose information. In ship construction, the joint of two planks in a vessel's hull is a *butt*, which is reinforced with a *butt* block; hence a *butt* is a coming together. A shed *butts* onto the main house. In logging, the first cut off a felled tree is the *butt* log; usually having no limbs, it makes the best boards.

❧ / Butter   To "call for the *butter*" is to have a thing almost ready, or to have arrived at a place. It is thus explained: Fishing skippers said they could locate fish by tasting the bottom mud on the Bank. When they presumed they were over fish, they would call for the *butter*. Cook would bring butter and some was smeared on the bottom of the sounding lead. Bottom mud stuck to the butter; skipper would taste; and *voilà*!

❧ / Buttonhole relation   A third or fourth cousin, at least; somebody distantly related but not close enough to bother about. Sometimes a family friend who is no kin at all, but is held dear. Similar to *woodpile cousin*. A less delicate version is an "arsehole relative," but this sometimes means somebody it is no honor to acknowledge.

❧ / By and large   From first to last, altogether, considering everything. The term comes from working a sailing vessel *by* the wind (on a tack), and running at *large* (before the wind). A vessel which worked well *by and large* was the *finest kind*. Interestingly, this sea term was worked into Maine's dog license law: Maine dogs which have their credentials may "run at large."

# A

/\\/\\/\\/\\/\\

❧ / **A** See *B, begin with*.

❧ / **ABAFT** Toward the stern of a vessel, rearward; usually shortened to "aft." 'Tis said a dry-land sailor, eager to sound nautical, once said "*abaft* the aft," and this caught on as a way to describe something which has fallen overboard and is bobbing astern. Thus to go *abaft* the aft can mean to fall in the drink.

❧ / **ABLE** Seaworthy. The word is general in nautical speech, and Mainers use it as people do everywhere. They do transfer it to onshore meanings where it suits, even to speak of an *able* horse ( a farmer would prefer *clever*).

❧ / **ABOUT** Originally, "*About* ship!"—an order to helmsman and crew to change tack, or to come *about*. People and situations, accordingly, can come *about*: "The school committee came *about* when they found so many people didn't like what they were doing." *About* is much favored by Maine people to express a definite intent, either positive or negative: "He asked me to sign his damn note, but I warn't *about* to!"

❧ / **ACADIA** The general area of Maine, New Brunswick, and Nova Scotia was encompassed in the Micmac

Indian name for the region, Acadia. However it was pronounced by the Micmacs, the French set it down as *l'acadie*, and if the British had not succeeded in taking the region over—thus introducing the names New England and Maine—the state would probably be *Acadia* today. The word remains only in the name of *Acadia* National Park, and in the pride of St. John Valley French who explain that they are *acadien* and not *habitant*. The St. John Valley *acadiens* are the same stock as the Cajuns of Louisiana, and *Cajun* derives from *acadien*. Because of the way the British dispersal of early French settlers progressed, *Acadia* came to be associated with Nova Scotia and New Brunswick more than with Maine, but, in the grant to the Sieur de Monts, Maine was equally a part of his domain.

❧ / ACCORDING TO  As much as anything, a variant of accordingly. Hearing this for the first time, strangers think Maine people leave out something. *According to* what? A board is cut *according to*; *according to* the way it must fit. Help are paid *according to*; *according to* each man's due. Used in whatever sense is at hand, *according to*.

❧ / ADAM'S OFF-OX  Used in the expression, "He didn't know me from *Adam's off-ox!*" A number of Biblical and pseudo-Biblical allusions run in Maine speech: "Older than Methuselah's billy-goat. . . poorer than Job's turkey. . . crazier than Gideon's geese (they swam across Fayi Pond to get a drink of water)." *Jacob's cattle* are explained under *beans*, and see *Samson pole*.

❧ / ADRIFT  Afloat, but meaning something that should be moored or in its right place. Hence, a flapping shirt tail, a barn door off its hinges, or a lady who doesn't do all her work at home. At Maine Maritime Academy the cadets use the term "gear *adrift*" for something they have found; particularly if 'tweren't lost until they found it. Gear *adrift* is up for salvage.

❧ / Adz  The craftsman's smoothing tool which, along with the broadax, played such a big part in Maine's shipbuilding story. References to it in everyday Maine speech are obvious as to derivation and meaning: "Migod, you should have seen him *adz* into that punkin pie!"

❧ / Aggravatin'  A favorite Maine word for petty annoyances, and often understatement for a major annoyance. A man watching another trying to extricate a truck from a mud hole may say, "*Aggravatin'*, ain't it?" A fellow who is a congenital pest is an *aggravatin' cuss*. You'll hear people say, "I've got an *aggravatin'* cough." Bothersome, but bearable. A dog may have an *aggravatin'* habit of chasing cats, but you'll seldom hear a Mainer say that a dog *aggravates* a cat, or that one thing *aggravates* another. Pronounced sort of as if *agger-vatin.'*

❧ / Aidge  Edge. With a coastal accent, *aidges* are put on knives, appetites, curt remarks. The lobsterman goes to haul at the *aidge* of day. Seiners go for herring at the *aidge* of night or the *aidge* of dark. A bo't is *aidged* out so it won't hit them rocks. (Some un-nautical remarks about an edge will be found under *edge*.)

❧ / Air Line  That part of Maine State Highway 9, between Brewer and Calais. The fine hunting region it traverses is said by Mainers to be "up on the *Air Line*." The route is not very straight, so there is no meaning of "as the crow flies." A sign in Brewer points to "*Air Line*" and every summer a fair number of *pilgrims* drive out that way looking for the Bangor airport.

❧ / All dressed up  Or, all rigged out. A vessel under full sail is in mind with this reference to glad rags. Sailors got *all dressed up* to go ashore, and woodsmen got *all dressed up* to go to town. There is a wryness to the Maine expression, "*All dressed up* and no place to go."

❧ / ALL DROVE UP    "Druv" up. Busy, overworked, and the standard excuse for not doing something else: "I was so *druv up* I never got to make the beds!" Probably the expression comes from the *droving* or driving of cattle. Among the minor town officials of each Maine community was the Field Drover (Driver), whose function was to round up stray farm animals and turn them over to the Pound Keeper (except pigs; the Hog Reeve did that). The business of chasing cows must have suggested *all drove up* to some early citizen who coined the metaphor.

❧ / ALL FIRED    To be *all fired* sure is to be certain in your self-estimation, but perhaps wrong in the eyes of your neighbors. To be *all fired* up is to be zealous, enthusiastic, and impatient to get at it.

❧ / ALL HUMPED UP    In full, *all humped up* like a hog going to war. The improbability of porcine belligerence suits the description of somebody advancing purposefully on an errand that won't amount to much. Possibly somebody mad as hops going in to complain in vain about an increase in taxes.

❧ / ALLIGATOR    A flat-bottomed scow or raft used on inland lakes for moving boomed logs. (Tow boats came later.) The alligator would be rowed out ahead of the *boom* of logs and anchored. A capstan or winch then pulled the *boom* up to the *alligator* by a cable. The *alligator* would be advanced to a new position and the process repeated until the *boom* had been brought to its destination. River drivers called the capstan the "headworks." Over the years of use the headworks were first operated by men, then a horse who walked in a circle, and finally by steam and gasoline. Comparing a man to an *alligator* has nothing to do with reptiles; it will mean he is slow, methodical, perhaps the kind who goes in circles with small gain.

❧ / ALL RIGGED OUT   See *all dressed up*. *All rigged out* in Sunday best is the *finest kind*. A gentleman *all rigged out* might tell you he is wearing his *other ones*.

❧ / ALL THERE   Another Maine peripheral approach for mental deficiency. One who is not *all there* is *lackin'*, underwitted, not too bright, a mite soft.

❧ / ALL USED UP   Tired, exhausted, perhaps aged before one's time. "He ain't a day over eighty, but he looks *all used up*." Clothing, tools, and about anything, as well as people, can be *used up*. This sense of obsolescence for *used up* differs from the simple meaning of thrift in the old adage, "Make it do, wear it out, use it up."

❧ / ALST   Perhaps *allst*. It means all or "everything that." "*Alst* I know is what they tell me." "*Alst* you do to fix that leak is buy a new bilge pump."

❧ / AMPLE   Favored Maine word to express satisfaction at table:

> "Have more potatoes, Cyrus?"
> "No, thanks, Helen, *ample* of everything."

A time-tested dialogue as old as Maine is between a deaf hostess and her gentleman guest. She speaks first:

> More vegetables, Jonathan?
> No, thanks—great sufficiency.
> Been a-fishin'?
> No, I say—I've got plenty!
> Caught twenty?
> No, no—I'm full!
> Broke your pole?
> No, no—*ample, ample!*
> Small sample—pass up your plate!

❦ / ANSWER   A vessel's response to her rudder in steering. She is said to be lively, cranky, sluggish, depending on how she *answers* her helm. In this sense of responding, Mainers often use *answer* when a verbal reply is not being considered.

❦ / AP'N   Correct Maine pronunciation of apron. *Nasty-neat* housewives used to wear two *ap'ns* at their kitchen work; if somebody knocked on the door they would whip one off and make a favorable impression with a spankin' clean *ap'n.*

❦ / APPLE KNOCKER   One of Maine's many names for a privy. This one means an outhouse so situated that apples dropping from a tree onto the roof make an obbligato to the business at hand.

❦ / APPLE PIE ORDER   A place for everything and everything in its place. Neat, but not *nasty-neat.*

❦ / APPLETREE-ER   A coasting vessel that doesn't get out of sight of land, or a skipper who sails one. Also applied scornfully to passengers who are seasick, and particularly those who make a big thing out of fearing they will be. The word is used in other contexts for timidity and extra caution. Cap'n Hosea Bibber wrote home that he was an *appletree-er* about the funicular at Vesuvius (afraid of height).

❦ / ARCTIC SMOKE   More often called *sea smoke* in Maine. Ocean vapors caused by winter air that is colder than the water. Vessels exposed to it, fishing boats in particular, can take on a coating of ice extreme enough to capsize them unless it is chopped or steam-hosed away.

❦ / ARSE BEHIND YER   Proper stance for proper work. If a lad is *gormy* about boring a hole, handling a line, and swinging a scythe, an older man will instruct him, "Here, put your *arse behind yer* and stand to it this way. . ."

🌻 / ARTISTIC PURPOSES    The full phrase is "mechanical and artistic purposes" and it comes from Maine's old dry law. Booze was outlawed except as prescribed by a friendly and understanding old family physician, or when it was to be used for "mechanical and artistic purposes." This latitude was often a blessing. In Maine conversations, *artistic purposes* means little more than devious intentions, a high-sounding substitute for something less than noble. Hank Woodbury, for example, used to go down to Boston on the *steamcars* for what he called *artistic purposes*.

🌻 / AS THE FELLER SAYS    An expression of disclaimer. The *feller* has never been identified, but he gets the blame and credit for a great many remarks: "It may rain but, *as the feller says*, it may not."

🌻 / ASH BREEZE    If the crew of a becalmed sailing vessel breaks out the sweeps and begins to row, the effort is called "making an *ash breeze*." Ash was the favored wood for oars. Hence, any make-do contrivance can be an *ash breeze*, and since outboard motors arrived the term has been heard inland for a paddle; an ash motor!

🌻 / AWAY    Any other place. To be *from away* is to be non-native. Aroostook County is an exception; up there to be *from away* is to be from "outside." There are niceties of distinction in the numerous Maine terms for non-Mainers which are best appreciated after attentive exposure; *from away* does suggest some effort to conform and belong. A man who has lived fifty years in your town and paid his taxes faithfully would hardly be called a *furriner*, and certainly not a *pilgrim*, but he will retain his non-Maine status of being *from away*.

❧ / AYEH   Or, *Eyah*, *Ayuh*, etc. The one word upon the entire face of the globe only true Mainers can say and use properly. It means "yes" or some variant thereof, and substitutes for the affirmative in a great variety of inflections. See *aye-yes* and *daow!*

❧ / AYE-YES   A possible explanation of the standard Maine *ayeh*. A generation or so ago a good many old Mainers would say *aye-yes*, a double affirmative that may have originated with the Scottish pioneers. A Scot might reply *aye*, and then out of deference to his non-Scottish audience add *yes*. A little imagination may suggest that over the years *aye-yes* could become *ayeh*. Compare the common use in Maine speech of *aye-yes*-nor-no for an indefinite and *weewaw* reply: "I asked him how he stood on the matter, and he didn't give me an *aye, yes,* nor no!"

# C

⁓⁓⁓
⁓⁓⁓

❦ / CABIN FEVER    Restlessness, and worse, that comes upon fire wardens and lone woodsmen who stay too long in camp. If not treated in time by a trip out to town, *cabin fever* may make one woods queer. The affliction also strikes offshore islanders during the winter.

❦ / CAGGED    To conk out (but see *caulk off*), to quit; "Hardly left my moorin' when the engine *cagged* out."

❦ / CALIBOGUS    A rum or brandy flip made with the usual spices, but unsweetened. Mainers use the word today for almost any kind of a non-temperance treat; even a can of beer.

❦ / CALK-BOOTS    Pronounce *cock;* the river driver's spike-soled foot gear. They were hi-cuts, coming up under the knee, very heavily constructed of excellent leather, and since they were meant to be worn in the water they were always kept well greased. The heels and soles were studded with about thirty-six steel spikes to each boot to give the wearer the footing he needed on rolling, pitching, bobbing long logs on the drive, or to make him secure on the booms and the sluicing platforms. About 1900, the Maine Legislature, reacting to howls from down-river dance halls, railroads, hotels, and other public places where calk-boots had torn up floors, etc., enacted a law forbidding the wearing of such boots other than in the line of logging duty. The enactment was followed by another howl from the river drivers, who held that wearing such boots was a status privilege and they were being abused. Holman Day fashioned a rhyme protesting the law, the last verse of which went:

> *For angels can just as well shed wings as*
> *a driver his spike-sole boots.*

❦ / CALL ON   For casual help. On a one-man farm there were many two-man tasks. A farmer needing an extra hand would *call on* his neighbor. *Calling on* is not the same as *changing work.* If payment is offered after *calling on*, a man would rightly reply, "Oh, no, that's all right; I may want to *call on* myself, some day." *Calling on* is also the term for asking welfare relief from the town; when a man couldn't swing his affairs and needed assistance, he would *call on.*

❦ / CALLED AFT   To die. A sailor not measuring up would be *called aft* to the captain's domain to be censured or punished; so a man would be *called aft* for final judgment. Railroad lingo has a similar expression; a brakeman deserving a reprimand is "called on the carpet." (Executive offices always had carpets on the floor.)

❦ / CALM AS A CLOCK   Composed, and particularly if relaxed and unexcited during general alarm. The old clock continues to tick away in the corner, regardless of household disturbances.

❦ / CAMP   The general word in Maine for a wilderness dwelling, no matter how elegant. It can be a one-room log cabin or the sumptuous retreat of land-owning executives. Not always, but in many instances Mainers will use *camp* for a building others would call a cottage. *Going to camp* does not mean tenting out in Maine, but moving to the cottage on the lake or in the woods for the season, or for a vacation. *Camp* also can mean a sizeable complex of buildings, such as a lumber or sporting *camp*.

❦ / CAMP COFFEE   Boiled coffee. The kind boiled in a pot or a No. 10 can over an open fire in the woods; but it is still *camp coffee* if made the same way on a range. People often ask, "Why does coffee always taste so much better out in the woods?" The answer is easy: camp coffee IS better! It's the best.

❦ / CAMP HUNTER   A *meatman*, which see. *Meatmen* in lumber camps considered *camp hunter* the preferred term.

❦ / CAMP INSPECTOR   A *chopper* who comes into *camp* to hire out, but for some reason doesn't stay too long, as if he were making an inspection visit. In the old days it didn't make much difference to the camp clerk, but with modern bookkeeping over social security, withholding forms, fringes, etc., it isn't much fun to do all the paper work and then find the *bahstid* lit out.

❦ / CAMPHOR BOTTLE   An early type of barometer, sometimes spelled "camphire." When the bottle became cloudy it foretold bad weather. This cloudiness gave the expression "feathers, streamers, and burgees," which is still heard to describe the making up of a storm.

❦ / CANOODLIN'   A Maine nicety for pleasurable dalliance atween the sexes, meaning mostly the casual kind— the kind in the *bushes* or behind the *chip pile*.

❦ / CANT   The sea term for changing a vessel's direction and the lumberman's term for rolling a log probably have a common origin. To walk with a *cant* is to have a list;

anything tipped and out of plumb has a *cant*. In logging, *canting* was done with the *canthook* or *peavey* (q.v.), and gave Maine its excellent expression for maximum felicity: "He's got the world by the tail on a downhill *cant!*" You can't have a much better *chance* than that!

❦ / CANT DOG   The *dog* is the hook that bites into a log on both the *canthook* and the *peavey*. (See *peavey* for a fuller explanation.) The similar hooks that hold a log on a sawmill carriage are also called *dogs*, and the word *dog* is used for numerous other mechanical contrivances that do the same kind of work. A man coming upon a crew at work, and offering to help them, may say, "Here, let me get my *dogs* into that!" It is the *dog* that gives the *canthook* and the *peavey* their *purchase* (which see).

❦ / CANTEL   See *quintal* and *kental*.

❦ / CANTHOOK   The tool for rolling or *canting* logs. It was a shaft or pole with a *dog* attached by a ring, and when the *dog* gripped into the log a man could exert great force by the simple principle of leverage. The *canthook* predated Maine lumbering, and was used in Maine until the *peavey* was designed, after which the *peavey* superseded it not only in Maine but throughout the lumbering world. The differences between a simple *canthook* and the more efficient *peavey* are discussed under *peavey*.

❦ / CANUCK   The word originated in Maine lumber camps for a French-Canadian working in the Maine woods. It did not mean a French-Canadian anywhere else, and when a British Columbia hockey team called itself the *Canucks* the word was far afield. Over the years, as *Canuck* took on an objectionable tone, the word has been superseded somewhat by *Kaybecker*. This is perhaps as good a time as any to set down the ethnic generalizations used in early Maine lumber camps:

Scandinavians were "squareheads."

Poles were "pole-locks."

Slavs and sub-Slavs were "bohunks." (Hungarians, Czechs, Slovaks, etc., were recognized much later.)

Non-French Canadians who came from Prince Edward Island, New Brunswick, and Nova Scotia were indiscriminately called *Pea-Eyes*, from the initials of Prince Edward Island. Newfoundlanders were "Newfies." French-speaking Canadians from Québec were *Canucks*.

🌿 / CAPE COD TURKEY    A salt fish dinner, usually codfish. (See *Kennebec turkey*.)

🌿 / CAPFUL O' WIND    A gentle sailing breeze, and thus one aspect of a pleasant day.

🌿 / CAPITAL    Top-grade, top-notch, first-class, *finest kind*. A *capital* ship was originally a warship of first rank in size and armament.

🌿 / CAP'N    In Maine usage, *captain* was the title of a merchant master mariner; *skipper* was reserved for fishing captains. Much of this difference has disappeared. Now even Navy crewmen speak of their commanding officer as *skipper*. No bilge rat would have offered that indignity in the days of sail. He wouldn't dast.

🌿 / CAPTAIN'S COMPANION    A chest or locker maintained in a ship captain's cabin for socializing in ports of call. It didn't do any harm to invite customs officers for a drink. These chests were made mostly by ship's carpenters to cheat the tedium of a long voyage, and they were beautifully constructed. There would be decanters for whiskey, gin, and rum, and an assortment of glasses riding neatly in felt-covered trays. Sometimes silver and pewter mugs instead of glasses. A similar handy item, intended to solace gentlemen on a stagecoach ride, was called a "traveler's companion." Both, if authentic, will fetch a pretty dollar at today's antique prices. Since Maine was traditionally dry, there was always snide comment about teetotalers who kept a *companion*.

❧ / CAR   A lobster car. A floating crate, often large enough to serve as a wharf or float, in which lobsters are stored to await shipment to market. The slatted sides permit free movement of tidewater to keep the lobsters healthy. Not to be confused with a *pound*, and not the same as a lobster *crate*; the latter holds 100 pounds of live lobsters for shipment to market. Strangers to the word are often amused to hear Mainers use *car* for a wheelless contrivance mostly under water.

❧ / CAREEN   A vessel under sail in a good wind, showing much of her windward bottom, is said to *careen*; this is also the term for grounding out a boat between tides for repairs. Mainers tend to use *careen* for *career*. A dictionary will show the difference in meanings. Whether a woman is *careering along* or *careening along* when she strides rapidly up the street is hardly worth a semantic argument; but if her bottom is prominent, *careening* is the correct nautical allusion.

❧ / CARIBOU   A northwest Maine and Québec cocktail, the drinking of which initiates one into Maine's famous *Caribou* Club. Everybody north of Greenville and west of Millinocket is a member. The only hint as to the ingredients in a *Caribou* came one time from M. Benoit Caron, proprietor of Boundary Motel at Ste. Aurélie, who told Felix Fernald, "A *Caribou* contains about everything except whiskey."

❧ / CARPENTER   In Maine, generally, a house *carpenter* (dentists are sometimes called tooth *carpenters*). A *carpenter* who works on boats is a shipwright, a ship- or boat-*car-*

*penter*, and a boat-builder. The ship's *carpenter* went to sea as a crew member, and besides being ready to make repairs if needed, he passed his time building *captain's companions*, ditty boxes, and sea chests.

❦ / CARRY    Preferred in Maine to portage; for carrying canoe and *wangan* around a falls or overland. The word appears in numerous place names—*Carry* Brook, *Carry* Island, *Carry* Pond, *Carrying* Place, *Carrying*place Cove, *Carry* Lake—some twenty-three altogether. The East, Middle, and West *Carry* Ponds were used by Benedict Arnold to move his army up the Kennebec in 1775. Perhaps Maine's best known *carry* is North East *Carry*, starting point for wilderness travel at the north end of Moosehead Lake. Until recently, North East *Carry* was a U.S. Post Office.

❦ / CAST ABOUT    Sailor's term for trying different courses when in doubt about a ship's position; thus, to consider various possible answers to a problem. It also means to look around, as to *cast about* for something to do.

❦ / CASTING BREAD    This refers to making yeast bread at sea or in the woods, as distinguished from making hot biscuits, muffins, johnnycake, etc. Of several explanations of the term's origin, the most likely one comes from the way Cook worked. He would mix his wet ingredients in a bowl, and then *cast* them into the open flour barrel, atop the flour. With his hands, he would work in as much flour as the mixture would take up, and then he would *cast* the dough on his board for kneading.

❦ / CATCH    Interestingly applied to punishment and instruction of a kind: "That kid'll *catch* it soon's I get my hands on him!" Also in the past tense: "Homer *caught* Hell when he got home."

❦ / CAT RIG  A fore and aft mainsail set on boom and gaff and stepped well forward, almost off the stem of the boat. A simple and easily handled rig for small harbor craft, and for young and learning sailors. Any simple contrivance or situation is a *cat rig*: "I *cat-rigged* a make-do."

❦ / CAT SPRUCE  A spruce with attractive bluish tinge, but having an odor suggesting a kitty pan. The coastal and island spruce which makes the Maine shoreline so beautiful from sea. Botanically it's the white spruce, *Picea glauca (Moench) Voss*. Sometimes called a skunk spruce.

❦ / CATCH A CRAB  To mishandle oars while rowing, so that there is a splash of water. Mainers transfer the term to any mistake, error, bungling, or *gormy* miscue.

❦ / CAUGHT  Frozen, as a water pipe. "If we don't get a fire started the pipes'll *catch!*" "The pump was *caught* this morning."

❦ / CAULK OFF  To take a nap. The term comes from the shipyard; a man's snoring is likened to the noise of *caulking* mallets. *Cork off*, *conk off*, and *conk out* are, of course, misuses of the correct imagery.

❦ / CAUTION  A noun for a person of comical bent: "That Madge, she's a *caution!*"

❦ / CEILING  The inside planking or sheathing of a vessel's hull, sometimes misspelled "sealing." Mainers like to drop final *g*'s, but they never do on *ceiling*.

❦ / CHAIN  A barrier on a private road to keep out the public, especially on wilderness lands. Some may be passed by paying toll; some require a company permit. Some are attended, others have locks, and authorized travelers are issued duplicate keys. A checkpoint. Some maps designate them as gates, but usually the barrier is a *chain* or cable that is dropped to the ground to let a vehicle pass over it. The French-Canadian woodsmen give the term a delightful "shine" sound.

❧ / CHALDRON, CALDRON   A measure of about thirty bushels, used for lime and coal. Mainers liked to call it *witch's chaldron*.

❧ / CHANCE   In the sense of opportunity, referring to the area where a chopper is cutting trees. Paid by board feet or cords, a man would have a good *chance* or a poor *chance* depending on the growth.

❧ / CHANCE ALONG   To coastal sailors, a *chance along* is a fair wind with favorable weather.

❧ / CHANGING WATER   When lobsters are not crawlin' (see *crawl*), the lobsterman who goes to *haul* and performs the maneuver of bringing up an empty trap to rebait and re-set will say that he has *changed the water* in his pots. Hence any unproductive and unrewarding activity is *changing water*.

❧ / CHANGING WORK   Exchanging work. A farmer would help his neighbor make hay, and in return the neighbor would help him cut firewood. There was good gentleman's agreement as to how much of one kind of work balanced off another. *Changing work* had an obligation to repay; see *call on*.

❧ / CHANTEY MAN   A seaman who could lead the crew in singing the rhythm songs that went with working a ship. Accordingly, someone with good voice who brightens up a party.

❦ / CHARLEY NOBLE   A galley stovepipe aboard ship: hence, any flue or chimney. The allusion is thus explained: "The First Lord of the Admiralty acknowledges your recent inquiry, and begs to state in reply that according to the records in the archives of His Majesty's Navy, an American Master Merchant Mariner, in the early 1800's, a Mr. Charles Noble of Nobleboro, of Maine, discovered one day at sea that his galley stovepipe was made of brass, and he gave an order that it should be kept bright." So, wherever a gleaming brass flue was seen at sea—there would be Charley Noble! This Maine-ism has gone the world around.

❦ / CHEW   Used for "talk" in many Maine expressions. To "*chew* somebody out" is to give him a piece of your mind. It can mean "protest": "He *chewed* a bit when he got the bill, but he paid it." Also it means to meditate: "After he *chewed* it over, he saw my point." (There is no connection here with the offensive "jew," to haggle over a price, to "jew down." The only time "down" is used with *chew* is in the phrase, "to *chew* anybody up and down." This means to bawl him out in good shape.) To *chew* the rag is to chatter idly, to gossip.

❦ / CHINA CLAY   The Portland waterfront has had active *china clay* docks for years, and many have wondered why so much *china clay* is imported to Maine when we have no potteries of consequence. *China clay* is used in the manufacture of high-grade printing papers.

❦ / CHINSING   The whole hull of a wooden boat is *caulked*, but a minor repair job of driving oakum or cotton into a small seam or crack is called *chinsing*. Thus, any small effort or temporary fix-it. To give a girl-friend a *chinsing* is exploratory.

❦ / CHIPS   After about so many hulls, any Maine ship- or boatyard accumulated a *chip* pile and it has become a romantic reference. To take your girl "behind the *chip* pile" is suggestive. (See *bushes.*) Less romantically, *chips* are the first step in converting pulpwood into paper. Forward-looking executives have already predicted the day will come when trees will be *chipped* in the forest and transported to the mill in pipelines. Considerable wood is already being transported in *chip* form, and the Maine Central Railroad operates a number of *chip*-cars.

❧ / CHOPPER    The Maine word for a lumberjack or timberjack. Even today, with chainsaws and tree-snippers, they are *choppers*. *Lumberjack* and timberjack originated to the west'ard. To have the "appetite of a *chopper*" is to be ravenous.

❧ / CHOREBOY    Even if he's an older man, the term for the errand runner and general utility hand in a sporting camp. Much like the *bullcook* of the lumber camp. He fills woodboxes, makes the mail and dump runs, and in former times when Maine was dry he usually could find the guest a bottle. The job was once remunerative in tips, and high school boys liked to get it for the summer, but the old-time camp that hired *choreboys* has been on the wane for some years.

❧ / CHOWDER    In addition to edible chowder, this word has the Maine meaning of wobbling, chattering, wavering, vibrating, and fretting. A drill that wobbles as it bores a hole is said to *chowder*, not only as to its wobbling but as to the noise it makes. Wind can rattle shutters until somebody will say, "The whole house *chowdered* all night."

❧ / CHUM    Chopped bait, scattered in the water to attract fish to the hook or net. Anglers for tuna have a meat grinder on the coaming and crank *chum* overboard as they troll. *To chum* is to entice, coax, wheedle. Also, Mainers like the word for a close friend of the same sex: "He and his two *chums* drove to Boston."

🌺 / CHURCH LOT  A reserved wilderness lot. When a Mainer says that he shot his deer on the *church lot*, out-of-staters may wince at a seeming violation of sanctity. When Mother Massachusetts first surveyed Maine wilderness townships and offered them for sale, four lots of 320 acres each were reserved for public use, income from them to go to educational and religious purposes. After Maine achieved statehood the four lots were changed to one lot of 1000 acres. Whenever such a township became populated enough to organize a government, these reserved lots were disposed of by the voters, and the money used for church and school. In townships still unorganized, the reserved lots are administrated by the State Forest Commissioner, and money received from stumpage or recreational leases goes to the common school fund. In many unorganized townships the reserved lots remain unsurveyed, and are simply an undivided portion of the area. In others, they have been set off, which is why one may prudently go hunting on a church lot. Edward Everett Hale's short story, "My Double and How He Undid Me," gives an amusing account of how one Maine *ministerial lot* was taken up. *Church lot, school lot,* and *ministerial lot* are variants of the correct term, *reserved lot.* The existence of many such *reserved lots,* whether set off or not, has attracted the attention of those seeking more recreational areas, and legislation may ensue which will change their status.

🌺 / CLABBIDS  Clapboards.

🌺 / CLAM (1)  In the perennial dispute between New England Clam Chowder and Manhattan Clam Chowder, the most important fact is usually ignored—two very different *clams* are at issue. Nobody in Maine has ever called a *quahog* a clam, or made a clam chowder from quahogs. New

Yorkers, contrariwise, think quahogs are clams. To a Mainer, the *clam* is the soft-shell and long-neck bivalve; he considers the *quahog* hard-shelled and short-necked. The question of adding vegetables to a Manhattan "clam" chowder makes sense to most Mainers; they realize a quahog needs all the help he can get. A chowder made from quahogs is, in Maine, a "quahog chowder." (For the pronunciation of *quahog*, consider this: R. P. T. Coffin, the poet, and his wife once did a charade at a party. They came in on all fours, side by side, grunting like two pigs. The answer: *quahog*.)

❧ / CLAM (2)  "As secretive as a *clam*," meaning to keep your affairs to yourself, is heard in Maine without probable derivation from the classical Latin adverb *clam*, meaning secretly, in private. It's just an interesting coincidence. The *clam*, as known to Mainers, produces many similes: as still as a clam, as cool as a clam, as moist as a clam, as thoughtful as a clam, tighter'n a clam (either well secured as with a lock, or close-mouthed). Consider, "He stuck out a *clammy* hand and sneered."

❧ / CLAMBAKE  Prehistoric Mainers held clam bakes 5000 years ago. Little circles of round stones where they cooked fish have been found in the shell heaps. The stones thus arranged were heated by fire, embers raked off, and the fish tossed on the rocks to cook. A covering of rockweed would hold down the steam. Today a piece of sailcloth is added, and the *bake* will include such far-fetched things as weenies, sweetcorn, eggs, potatoes, &c. If only lobsters are baked, the term *clambake* still applies, but clams should always be used because it is their juices that make the best steam. The first *clambake* on record as being attended by Englishmen was held at Popham Beach in 1607. The term *clambake* is sometimes erroneously used for a *shore dinner* (see *shore dinner*). A *regular clambake* (see *reg'lar*) is used in Maine speech for any kind of hi-jinks fun, even for a schoolhouse dance or a close basketball game.

❧ / CLAM DIGGER'S HANDS   A unit of heat measurement, like the BTU and the calorie. As cold as a *clam digger's hands* is about as cold as you can get unless you add ". . . in January." (See *cold as a dog* . . . ) "Affable? The Helleewas! He give me a look as cold as a *clam digger's hands*." Another occupational simile used by Mainers in the same way is "cold as a well-digger's elbows"—although sometimes a word for the human posterior is substituted for elbows.

❧ / CLAM, HAPPY AS A   The ultimate in jubilation and contentment. The full expression is *happy as a clam* at high tide. When the tide is full, nobody is digging clams.

❧ / CLAM JUICE   Marketed as *bouillon*, it is called *clam juice* on the Maine coast. In canning clams the excess sea water from the cooking was formerly run back into the tide, but a thoughtful packer once put some in jars to see if it would sell. It did. It is said to have efficacy as a morning-after pick-me-up, and often is a breakfast substitute for fruit juice. It is also a superb condiment for lobster stew and fish chowder; add some (not too much!) to your next effort and see the difference!

❧ / CLEAN BILL OF HEALTH   The certificate required from the port health officer before a vessel could depart, and making it easier to be certified at the next port of call. In present usage it means free of blame and complicity, a clear record. "They thought the Wilkins kid was stealing things, but after an investigation the police gave him a *clean bill of health*."

❧ / CLEAR GRAVY   Extra profit, or an unexpected bonus. *Gravy* as an embellishment is standard (compare "gravy-train") but adding *clear* seems a Maine-ism.

❧ / CLEARN   Extra fillip for *clear:* "He's a hundred percent honest *clearn* through."

❧ / CLEVER   To describe intelligence in a farm animal; clean and *clever* is the kind of animal to buy. The word *smart* is avoided by Mainers in this sense; it suggests *smart-alecky.*

❧ / CLIM   Preterit of *climb:* "He *clim* a tree." Certainly to be preferred to *clomb,* and easier to handle than *climbed.*

❧ / CLIMBING MARCH HILL   Winter-weary Mainers, hopeful of spring, come through February to *climb March hill;* after the middle of March things are down-hill. Fannie Jordan once said, "Seems-if I February all right, and *climb March hill,* I last out the year."

❧ / CLIP AND CLEAN   Completely: "The jolt took out his front tooth *clip and clean.*"

❧ / CLIPPER   The famous clipper ships contributed much lore to Maine and much imagery to the speech. "She's a *clipper!*" means she walks well, wears her clothes well, carries her head high, etc. But there is much misunderstanding about clippers. Their period of usefulness was relatively short and they were limited to cargoes where speed was more important than tonnage. They were three-masted, fore and aft rigged with spanker, and their height of sail was lofty. Their length was disproportionate to their beam and the hulls were deeply designed to accommodate the high stand of sail. The Maine shipyards soon sophisticated the design into the extreme *clipper,* and then into the *Down-easter* (which see). Most lingering Maine references to *clippers* allude to women and similar things of beauty—fast, trim, neat, tall, showy, dressy, clean, etc. *Clipper* days are hardly more than the "good old days."

❦ / CLOSE THE DOOR   Said of somebody who falls overboard and goes completely under: "He went right in and
*closed the door!*"

❦ / CLOVE HITCH   The same knot the Boy Scouts
learn in the first lesson, ideal for making a line to a *spile* or
a tent-stay to a stake. In Maine transferral, it denotes a situation not easy to get out of: "She got a *clove hitch* on the
poor *joker*, and it looks like wedding bells!"

❦ / CLUB   To anchor a ship. Also a short boom used
on a headsail. A jib or forestaysail may be *club*-footed so it
can be handled by a single line instead of one on each side
of the mast. Easily transferred to crippled feet on a person.

❦ / COASTER   A ship that carried cargo port to port
along the coast, as distinguished from one that crossed
oceans. However, the term included West Indies trade. A
*coaster* was not deep-water bound. Also, the captain or
crewman of such a vessel. To Mainers, *coasting* for moving
along leisurely does not derive from sliding on snow.

❦ / COCK   See *calk-boots*. One folklorist with poor
ears suggests Mainers call their calk-boots *cork* boots, but
*cock* is more like it. See *cod* for a clue as to how this sound
should come out.

❦ / COCK SHOP   A lumbercamp office. The beautiful
forest-based pileated woodpecker is known as cock-o'-the-
woods, so the beautiful boss of the operation would be in
the *cock shop*.

❦ / COD   The name of this important food fish is
pronounced identically in Maine to denote a string (cord);
128 cubic feet of firewood (cord); or several harmonized
musical notes (chord). It is also what the crow did.

❦ / CODDE  Found on old charts and in history books, it's a bend or a curving cove in a tidal river.

❦ / COD END  The bag end of a trawl net. If somebody gets bagged in the *cod end*, he's caught up for fair.

❦ / COD HEAD AND MACKEREL TAIL  To describe a vessel broad in the bow and tapering to a slim stern.

❦ / COILED HIS ROPES  Died. A good seaman coiled his lines neatly after work.

❦ / COLD ARSE  An island off Port Clyde, so named by vivid-speaking Mainers to explain the condition of a fisherman who was marooned there one winter night.

❦ / COLD AS A DOG AND THE WIND NORTHEAST  A most excellent term to show the magic and charm with which Mainers adorn their speech, and the title of a book by Ruth Moore. There is nothing in God's great world so cold as a short-haired dog faithfully sitting with his tail on the ice as he gazes after his beloved master, who has told him to stay. Stay he does, shivering until his master is out of sight, and still shivering he sits there quite a time in hopeful presumption his owner may turn back—or perhaps change his mind and take him along. To describe anything as being cold as that dog is a pinnacle of vivid speech and poetic beauty. But even this lily may be artfully gilded! The northeast wind is Maine's *narsty* blow; the one that brings the blizzards and the ripping rainstorms that peel shingles from the barn. That dog, now, is really cold.

❦ / COLLOPS, COLLOPES  Pieces of clear meat without bones or fat; similar to and probably derived from cutlets.

❦ / COMBUSTIBLE  A gale of wind approaching hurricane velocity.

❦ / COME-ALONG   A block-and-tackle or winch used horizontally to move heavy objects over the ground, such as a building or a boat in its cradle.

❦ / COME DAY, GO DAY, GOD SEND SUNDAY   Used in the beginning to describe an indifferent seaman who looked forward to the lighter labors of the Lord's Day, this phrase is now used for clock-watchers and whistle-listeners.

❦ / COME UP ALL STAVIN'   To survive and endure some misfortune, but not scot-free: "Watch out with that bike, Sonny, or you'll *come up all stavin'*!" A contraction of *stave in*, to puncture and break the planks of a vessel or the staves of a cask, and also used in the past tense, *stove*: After a whale capsized a boat the log entry said, ". . . dory slightly stove."

❦ / COMEUPPANCE   A happening, and not a happy one. One's just deserts. "Myra's rich aunt died, and Myra sure got her *comeuppance* when it turned out the old lady left everything to a church!"

❦ / COMFITS   Confections with centers of fruit or nuts and coatings of many layers of sugar. In early Maine days *comfits* were candies of any kind. "Just like takin' a *comfit*" describes a pleasant, easy-to-do experience.

❦ / COMFORTABLE   Pronounced *cum-f't'bl*. A variation for comforter, a quilt or puff for winter sleeping, but not a blanket. It's about fifty-fifty that Mainers will say comforter or *comfortable*.

❦ / COMMON   When Mainers say somebody is *common*, they mean he is unpretentious, a real sort who doesn't put on airs: "Real *common*, same as us." It is high praise.

❧ / COMMON TALK   No longer gossip because everybody knows it: "They're always lovey-dovey in front of people, but it's *common talk* they don't get along."

❧ / CONNECTIONS   Relatives in general: "He's got cousins, aunts, and assorted *connections* all over Knox County." The word is also used as elsewhere for useful contacts in social and business affairs.

❧ / CONSTABLE   Usually given the English sound of *cun-st'bl*, this is still the basic law officer in the *township*. He may be dignified as chief of police, but in town affairs he remains in the records as *constable*. In addition to his duties as peace officer, he performs some civil work: he posts the notices for town meetings.

❧ / CONVENIENCE   Maine has many euphemisms for the toilet and matters related thereto. Some are considered in their proper places in this lexicon. The *convenience* is the backhouse, privy, outhouse, roost, retreat, observatory, nook, cubicle, sacristy, chapel, throne-room, meditation chamber, etc. It may also be the pot; i.e., mug, jug (chamber mug and thunder jug), receptacle, receiver, utensil, vessel.

❧ / COODLE   A word of unexplained origin, this is a small cove or *backwater*, most often one used by a sawmill for storing logs. (Worms won't get under the bark if pine logs are kept floating.)

❧ / COOKEE   An assistant to a lumber-camp cook. He serves at table, washes dishes, and aspires to becoming a cook. In the days of lumbering on snow, the *cookee* was the cock-crow; he awakened the men by hammering on his "come-and-get-it"—a sawblade or length of metal used as a dinner-gong. He was expected to have some merry jingle to put the crew in good pre-dawn, sub-zero humor, and would call out as he banged, "Wake up and hear the pretty birdies sing!"

❦ / COON CAT   The Maine *coon cat* was sometimes thought to be a cross between a cat and a raccoon. The truth is that Maine captains brought home all manner of cats from around the world, and the *coon cat* is a descendant of Angora cats brought from Turkey. Cat fanciers like the Maine *coon cat*, but he's common enough so most Mainers aren't that much impressed.

❦ / COOP   The chicken-coop of more southerly states will likely be called a hen-pen in Maine. Although a Mainer may use *coop* for closing up his poultry, he will certainly use the word to describe his being *cooped* up all winter with a lame back.

❦ / COOPER   The *oo* sound is shortened in Maine speech; about the only approximate phonetic attempt might be *koup-peh*. The same for the related word, hooper, and also for the proper names. The earliest Maine forest-based industry was a cooperage at Pipestave Landing on the Piscataqua River, and in active trading days barrels were mighty important in handling fish, molasses, and rum. In the early 1800s the new potato acreage in Aroostook also needed barrels. From the way barrels are set up and hooped together, a man briskly doing nothing much is often compared to a "*cooper* goin' 'round a bar'l."

❦ / COOT   On the Maine coast, the American scoter, a saltwater duck whose habits give us numerous similes, and whose athletic flesh is legendary. He will not fly over land, so will wing miles down one cove and up another to reach a spot 50 yards over a neck of land; hence, to be "crazy as a *coot*" is not complimentary. *Coot* are edible and in the hands of an understanding coastal cook can be rendered delicious, but the old Maine recipe for cooking a *coot* runs, "Put an ax in the pot, and when you can stick a fork in the ax the *coot* is done." Sometimes, ". . . then throw away the *coot* and eat the ax." Before conservation laws were taken seriously by Maine fishermen, many barrels of *coot* were salted down each fall for winter use. In shooting most ducks, some stealth is required, but if you stand in a skiff on the open ocean and wave your hat and shout, *coot* will fly over to see what's going on. A much loved elderly man may be referred to by his friends as "an old *coot*."

❦ / COPPER   To sheathe with copper sheeting, but more likely, to apply copper-content paint to the hull of a boat below the water line. This discourages marine growth. Groundin' out for *copperin'* is done periodically by fishermen, who don't usually *haul* their boats for winter, as the Mahogany Set does, and since the copper paint can be applied to the damp hull and the boat refloated at once, it's usually a one-tide job.

❦ / CORDUROY   From the ribbing on corduroy cloth, a road or bridge in the Maine woods made with logs laid crosswise of traffic on stringers. On log-hauls, the bumpy surface would be covered with dirt, snow, and ice, and rendered excellently smooth, but otherwise *corduroy* construction would jounce travelers out of their socks. To "hit the *corduroy*" is to experience a wild surprise, even to get your *comeuppance*. Holman Day has a verse about an old codger riding in a buggy with a pail of molasses between his knees, and when the horse hit the *corduroy* the old man wound up in the ditch with his head stuck in the bucket.

❦ / CORFISH   Whole cod pickled in brine; the "soft cure" of early English colonists and Maine's major export for a long time.

❦ / Corn shop   Now a completely lost industry. Maine once packed tremendous quantities of cream-style sweetcorn; almost every town had a *corn shop* and some had several. In late August and early September the *corn shop* was right *out straight*, and its activity was extremely important to the Maine farming community.

❦ / Corn sweat   Today, a *corn sweat* is an effort by cajolement and insistence to persuade somebody to your way of thinking: "The folks on Birch Hill really put on a *corn sweat* to get their road paved." The expression comes from an old home remedy for a fever. Steamed or boiled ears of yellow corn were laid alongside a patient with a fever, and when the patient was well covered with blankets he'd burst into a sweat in no time. Just for fun, see *fish draft*.

❦ / Corn weather   Hot July and August weather, just right for forcing the sweetcorn so important to Maine farmers. *Corn weather* is when the farmer sleeps "nekkid," without even a sheet. 'Twas said he could lie abed and hear the corn grow.

❦ / Corner   Certain Maine towns where the business section formed at the meeting of highways (a *corner*) have retained this term for the complex of stores, post office, barber shop, etc. "Going to the *corner*" means going to the *store*.

❦ / Corporation   A village *corporation*. Sub-division of a Maine *township*, created to provide special services. The Bustin Island Corporation exists in Freeport to handle the affairs of islanders apart from the affairs of the rest of the town.

❦ / Corpse candles   St. Elmo's fire; a slow discharge of atmospheric electricity making a glow at mastheads of vessels and other tall objects. The macabre attitude of Maine mariners to the glow, making it a bad omen, is inconsistent with the older name of St. Elmo's fire. Early Mediterranean sailors believed the glow proved their patron saint was on guard.

❧ / COUNTER A legal lobster, or *keeper*. Maine's double-guage law permits keeping only those larger than 3 3/16ths inches from eye socket to base of tail, but not over 5 inches. The "shorts" and the "breeders" must be returned to the ocean, so a Maine lobsterman catches many more lobsters than he may *count*.

❧ / COUNTY, THE Aroostook is the only Maine county which stands by itself with a *The*. People live in York County, and in Somerset County, but Aroostookians live in *The County*. Known also as the Inland Empire and the Potato Empire. Aroostook is very different in many ways from the rest of Maine, and has much lore and many expressions deriving from her peculiar economy and her isolated geography. No doubt the Queen of our shire fleet. Aroostookians all agree the *The* is merited.

❧ / Cow BEEF See *bullbeef*. The Superannuated Maine dairy cow, readied for table, was not always a blessing.

❧ / Cow PUNCHER A doctor of veterinary medicine, except that in earlier times the "doctor" may have been a presumptive title. The term was used in Maine long before they had cows in Wyoming. The first stomach of a cow is called the rumen, and sometimes from eating apples or perhaps some fermented grain or pomace a cow would bloat, a condition known as impaction of the rumen. Standard treatment was to "punch" the cow with an awl or the small blade of a jackknife. This released the gas, and bossy would soon recover. As recently as the 1920s a Maine veterinarian was referring to himself pleasantly as "one of the last real old *cow punchers* left in the state!"

❦ / Cow's TAIL    The frayed ends of a rope, looking very like a cow's tail. The straggly hair of a child may be called a *cow's tail. Irish pennants.*

❦ / Cow, THE    Maine woods levity for the ubiquitous can of evaporated milk; as in the table request, "Please pass *the cow!*" Lack of refrigeration made the old-time woodsmen rely on tinned bossies. When *the cow* is called for, the standard reply is, "Send down the milk, the calf's blattin'!"

❦ / Cow's TONGUE    From the rough and smooth sides of a cow's tongue; a two-faced person. A hypocrite. Also, a gruff old codger who is soft-hearted.

❦ / Cow TRADE    From the traditional dickering that went on when two farmers swapped cows, a term for any kind of a deal, and particularly one befraught with chicanery. A man who is a sharp trader in any commodity will be described as "knowing his way around in a *cow trade.*"

❦ / Cow YARD TAR    One of many Maine-isms for a saltwater farmer. A fisherman who grows a good garden or a farmer who goes clamming. "Hayfield lobsterman" and "straw-sailor" are similar terms. Depending on context, these terms may be either complimentary or not, and the combination is so important to Maine that the farmer and the sailor share prominence on the official state seal.

❦ / CoyDOG    A coined Maine word to describe an animal found in the woods—this one real. Western coyotes came via Canada, and crossing with domestic dogs they entered Maine along the Québec border. When first sighted they were thought to belong to the *Shagimaw* and *Fillieloo* category, but biologists studied the cranium structure and confirmed that they truly are coyote-dogs, or *coydogs*.

❦ / CRACKED  A bit foolish; interchangeable with *warped*, and quite likely deriving also from lumbering, where a weather-crack reduces the quality of lumber. But perhaps from *cracked* crockery.

❦ / CRADLE  Besides its usual meanings, this is a term Mainers use for a Y-shaped rope hitch when towing a canoe. A line directly off the bow causes a keelless canoe to sideweave; the *cradle* does the towing from the forward gunwales just abaft the bow, and the craft will follow steadily. Lobstermen also use a *cradle* hitch to attach warps to their traps to gain a direct pull.

❦ / CRANK, CRANKY  Said of a vessel which doesn't handle properly, whether from poor design, dirty bottom, poorly stowed cargo, or whatever. Thus, a baby who fusses, and an older person who doesn't like to conform.

❦ / CRATE  A container, and its amount. A lobster *crate* is designed for 100 pounds, and a *crate* can thus mean 100 pounds. Transferred to many metaphors: "He talked for an hour, biggest *crate* of hogwash I ever heard."

❦ / CRAWL  An important word if you would converse with a Maine lobsterman. Lobsters, moving on the ocean floor, are said to *crawl*. So you do not ask a lobsterman if he is catching any lobsters; you ask him esoterically if they are *crawlin'*. "They *crawlin'* good?" will always be answered in the negative by any pure-bred Maine lobsterman. (See *daow!*)

❦ / CREATURES  The womenfolks. English-speaking Mainers borrowed this from the archaic French of the St. John Valley, where it is still the generic word for the ladies

—*les créatures*. As used by the Acadians, it is familiar and never employed slurringly, although it obviously has an undertone of masculine superiority. (Incidentally, *créature* in French is a feminine noun, and in the old dictionaries is defined as *tout être créé*.) In English, as in French, the word will be heard in some such sentence as this: "Run and tell the *creatures* (i.e., your mother, aunts, and sisters) that Uncle Josh is staying for supper!"

❦ / CRIBBER    A horse who stands in his stall in meditative abstraction and absently chews on the woodwork. (Maine farmers use the word *crib* for a manger or feed-box: "Clean the *orts* out of the cow's *crib*!")

❦ / CRIBWORK, CRIB WHARF    Logs laid alternately as if making a cabin—but not notched so they come closely together—is cribwork. The interior is filled with rock and earth to make a wharf or pier. The same construction was used for *boom* piers on fresh water.

❦ / CRICK    A *creek*, if a Mainer uses that term for a brook; but otherwise a muscle hang-up: "I got a *crick* in my neck and couldn't turn my head."

❦ / CROWD    A word much loved by Mainers for "force" in various degrees. To *crowd* your luck is to hope for more than is likely to accrue. Workmen will *crowd* a cupboard into a kitchen corner to leave more wall space by a window. Groceries will be *crowded* into a bag. A boss may *crowd* his help by giving them too much to do: "I'll do better work if you don't *crowd* me!" (See *crowder*, below.)

❦ / CROWDER    A horse who resents the farmer's intrusion into his stall, and leans against him. When a farmer takes down a bridle, the horse knows very well he's about to work, and in his smarty way he waits until the farmer is between him and the wall, then acts accordingly. The farmer is thus *crowded*. The remedy for a *crowder* is to carry a short stick about five inches longer than you are wide, and let the fool horse *crowd* that! There is no evidence that a *crowder* ever *crowded* a stick twice.

❧ / CROWN   A forest fire so intense it travels through the tops of trees is said to *crown* out; the most difficult of woods fires to bring under control.

❧ / CROZE   The groove on a barrel stave which fits the *head*. Shook for casks was shipped knock-down, with "staves croze, hoops shaved, and headings ready." A person who won't conform, or fit, may be said to be having a mite of *croze* trouble, and as the allusion comes from a lost past the word is sometimes thought to be a misuse of craze or crazy.

❧ / CRUISE   Apart from nautical application, *cruise* is the word for inspecting a stand of timber for management purposes. A lot is *cruised* to estimate yield by varieties, to lay out roads, and to select a spot for a camp. The man who does this is a *cruiser*, sometimes timber *cruiser*. L. L. Bean, whose "Maine Hunting Shoe" made him a fortune, also offered a "Maine Cruising Shoe," a lighter boot meant for timberland use. More than a few customers presumed this was a shoe for yachting.

❧ / CRY-BABY   A soft sugar cookie with a filling of mince-meat, raisins, nuts, jam, etc. A filled cookie. (See *Jonah*.)

❧ / CUDDY   A storage space forward in a small boat, never so large as a cabin or a house. Thus, any cupboard or closet usually thought of as a catch-all. Mainers usually call it a cuddy-hole.

❦ / CULBERT   Culvert.

❦ / CULCH, CULTCH   This word's basic meaning is the debris to which young oysters attach themselves but in Maine it has always meant rubbish, junk, and any accumulation in attic, shed, and cellar. It may or may not have value. Children may be told to pick up their *culch* and get to bed. Reading matter in bad taste is *culch*. Po' white trash can be *culch*. A poor cook's unsavory offering is *culch*. Silly speech is *culch*. Many times Maine attics have yielded *culch* which antique buyers are happy to pay for. A much used and variously applied Maine favorite.

❦ / CUSS   A contraction of curse; to *cuss* somebody out. *Cussid* ("I can't get the *cussid* thing to run!") is thus accursed. The word is also used for a person: "He's a congenial *cuss*," or, "You can't fool an old *cuss* like me!"

❦ / CUT BAIT   It means an alternative, but a sort of choice without a difference. Aboard a fishing boat, everybody must *fish or cut bait*, or otherwise go ashore. Do one thing or the other.

❦ / CUT CAT   The catastrophic consequences of feline castration, appearing in many, many Maine expressions: As frustrated as a *cut cat*, as lazy as a *cut cat*, as fat as a *cut cat*.

❦ / CUTOFF   A short cut: "Take the *cutoff* at the schoolhouse." Also, a tract of timberland which has been harvested. Sometimes called a cutover.

❦ / CUTWATER   That part of any vessel's prow that cleaves the water, but more particularly the molded brass or copper on bow and stern of a canvas canoe. Old-time canoe makers had a crank machine for turning them out, but the art is long lost. Canoe buffs who restore a beautiful old cedar canoe can still get all the parts they need except authentic *cutwaters*.

❧ / CUT YOUR FOOT   On the farm, to step inadvertently on a pasture cow dropping or flap is to *cut your foot*.

# D

∧·∧∧·∧

❧ / DAB  This once referred to any of the saltwater flatfish, but is now reserved for the smaller flounders. Accordingly, a *dab* is small; a small quantity. "I'll take a *dab* more potatoes, if you please." A *doit, smidgen, dollop.*

❧ / DAMN'S-ODDS  Used frequently in Maine speech, with this meaning: "It don't make no *damn's-odds* who you be, the answer is NO!"

❧ / DAOW!  Impossible to toss this off unless to the manner born. It is the coastal Maine emphatic for NO!

(Some years ago the federal boys had some Maine lobstermen in court for price fixing, and one of the Washington lawyers asked a witness a sort of foolish question. The answer was, "Daow!" Court was recessed so the lawyers could find out what this meant, and how to spell it.)

❧ / DARST, DURST, DASST  Dared in the sense of challenged: "He *darst* me to hit him, so I did." Also in the sense of being rash: "Never *darst* talk back to the cap'n."

❧ / DASH  The word for a horse race on ice. A sport mostly in Maine and New Brunswick, regular track horses are used with wheeled sulkies. Instead of a half-mile oval track, a straight course on smooth ice is used, a quarter of a mile long. A *dash* record set by Hal L, owned by Linwood Seeley of Fort Fairfield, in the 1920s still stands: 27 seconds.

❦ / DEACON    Verb; to arrange the apples on the top of a box or barrel so the customer presumes the same quality runs to the bottom. Thus, to put on a good front, perhaps with a mild effort at cheating, but at least giving an impression without backing it up: "He *deaconed* his barn by painting the side towards the ro'd." Perhaps an alleged sanctimoniousness of deacons is behind the term.

❦ / DEACON-SEAT    Because the deacons usually sat down front in church, the *deacon-seat* became the bench nearest the fire in a lumber camp. Sitting on it in the evening led to yarnin', and many a whopper took shape on the *deacon-seat*. A good tall story is a *deacon-seater*; the *Shagimaw* is a *deacon-seater*. (See *stretcher*.)

❦ / DEAD    Not always with reference to death, *dead* appears as an emphasis word in many Maine expressions. *Dead* ahead is directly ahead. *Dead* right is absolutely right. Aboard ship, a navigator not *dead* sure of his *dead* reckoning may fetch up *dead* wrong. (Whereupon, he is a *dead* duck!) To have anybody *dead-rights* (usually *dead to rights*) is to catch him in the act without a defense.

❦ / DEADFALL    Two meanings for this. First, a forest tree that died standing and has now fallen to the ground, but not a *blowdown*. Secondly, a non-mechanical trap for wild animals much used by early Mainers when gunpowder was hard to come by. A log was triggered so it fell when the animal touched the bait. To be caught in a *deadfall* is to be trapped indeed, as when one is discovered in a lie.

❦ / DEADWATER    Still water, used for that part of a stream which is sluggish. Dead River is so named from the *deadwater* in some stretches, although parts of the stream are lively enough. Like *branch* (which see), Mainers use *deadwater* for a wild land area as well as for the stream: "We were hunting on the Canada Falls *deadwater*."

❧ / DEALS   Lumber precut to specific measurements for its particular market or purpose. In general it means boards sized at the mill. Much of the lumber Maine vessels carried abroad, especially to the West Indies, was manifested as *deals*.

❧ / DEAR   Dropped by newer generations, this was a word old-timers used in talking to one another, and it had none of the sweeter meanings. It was hardly more than a substitute for "you-there!" or "old chap." Presumably it began as a whimsical salutation, and survived without any meaning of endearment. If some old *joker* comes out to pump gasoline in your automobile and says, "Do you want the high test, *dear?*"—you've been forewarned.

❧ / DECK   Besides the nautical meaning, this word applies to piling pulpwood. After being *yarded* from the woods, it is *decked* along the road for later *hauling* to the mill.

❧ / DEESTRICK   The way Mainers like to say district, but with special reference to the old-time local school districts. Older folks will often snort at new-fangled educational theories, and tell you they learned a good more in the old *deestrick* schools.

❧ / DELUDED   Diluted, as to rum and whiskey. This Maine way to say diluted seems logical under these circumstances.

❧ / DEMOCRAT HOUND   An otherwise intelligent animal who takes up the wrong scent, as when a rabbit hound chases a fox. The term originated before Maine was a two-party state.

🌿 / DENTIST   The *dentist* was the traditional excuse for going out of the woods for a day or two. Choppers who had a yen to disport in town would tell the boss they had toothaches. Also used by *choreboys* and waitresses in sporting camps. One year a logging camp at Roaring Brook got snowbound and ran out of supplies, and for weeks on end the crew had to eat salted trout laid down by the *meatman*. Trout is a delectable food, but it isn't something you can take meal after meal. Since criticism of camp fare is forbidden, Martie Holbrook got around the interdict by asking for a couple of days off. The boss said, "Don't tell me you gotta see the *dentist*!" Martie said, "No, I thought if you'd give me the chance, I'd swim upstream and spawn."

🌿 / DEPOT   Pronounced dee-peau; the Mainer's word for a railroad station. A train comes into the *depot*.

🌿 / DEPOT CAMP   The base *camp* in a multiple-*camp* operation. The term is even used for summer people: "They come every summer; been comin' for years—but their *depot camp* is in New Jersey."

🌿 / DESPIZABLE   Pronounced des-spize-a'bl, it is the Maine improvement on despicable, but with a stronger meaning.

🌿 / DEVIL'S HALF ACRE   That part of old Bangor where choppers and river drivers disported. The vicinity of lower Exchange Street, now re-urbanized.

🌿 / DIMITIES   Sails on a ship, from the cotton cloth so named. "Put the *dimities* to her, boys!" would be a command to *crowd* the canvas. Female petticoats (remember petticoats?) showing in a wind were *dimities*. Sometimes a laundry on the line will be called *dimities*.

❦ / DINGDHI   Spelling may vary; it is not often written but it is spoken frequently in Maine; *ding-die*. It means anything; a dingus, a doodad, a doohicky, a fid, a cover, a catch, a lever. "Heave me that *dingdhi!*" can mean a wrench, a carburetor, a coffee pot.

❦ / DINGLE   Conjecture about the origin of this word will doubtless go on and on. It means a shed and storage area adjacent to the cookshack in a lumber camp. In old Scottish and English usage the word means a cleft between hills, a shady dell, and is said to be chiefly poetic:

> "I've an ingle, shady ingle,
> Near a dusky, bosky dingle . . ."

It is not unreasonable to presume the low geography of a shady *dingle*, between two hills, conveyed an idea to the first man who noticed that the cookshack storage shed was a small building between and connecting the larger cookshack and bunkhouse. One of the last old-time lumber camps to demonstrate how the *dingle* sits between two other buildings burned in 1970 at Township 6R14, Caucomagomoc Quadrangle, so we may not look upon its like again. *Dingle* is now used for any storage or utility shed at a woods *camp*, provided it is strategically near the kitchen, and it has also been used for a porch and a piazza on a woods camp or cottage. It can mean a pantry or closet space off a kitchen. A swing-*dingle* is a *go-devil* (which see), perhaps because it brought groceries into camp which were then stored in a *dingle*. Conjecture aside, *dingle* is a word well understood by all Maine woodsmen.

❦ / DINGLEFUZZIE   Nothing to do with a *dingle*, this is a word for somebody whose name you can't come up with, like Whoozit or Whatsisname. "*Dinglefuzzie* stopped in while you were gone; he wouldn't tell me what he wanted."

❦ / DINGLE MAUL   Also *dingmaul*. A wooden hammer or mallet for securing the *dogs* of a sawmill carriage into the logs. It appears in speech as a hypothetical weapon (much like a *sled-stake*, which see): "The news staggered him as if he'd been clipped with a *dingmaul*."

❦ / DINNER   Traditionally, the Maine *dinner* is served at noon. Lunch is reserved for a snack, a picnic, and a bedtime piece of pie. Supper, of course, comes at suppertime. What others call a lunch-box is still generally known in Maine as a *dinner*-pail or *dinner*-bucket. Workmen who do not come home at noon carry their *dinners*. There have been times that Mainers, invited to *dinner*, came at noon and astonished their *outlandish* hostesses.

❦ / DIPPER DUCK   Any of the ducks that dip to feed under water, staying for a time and reappearing at a distance.

❦ / DIRTY WATER   Long before ecologists brought us a new vocabulary, *dirty water* was the Maine term for any stretch of sea with shoals, ledges, and rocks that called for close attention to charts and a keen lookout. Most yachtsmen consider a good part of Casco Bay *dirty water* in the sense that it challenges their sailing skill and lends charm to their outing.

❦ / DISENABLED   Variation for disabled, for emphasis.

❦ / DITE   The word is *doit*; once a Dutch coin of small value and hence a wee bit. Mainers who have forgotten the derivation usually spell it *dite* or *dight*. Men adjusting a timber will say, "Shove it my way a *dite*!" A *dite* more of smashed potatoes at supper will be just a touch. Smidgen, dab, pinch, whisker, and words of that category are usually interchangeable with *dite*.

❦ / DOCTOR   The verb: "He had it bad enough to *doctor* for it."

❧ / DODDLE    Probably from dawdle; but Mainers use it for stagger and reel. Also to fiddle around, tinker, *putty* (which see), and make waste motions.

❧ / DOG    The sharp hinged hook on a canthook or peavey which bites into a log. Also the same kind of device on a sawmill carriage. To *dog* a thing is to get a good grip on it and to be in control of it. (See *cant dog* and *dingle maul.*)

❧ / DOG FIGHT    A fine example of the Mainer's native knack for transferring a picture from one context to another. A fight between two dogs is noisy, absurd, irrational, and hardly an attraction with sporting and social flavor. The Maine mind was able, however, to imagine the *dog fight* to be a gauge of sartorial judgment, as if one should choose the clothing he wears to a *dog fight* just as much as he chooses the outfit he will wear to a wedding. This unlikely juxtaposition of unsimilar situations is used often in Maine speech, in this fashion:

"What did you think of Rob's red necktie?"
"That god-awful thing! I wouldn't wear it to a *dog fight.*"

❧ / DOGFISH    A *summer complaint.* The *dogfish* is a small shark that feeds on edible fish and is the bane of the handliner. About the time a haddock should be taken, the *dogfish* moves in and spoils everything. Seasonal visitors arrive about the same time.

❧ / DOG SHORE    The props and blocking that hold a boat upright on the ways while it is being built are called *shores.* These are knocked away to let the finished vessel slide into the water. The last prop to be knocked away, giving the vessel her freedom, is the *dog shore.* Because there is some danger in knocking away the *dog shore,* a nimble and alert man does it. So, a man fit for *dog shoring* will have more than ordinary ability. The main prop or crux of an argument or discussion may be its *dog shore*.

❧ / DOG WATCH  Properly, *dogwatch*. The four-hour watch aboard ship became two watches of two hours each between 4:00 and 8:00 P.M.—the first and second *dogwatches*. Now and then Mainers toss off *dogwatch* for suppertime or the cocktail hour.

❧ / DOIT  See *dite*.

❧ / DOLLOP  A sea that comes over the rail and breaks on deck. Hence, a serving of food, usually a second helping, which the hostess figuratively slaps on your plate with a spoon. The amount is never precise, and one can just as properly ask for a *dite*, a *dab*, a touch, etc.

❧ / DONKEY'S BREAKFAST  A sailor's mattress, from the hay or corn shucks in the tick. A less than comfortable bed.

❧ / DOOGING  Pronounced *doogin'*. The paying out of a baited trawl line as it is set from a dory. See *tub* for an explanation of the little stick used in this job. The paying-stick was called a *dooging-stick*, and from the swiftly moving action necessary as the trawl unwound from its tub, Mainers transferred the term with their usual imagery. Children dancing and prancing about to the annoyance of elders may be told to quit their *doogin'*. Rapt attention to any job being done, even to the extent of a "brown study," can be *doogin'*, from the way a man setting trawl is oblivious to all else—as he well should be.

❧ / DOORSTONE  The granite, etc., block doorstep at the front entrance of an old-time Maine home, especially along the coast. Incidentally, the *doorstone* of a certain "tavern" that once graced Bangor's *Devil's Half Acre* was taken to

Chesuncook Dam to become the base of the memorial to the Maine river-driver. It is well worth a trip beyond Moosehead Lake to see this memorial; it stands before the old Chesuncook Dam boomhouse, a short side-trip off the Baxter State Park route, between Kokadjo and Ripogenus Dam.

❧ / DOORYARD VISIT   Or dooryard call. Although still used with automobiles, this meant a buggy visit when the occupants didn't descend to come into the house. It was a neighborly call, in passing.

❧ / DORYMATE   In the old days of handlining, two men would fish from each dory, and there was an essential quality of compatibility. Being *dorymates* implied something more than simple friendship, because one not only had to get along with and put up with his *dorymate*, but depend on him often for survival. "Closer than *dorymates*" is a relationship of the strongest kind.

❧ / DOUBLE-ENDER   Any boat with bow and stern alike. The original *Rangeley boat* was a double-ender, but most of the surviving models have had the stern squared off to accommodate an outboard motor. Phil Johnson used to tell tourists that a *double-ender* is "a bo't that leaks over the side as much as it takes in at the seams." (Phil was phunnin'.)

❧ / DOUBLE RUNNER   Traverse sleds, either for hauling logs or for fun coasting. One of the sleds is properly termed a bobsled, but when teamed up with cross-chains or ropes to make the rear sled track with the front, *double runner* was used, and sometimes double bobsled.

❧ / DOUGHBOY   Very old word asea and ashore for dumplings, and sometimes improperly used for *John the Baptists*. Perhaps derived from buoy because they float atop the stew. Some of the dictionaries suggest *doughboy* came from certain buttons on Civil War uniforms, but Mainers were eating *doughboys* on *pot hellions* long before 1861.

❧ / Douse To strike or dip colors, to lower or take in sails, to slacken a line, and to put out a light or a fire. It suggests a quick, forthright act; when *dousing* a fire it is completely drowned out. Clam diggers also speak of *dousing* their hods, to rock them in tidewater to wash off mud and sand, a plausible derivative from the usual meaning of drench. In this latter sense *douse* is often interchangeable with *souse*, which see.

❧ / Down East Coastal Maine and the Maritime Provinces, in relation to Boston. A quotation from Lew Dietz in the first issue of *Down East Magazine* may help:

> *Cleared away and sailing in a northeasterly course out of Boston, the first landfall is the dark and jagged coast of Maine. That's where* Down East *begins. In the great hey-day of sail, windjammers took advantage of the prevailing westerlies on the run to Maine and the Maritimes. They sailed down-wind with the canvas bellied taut and shrouds singing. Down-wind to Maine became a manner of speaking, slipping with time into the salty brevity of the term* Down East . . .

There was always, however, a distinction between down Maine and *down east*. A coaster out of, say, Boothbay Harbor, who was going to Stonington would not consider that a trip *down east*, but only "to the east'ard." He would think of *down east* as being at least St. John. People from Prince Edward Island, Nova Scotia, and New Brunswick who have moved to Boston will make visits home and say they are going *down east* without reference to Maine at all. Maritimers consider themselves "far downers." When *down east* is applied to Maine, it is mostly a tidewater matter. Inland Mainers keep the customary map directions and go *down* to Boston. Arthur G. Staples, long the dean of Maine journalists, wrote a book he called *Up In Maine;* poet Holman Day also used the phrase "up in Maine." But the usual explanation, always offered inquiring tourists, is that one sailed down-wind from Boston to Maine, and then beat back up-wind on the return.

❧ / DOWN-EASTER   Howard I. Chapelle has written that the *Down-easters* "were, without doubt, the highest development of the sailing ship." Historian Rowe said, "*down-easter* was a term of fixed and no uncertain meaning. It conveyed a picture par excellence of a full-rigged wooden ship or bark with her canvas spread in the wind, designed, built and launched in a shipyard on the coast of Maine, and more often than not commanded by a Maine captain." The *Down-easter* followed the *clipper*, and added a good quarter century to the era of sail. Their similarities and their differences need not be enumerated here, but essentially the *clipper* was designed for the Gold Rush trade, and her lines and rigging were altered to make the Down-easter, which carried the heavier burdens of California wheat to Europe. Historian Rowe makes the point that while "down east" is a never-never land always east of where you are, the *Down-easter* was wholly and truly Maine. The period of the *clipper*, which was not wholly Maine, waned in 1859 after only 13 years, after which the *Down-easter* kept sails at sea until steamships took over. Because of the similarity of the two types, many people presume *Down-easters* were clippers; the famous marine paintings of Charles R. Patterson do not show clippers—they show *Down-easters.*

❧ / DOWNHILL SIDE (OF MARCH)   (See *climbing March hill.*) The vernal month, March has a hump in the middle. The latter part is all *downhill.*

❧ / DOWN SULLA   The Maine cellar was the storage vault of winter goodies, and this included the cider barrel. When a man invites a friend to see his *sulla* it is the equivalent of, "Can I buy you a drink?" *Down sulla* is the opposite of "up attic." (See *upstair.*)

❦ / Doze   A word peculiar to Maine for a certain kind of rot in wood, usually firewood. The fiber changes color, becomes not quite punky, but the stick doesn't disintegrate, so that an unprincipled farmer may sell *dozey* wood, and the customer won't know it until he tries to get heat out of it. Beech and gray birch are most susceptible to *doze*, and of the softwoods hemlock is often infected. Carpenters often use *doze*, perhaps not with accuracy, for rot that appears in construction timbers, both in buildings and in boats. Likely this use of *doze* derives from a person's dropping off for a nap, because the wood seems palpably to go to sleep.

❦ / Dreen   Drain. The kitchen sink *dreens* into the cesspool. A meadow *dreens* into the brook. Coffee is *dreened* to the last drop. Clam diggers like a low *dreen* of tide.

❦ / Dressed full   A ship with all flags flying, as for a launching or a regatta; hence, a newly painted house or anything handsome or frilly. Glad rags for Sunday-go-to-meeting would be *dressin' full*.

❦ / Dressed like a deacon   All rigged out, all decked out, all duded up. See *deacon* for a discussion of the derivation. The pious deacon has always been a low-comedy personality in Maine affairs.

❦ / Dressing   Barn manure when applied to the land. Enrichment!

❦ / Dress-suitcase   Older Maine people seldom say merely *suitcase*. The term is mostly inland, because there was some nautical superstition about suitcases aboard ship.

❦ / Dri-ki   Or, *driki*, an Indian word the palefaces first wrote. Dri-ki is the dead forest growth standing in a beaver bog. When the beavers raise the water with their dam, the trees can't survive, but they stand there in stark nakedness for decades. When man began building dams on Maine rivers, his back-flow also killed trees and made dri-ki, but Maine finally passed a law requiring land to be flooded in this way to be lumbered off first. When *dri-ki* finally falls it may float away and become driftwood, but the two words are not synonyms inasmuch as true *dri-ki* remains pretty much where it grew.

❧ / DRIVE   Both noun and verb; the whole business of bringing a harvest of lumber or pulpwood from the forest down a spring-swollen river to the mill. Men work the *drive;* the logs are *driven;* the man who works on a *drive* is a river-driver. Maine's extensive vocabulary of *drive* terms and expressions is moving into the past tense as trucks and highways supersede use of rivers.

❧ / DRIVE A NAIL ON SUNDAY   That would profane the Lord's Day, and aboard ship was unlucky. A vessel on which "no hand is asked to *drive a nail on Sunday*" was taking a landward phrase to sea, and it meant the labors were light on Sundays. With a thought to the Maine facility with imagery, it is pleasant at this point to imagine a quiet, pious community observing its Sabbath while one non-conformist citizen attempts to hammer a nail secretly.

❧ / DROGHER   A name for vessels that carried very heavy cargoes, particularly the *stone boats* that handled construction and memorial granite from the island quarries. When one of 'em developed a leaky seam, it'd go down kerplunk, so "to go down like a *drogher*" means an abrupt end to something. (The term *stone boat* is also applied to the farm drags for moving field rocks, but these farm drags are not called *droghers.*)

❧ / DROP A STITCH   From knitting, where a dropped stitch leaves its own evidence; a *crick* or catch in the back or neck which is painful and annoying. "Henry *dropped a stitch*, and can't stand up."

❧ / DROPPED EGG   Maine for poached egg, usually on toast.

❧ / DROPPER   In fly fishing, a second fly on the leader, a short distance behind the first. Sometimes trout will ignore the lead fly but hit the *dropper*. Accordingly, to have somebody "take your *dropper*" suggests you have been artful in your persuasion.

❧ / DROWN-DED   Preferred to *drowned*: "Henry *drown-ded* the kittens."

❧ / DROWN THE MILLER   Often *drownd*: "Don't *drownd* the miller!" It is almost always heard in this negative imperative, because it means to over-water the rum or whiskey, which is never taken to kindly.

❧ / DRUMMER   A traveling salesman, perhaps because he fared forth to "drum up" business. Another Maine term for a *drummer* is "runner."

❧ / DRUTHERS   Heard elsewhere as in Maine; a favorite way of indicating a choice: "If you was to have your *druthers*, which would you *druther*—the pear or the peach?" A portmanteau word that suggests would, rather, and other.

❧ / DRY GALE   A wind of gale intensity, but as it comes from the northwest it brings neither rain nor snow. (See *blow*.)

❧ / DRYING DAY   A pleasant day with dry air that quickly makes the laundry on the line smell sweet and good. Usually with good; "Good *dryin'* day today!"

❧ / DUDE CRUISERS   Exactly the same idea as in dude ranches. Coastal schooners converted to passenger accommodations for vacationers. Also known as "skin boats" because of the sun bathing by folks aboard. Fishermen and coastal people keep a wry attitude toward *dude cruisers*; the very popular *Victory Chimes* suffers some small indignity by being known to the lobstermen as "Jingle Bells."

❧ / DUFF   A thick flour pudding steamed or boiled (sometimes in a bag) and well fixed with raisins, which were called plums. Plum *duff* distinguished Sunday from the week aboard ship. In recalling poor fare on a banker, Lem Mortimer says, "We'd get salt-horse hash for six days, then Cook would put the raisins to it and call it *duff*." *Duff* thus means a little something extra or different. In the Maine woods, *duff* is the top turf of the forest floor. Before a lumber camp was erected, the *duff* was cleared away for fireproofing.

❧ / DUFFER   Another word for chap, party, character, fellow, and so on, but with kindly tone: "He's a pleasant old *duffer*." Not necessarily in a golfing context in Maine usage.

❧ / DULSE   A coarse, reddish seaweed of the Maine and Maritime coasts which makes a snack or confection when dried. Some say it was named *dulcet* (sweet) by Champlain's sailors, but the word really comes from the Gaelic *duileasg*. *Dulse* is not to be confused with Irish moss (see *moss*). In eastern Maine, tourists will find *dulse* in the stores. Might like.

❧ / DUMBIE   A lobster that has lost one or both claws, but the word isn't heard so much as *pistol*. (See *pistol*.)

❧ / DUMP MASTER   Caretaker at a town dump. Since ecology awareness, this low-grade job has assumed some prestige, and Mainers had to invent a term for the official custodian. Although all towns now have a *dump master*, the title is not legal and statutory, as is the *harbor master's*.

❦ / DUTCHMAN'S PANTS   The first showing of blue sky when a storm clears; it augurs fair weather. "There's enough blue sky to make a *Dutchman* a pair of *pants*."

❦ / DYNAMITE   Nitroglycerin pills as prescribed by a physician for heart conditions: "He took his *dynamite* and went right to bed." (See *powder*.)

# E

❦ / Edge   See *aidge*. To be *edgy* is to be uneasy and also to be touchy. After several incendiary fires, a town was said to be *edgy*. To be *on edge* suggests nervousness, perhaps unreasonably: "Mom's been *on edge* all day today; somethin' buggin' her." Edginess suggests a disposition to quarrel, somewhat like having a chip on your shoulder.

❦ / Edgings   Similar to sawmill slabs, but the bark *edges* of boards rather than from the whole log. Shook and bolt mills make a lot of hardwood *edgings* and wire them in bundles to sell as kindlings and *biscuit wood*. Thus a customer will buy a bundle or a load of *edging*. (See *sticking*.)

❦ / Eel rut   A very small harbor or tidal inlet that *dreens* out at low tide. So called because an eel crossing mud leaves a small track that reminds one of the residual tiny channel in a cove that drains completely.

❦ / Eeyaw   A variation of *weewaw*; lopsided, askew, aslant. A sagging shed is *eeyaw*; poorly woven cloth goes *eeyaw* on the machine and makes the seamstress unhappy; a framed picture hanging askew is *eeyaw*.

❦ / Eleven-foot pole   The standard Maine device for touching somebody you wouldn't touch with a ten-foot pole. Coastal Mainers have embellished the old ten-foot pole wheeze to the extent of changing *pole* to oar: "I wouldn't touch him with a ten-foot sweep!"

❦ / ENDS   Only at Bowdoin College. Winthrop, Maine, Appleton, and Hyde dormitories were originally built with north and south *ends* divided by fireproof walls. Accordingly, *ends* became the Bowdoin word for dormitories. To go to the *ends* is to go to your room.

❦ / ENTREPRENEUR DE BOIS   Good French, but now good Maine. The man (usually from Québec) who contracts with a Maine timberland owner to harvest lumber. The job includes hiring a crew and, as most of his workmen will be fellow Canadians, the operation will have a French flavor. Some of the *entrepreneurs de bois* have become legendary Maine characters; one such is Adelard Gilbert of St. Georges, County Beauce, whose retirement party after a lifetime with the Great Northern Paper Co. was a social event not soon to be forgotten.

❦ / ESSENCE PEDDLER   A skunk.

❦ / EVER AND NEVER   *Ever* and *never* appear in Maine speech to indicate incredulity. When something nobody could possibly foresee happens, one will say, "Well, did you *ever!*" and the answer can be, "No, I *never!*"

❦ / EVERY HAIR A ROPE YARN   Part of an old description of a very tough seaman: "*Every hair a rope yarn*, every finger a marlinspike, every drop of blood pure Stockholm tar, etc." Lingering phrases for a good man at his work.

❦ / EXERCISE   The special Maine usage is heard in some such sentence as this: "He was *some exercised* when he found his apples had been *swiped*." To be agitated and concerned, even to great anger. In this sense, the word is seldom heard other than as a predicate adjective; one does not similarly *exercise* another person.

# F

/\.\.\/.\/.\

❧  /  FACET    Maine plumbers like this pronunciation of
faucet. As with *hurth* and harth amongst Maine masons,
you'll find the plumbers about fifty-fifty *facet*-fawcet.

❧  /  FAIR    Used by Mainers to understate excellence,
*fair* usually means superb, wonderful, *finest kind*. "That's a
*fair* piece of pie!" is equivalent to "That's the best pie I ever
stuck a tooth in!" *Fair* is not used much in Maine to describe complexion; "light complected" is more likely.

❧  /  FAIR AND SQUARE    A term used universally for
something just and upright without thought about its origi-
nation in the Maine boatyards. (See *faired*, below.) A timber which had been adzed and broadaxed to specifications,
smoothed or *faired* until it was just right, was *fair and square*.

❧  /  FAIRED    Smoothed, leveled, evened up, planed.
Sometimes spelled *fared*. Ship timbers were most often
*faired*. Inland carpenters didn't use the term so much unless
they had had boatyard experience. "You can't *fair* a rough
floor by castin' a rug on it!"

❧  /  FAIR WATER    Fresh water for cooking. *Fair water*
is also an easy-going stretch with no navigation problems.

❧  /  FAKE DOWN    To coil a rope is to *fake* it *down*.

**❧ / FAMILY JEWELS**   A gentleman's private parts. They are usually referred to in the past tense: "He fell off the load, came down astride the fence rail, and lost the *family jewels*."

**❧ / FANCY WORK**   Maine ladies' term for needlework, tatting, crocheting, etc., of a polite and sociable nature. It means articles to be sold at the church fair, where there is always a *fancy work* table. One does not bring socks to darn when making a chat with a neighbor over tea, but will bring a doily or needlepoint for gentility. There is the old story of Satchel-eye Dyer who brought his bride home from their wedding, and they sat together in the kitchen lamplight to await bedtime. He was picking over dry beans, and he looked up to find his wife's hands idle. He said, "Didn't you bring no *fancy work*, somethin' to do?"

**❧ / FARM**   Besides its agricultural meaning, *farm* has a lumbering context in Maine. The early woods operations used many horses, and, as lumbering was done on winter snow, *farms* were cleared for pasturing the animals all summer. These *farms* became regional offices, storehouses, and general headquarters for all timberland activity in a region. Pittston Farm, Grant Farm, Michaud Farm were not *farms* in the sense that they grew crops. The term *farm* lingers for a place, an area, a headquarters.

**❧ / FAR PIECE**   Considerable distance. It's a *far piece* from Liverpool to Hong Kong! Also the distant part of a Maine farm which folks to the west'ard might call the "back forty." A man going to work in the *far piece* would carry his *dinner*. (*Far* is sometimes *fur*, and *farthest* is often *fartherest*.)

**❧ / FARRIER**   In a state where forgers spent all their time making mast rings, logging sleds, and tools for the quarries, the master ironworker often shod no horses and might even not know how. A *farrier* shoes horses, and

Mainers have tended to keep the distinction with care.

❦ / Fast   The many Websterian nuances of this word suit Maine usage, but the nautical meanings survive in Maine more than they do in some other places. Regionally, it may be pronounced *fahst*. *Fast* is used for tied, secured, nailed, buttoned; things get stuck *fast*; racehorses are *fast* but so is a young lady who steps out; in harpooning, a fisherman gets *fast* to a horsefish; and, in Maine, Daylight Saving Time is usually called *fast* time.

❦ / Fat   Numerous similies prevail, from *fat* as a hog to *fat* as they come. *Fat* and sloppy explains itself, but it sometimes is heard as *fat* and slutty. *Fat* can mean prosperous.

❦ / Fathom   As used in Maine, fathom is also used about everywhere in its nautical measurement of six feet. It does have some localized transferrals in the sense of "understand": "It's hard to *fathom* Joe sometimes."

❦ / Favor   It has been said a Maine man will come to work for you more willingly if he thinks he is doing you a *favor*. Thus, "Wonder if you'll do me a *favor?*" is preliminary to engaging a plumber, carpenter, etc.

❦ / Fay-muse   Maine way to pronounce Fameuse, the original name of the Snow Apple that originated in France.

❦ / Fearnought   A heavy woolen cloth suitable for winter wear. Also, a jacket made from it: "Cold enough today for my *fearnought!*"

❦ / Feather white   A wind-whipped sea, all whitecaps, is said to be *feather white*. Hence, some degree of agitation in a person: "He came all *feather white* to give me a piece of his mind!"

F / 89

❦ / FEELING NO PAIN   Happily in one's cups until don't-know-care-whoozit. Able to get home, barely. In court testimony a witness said, "I don't know if he was drunk when he hit the tree, but when I saw him early in the afternoon he was *feeling no pain*."

❦ / FEELING STONES   Sometimes executive stones. Sea-washed small pebbles from certain Maine islands become so smooth it is pleasurable to rub them idly with the fingers. A solace to high-strung businessmen. Ye Olde Giftie Shoppes sell a lot of them every summer.

❦ / FELT   To "hit the *felt*" is to turn in for the night. The heavy blanket on paper-making machines, which gathers the fibers of the wet pulp and begins the process of manufacture, has always been known as a paper-mill *felt*. After so much use it loses its efficiency on the machine, but is still a dandy piece of cloth that can be cut into bedsize blankets. Woodsmen admired *felt* blankets, and they were standard bunkhouse bed-covers.

❦ / FENCE VIEWER   A minor town official whose duties have largely become obsolete. In early days there was frequent dispute between neighbors as to how much of a line fence each should build and maintain. The board of three *fence viewers* would adjudicate. The *fence viewer* was not meant to be a surveyor; he was concerned only with construction. Although his day is done, the *fence viewer* is still a statutory town officer, and some towns still appoint them; an empty honor. A man who is busy as a *fence viewer* will not be doing much. Most of the other town officers in the same category have lapsed the same way: *scalers* of bark, surveyors of shook, inspectors of spirits and vinegars, field drovers, *pound* keepers. The *harbor master* (which see) does survive.

❦ / FERRULE   The big dictionary gives all the meanings of this word except the one that has been common in

Maine from earliest days—a stick to whip children, and in particular that wielded by a schoolteacher. No doubt a metal *ferrule* on the end of a cane explains the matter (figure of speech using a part for the whole). If the cane itself were used in the beginning, the *ferrule* later became a hardwood stick about 18 inches long, and its contour a little bit rounded, oval. It smarted like the dickens. To put the *ferrule* to somebody is to spank him, and occasionally a spanking or merely a sharp talking-to or dressing-down will be called a *ferruling*-out. Before schoolmarms were told not to manhandle their pupils, lady teachers often asked difficult boy students to "hold up your hand for the *ferrule*." A boy would hold his hands before him, palms up, and she'd whack him a good one.

❦ / FETCH   A favorite Maine word in many meanings. *Fetching* is to be pretty, as a *fetchin'* young lady, but Mainers construe it into a negative: "Now, ain't you *fetchin'*, with mud all over your dress!" To *fetch* the turf is to bring a vessel into port, or successfully round a headland; it derives from the nautical meaning of *fetch*, to reach or arrive. The standard sense of to go, to get, and bring back (a dog *fetches* a stick) is not precise in the Maine usage of "He dared me, and I *fetched* him one!" or "He got there first and *fetched* the job." I.e., landed him one, landed the job. A *fetchin' up* has two Maine meanings. First, a child shows his *fetchin' up* by his manners in public: "Show your *fetchin' up*—stop spilling your milk!" Secondly, "He *fetched* up on a dead-end road." *Fetchin' up*, as applied to a child, is often shortened to *fetch-up*; "Now, be a good boy and show your *fetch-up!*" It is also a verb; "They took two state children to *fetch up* along'th their own."

❦ / FEW WORDS   Standard for an invocation: "Parson Potter will now say a *few words*."

❦ / FFO   Fly-fishing Only, a Fish & Game abbreviation. (See *usual manner*.)

❧ / FID The upland *fid* is a metal pin used to shorten chain. One link is thrust through another, and a *fid* inserted. Ruel Norton once fidded a chain with his thumb, but only once. A farmer sometimes calls his *fid* a toggle, but the lobsterman's *toggle* (which see) is never called a *fid*. On shipboard a *fid* is a small, wooden *marlinspike*.

❧ / FIDDLE A frame or railing to keep dishes from sliding off a ship's table in rough weather. *Fiddle*, when used to describe the shape of a bow on a vessel, means the same as *clipper* bow, the distinctive sharp bow of the clipper ships.

❧ / FIDDLEHEAD The curved ornamental carpentry on a ship's bow, suggesting the scroll of a violin. This same scroll gives the word *fiddlehead* to the tightly curled springtime shoots of the ostrich fern, used as greens. Micmac Indians introduced *fiddlehead* greens to the palefaces of Maine and New Brunswick. Going *fiddleheading* ranks with goin' smeltin' as a Maine vernal outing of ritualistic importance. Once wholly a home delight, *fiddleheads* are now quick-frozen for market sale; if you've never tried 'em, you're *livin' short!*

❧ / FIERCE A fairly mild Maine adjective, seldom meaning ferocious. It can mean agitated, as in "He was some *fierce!*" But mostly it qualifies only slightly: a *fierce* (big) hunk of pie, a *fierce* (forced or unmeant) smile, a *fierce* (heavy) fog. It comes trippingly on the tongue when Mainers use it in their own way.

❧ / FIGHT It can mean fisticuffs, but as used in Maine it is often a minor difference of opinion, even a debate or dispute. "Me and Marge had a helluva *fight* over the wallpaper!" They didn't come to blows. "There'll be a big *fight* in town meeting over the fire truck!"

❦ / FILER   An important man in a lumber camp; he filed saws, and made ax handles in idle moments. His separate shop was usually where he could keep an eye on the goings-on, and he was supposed to know everything. He remains a corroborating expert: "If you don't believe me, ask the *filer!*" This has about the same underlying thought as "tell it to the Marines!"

❦ / FILER'S TWO INCHES   A new expression in Maine lingo, coming into use since the invention of the chainsaw; it means a gratuitous extra amount. Hardwood bolts for the turning mills were always handled in four-foot lengths, but the buyers found poorly filed chainsaws were "running" in the cut, and a man might start at 48 inches, but finish a couple of inches one way or the other. To be sure they got full 48 inches, they insisted on 50-inch bolts. Thus the *filer's two inches.* (Figure it out: poorly filed chainsaws waste $5\frac{1}{3}$ cubic feet of every cord!)

❦ / FILLIELOO   Commonest of the imaginary feathered friends of Maine. Some say he doesn't care where he's going, but flies backwards so he can see where he's been. A more plausible explanation is that he flies backwards to keep the wind out of his face. His limited range (only in Maine) is explained by the great time it takes him to get anywhere; he flies always in slow motion.

❦ / FILLIT   Plenty of Mainers properly say *fil-lay* for filet and fillet, but in the fisheries *fillit* is the right sound. Redfish are *fillited*, chowder is made from haddock *fillits.* The knife used is a *fillitin'*-knife.

❦ / FILLS   Maine word for thills or shafts on a buggy or wagon. A horse is backed into the *fills.* If shafts is used in place of *fills*, it is pronounced "sharves." Nova Scotians like shafters for shafts, and occasionally you'll find a Mainer who has picked that up, but it was more common in the days when many *Pea-Eyes* worked in the Maine woods.

✤ / FILL TO THE NORTH   A small superstition of old sailing masters was that when outward bound from a dock or anchorage, it propitiated the voyage if the sails were first *filled to the no-thard*. Hence, to take a farewell snort is to *fill to the north*. A stirrup cup.

✤ / FIND A HOLE IN THE BEACH   To anchor in an emergency harbor because of storm or fog. To find a place to put up for the night when traveling; a motel.

✤ / FINEST KIND   Spoken as one word to designate the very best. Whatever it is, the *finest kind* cannot be surpassed. The *summer complaints* have picked this up and work it to death. Ask a tourist how he slept if you want to hear him say *finest kind*. (Newfoundland may have a prior claim to *finest kind*, and the Maritimers use it as much as Mainers do.)

✤ / FIR   The common *fir* tree of Maine, known elsewhere as balsam and balsam *fir*. Good for fenceposts and Christmas trees and for pulpwood, but not esteemed by Maine carpenters for construction; it splinters terribly when nailed. But Maine carpenters have another meaning for *fir* which seems to be unique. It means to gain thickness where needed; if a stud doesn't line up with the wall it will be *firred* out by nailing on a strip the right thickness. Placing battens for sheetrock and panels is also called *firring;* a room is *firred out* by strips placed exactly right to take the nails of the paneling. It is unlikely this use of *fir* derives from the *fir* tree, since Maine carpenters use spruce.

✤ / FIRE   Phosphorescence in salt water at night. Fishermen can establish the presence of fish by thumping a boat's side and watching the *fire* of the startled fish as they dart away. A school of herring can be followed by their *fire*.

❦ / FISH DRAFT   Some say this came into Maine from Nova Scotia; it is a home remedy guaranteed to break up a high fever. The patient is warmly wrapped in bed with his feet sticking out at the foot. Then a salt fish is bandaged to the flat of each of his feet, and these are supposed to "draw out" his fever. The late Dr. Harvey Howard used to tell about the first time he encountered a *fish draft*. Called to attend a patient, he came into the bedroom to discover the ludicrous tableau of a delirious citizen with his prominent feet thus adorned, and his professional manner deteriorated into hilarity. Asking "What the hell is THAT," he was reprimanded by an old woman who assured him the *fish draft* always worked. Dr. Howard said he pulled the patient through, but the old lady always believed she did it. (This is perhaps a proper place to add that salt pork had some efficacy in "drawin' p'izen" from an enflamed wound. For a nail hole in a foot, threatening blood poisoning, tie on a small piece of salt pork; and it will draw every bit of p'izen right out!)

❦ / FISH PEAS   Spawn, roe, caviar, haddock eggs, but usually when they are still massed within the membrane.

❦ / FISH WARDEN   The enforcement officer of the Department of Sea & Shore Fisheries. This distinguishes him from the Game Warden, who is the officer of the Department of Inland Fisheries & Game. The inland wardens also police freshwater fishing, but are never called *fish wardens*. A Maine *fish warden's* jurisdiction not only extends to sea, but he can make inland arrests if, say, he finds a restaurant in Stratton that is serving short lobsters. (Not that one ever did, of course.)

❦ / FIT (1)   A vessel *fitted* out is ready to sail, and a comparison is found in the Maine use of *fit* to refer to readiness: "He was *fit* to go." Probably something of the same derivation, although oblique, is in the expression, *"Fit to be tied."* A man who is *fit* to be tied is angry about something; probably there was an inference in the beginning that if you didn't tie him up, he might do some damage.

❦ / FIT (2)   The term for sawing and splitting firewood to make it stove size. *Fitted* wood is what ultimately goes into the woodshed.

❦ / FIT AND FIT   As the Kilkenny cats. Fought and fought, in the sense of prolonged, continuing strife (see *fight*). "Them two *fit and fit* as kids, then they got married and they've *fit and fit* ever since."

❦ / FITTEN   Fitting, proper, seemly. "Not *fitten* for a woman her age to be haulin' well water!"

❦ / FIVE FRUIT   A one-time sody-fountain flavor developed by a Portland wholesaler and for many years the favorite of Maine. An extract presumably compounded of five flavors, it was served with carbonated water. Some think if it had been shrewdly marketed, it might have become as famous as "Coke." The five fruits were never identified. "Can I buy you a *Five Fruit?*" is still heard occasionally as an invitation.

❦ / FLAKES   The wooden racks on which split fish are dried after salting; hence, a corpse laid out is "on the *flakes.*" The *flake* yard is the area where *flakes* are arranged.

❦ / FLAPDOODLE   Persiflage, idle and nonsensical *palaver*: "I asked him what he was doing on my wharf, and he gave me a crate of *flapdoodle* about lookin' for a dog."

❦ / FLAPJACK Heard today mostly in the plural, *flapjacks* are griddlecakes, but in the dawn of Maine lore the word was *flapjack*, in the singular, and it meant the batter from which griddlecakes were to be made. *Jack* was a term for the batter or dough (see *blackjack*). Since sea- and woods-cooks couldn't be bothered with spatulas, but flipped the spider to turn the cakes, *"flip"* is the key word—and it became *flap*. In the Maine home, where traditional flapping of pancakes is not so much admired, *flapjacks* are usually called griddlecakes, and an attentive ear notices that when blueberries are added they become blueberry pancakes.

❦ / FLASH The last thing seen of a vanishing deer. The white tail of the Virginia deer (the variety we have in Maine) gives it the name of White Tail. In running, this white tail is prominent, and Maine gunners often call it a "flag" as well as a *flash*. To be "gone in a *flash*" is thus explained; and a *flash* shot is a vain, tardy shot more often made from excitement than with any hope of success.

❦ / FLAT-ARSE CALM Absolutely no motion of wind and water. Coleridge achieved tediously the same perfection of description in several lengthy stanzas of *The Rime of the Ancient Mariner.*

❦ / FLATFORM Possibly from *platform*, because that's what it is. A boarded area usually at a back door but not connected to the house or foundation. A walkway where mud and snow may be stamped off boots.

❦ / FLATUS A considerable variety of colorful, expressive, and highly poetic imagery adorns Maine speech in the general context of the precipitous *flatus*. Because of the gentle manners of the editors of this volume, examples of this are tastefully omitted, so that readers will not have the opportunity to compare the Maine kind with those of

F / 97

such adroit authorities as Chaucer, Shakespeare, Plautus, Boccaccio, and the daintiest authority of all, the demure and lovely Scheherazade. It is suggested that persons feeling an academic desire to pursue this area of scholarship do their own research in the field, which will not take very long.

❧ / FLEMISH   A figure-eight knot, but more likely the neatly coiled circle of rope on the deck of a boat. Both verb and noun; to *flemish* a line is to make a *flemish*.

❧ / FLINDERS   Slivers, shards. "My truck hit that chicken crate and stove it all to *flinders*."

❧ / FLIP   A popular old-time Maine beverage, not of temperance. Today the word is not precise; it means a drink of some kind and is more or less a synonym for *snort*. *Flip* was a beer spiked with rum, sweetened, and mulled.

❧ / FLIRT o' SNOW   A light flurry, not enough to "make" any. Not so much as a *robin snow*, even.

❧ / FLOAT   The distinctions amongst *float*, pier, wharf and dock lie in the construction and use of each; they all serve the same purpose of connecting land and boat. (See *landing* for another word in this group.) Most Maine *landing* places used by fishermen and pleasure craft have a dock or pier either on piles or cribwork and then a *float* (reached by a slanting ramp or runway) that conveniently rides up and down with the tide. The entire installation serves as a wharf. Thus, if somebody says, "Harry's on the wharf," it doesn't matter if he's precisely on the pier or the *float*.

❧ / FLOOT   Perhaps *flute*, but no reason to think so. This appears only in the Maine expression to denote a complete and absolute collapse. "He fell flat on his *floot*" can mean he tripped and went down, or it can mean he ran for office and was soundly defeated. No doubt the originator was striving for alliteration.

🌿 / FLORIDY  The state. Mainers like to give the *y* sound to a final *a* in place names. *Floridy*, A'gusty, Alny. (See *sody*.)

🌿 / FOG MULL  Heavy fog, often with a drizzle but without wind. A man dazed or in his cups is described as being in a *fog mull*, rather than the customary description in other places of being "in a fog."

🌿 / FOOL HEN  The spruce grouse (see *pa'tridge*). A northern Maine game bird unwary enough to be called foolish.

🌿 / FORE-AND-AFTER  The general term for sail rigging that is not "square-rigged." Schooners and ketches are *fore-and-afters*. But the term is held over in Maine speech for something that is trim, or perhaps a mite new-fangled and stylish. In this sense, "schooner-rigged" will more likely be heard: "Schooner-rigged and face washed, little Charley took his first day at school."

🌿 / FORT, THE  Localism in Aroostook County for the town of Fort Fairfield. A person returning from Fort Fairfield will say, "I've been over at *the Fort*." The name comes from a fort erected there for the Aroostook War, and named for Governor John Fairfield (1839).

🌿 / FORTY-FIVE  Also heard as *forty-fives*; a card game dearly loved in Aroostook County, introduced from the Maritimes. They have winter tournaments that go on and on.

🌿 / FOUL  The coastal uses of *foul* for snagged, tangled, barnacled, and the like come over into upland speech with some interesting expressions. A dog gets *a-foul* of a skunk. A man may get *fouled* up in his thinking.

❦ / FOUL BIGHT   A poor harbor exposed to the open sea, usually with poor anchorage or holding grounds. "Cape Neddick Harbor is a *foul bight* southward of Weare Point and less than a mile northward of Cape Neddick."

❦ / FOUND   Room and board in addition to wages. The term comes from seafaring, but was picked up for use in the lumber camps and in turn in sporting camps. A waitress will be paid so much a week and *found*. On the farm, a hired man who lives in will get wages and *found*. Newer tax and minimum wage regulations are bringing an end to this long-accepted Maine manner of engaging help; employers find it difficult to compute *found* to the satisfaction of tax collectors.

❦ / FOUR CORNERS   The usual Maine term for a crossroads. (In Somerset County a place where three roads intersect in such a way that three *four corners* are formed close together is known as Twelve Corners.)

❦ / FRENCHMAN   The general reference word in Maine today for people of French-Canadian background. Over a third of Maine's populaton has such a background. It is not really a deprecatory term as used, but some *Frenchmen* have suggested the substitute term Franco-Americans. The word *Canuck* originated in the lumber camps, and at first meant only a French-speaking Canadian working in the Maine woods; it was not intended to include those in other parts of Maine, or the Acadians of The Valley. The offensiveness of *Canuck* is supposedly diluted by a shift to *Kaybecker*, but, as used in the woods, *Kaybecker* still does not include *Frenchmen* resident down-state. Recent popularity of the Old Orchard Beach area as a Canadian vacation resort has definitely expanded use of *Frenchman* into the category of *summer complaint*. Time has made the *French-man* a niche in the Maine scene, and some of his contributions to lore, life, and legend are included in this compendium.

❦ / FRENCH TOAST   This means a silly complaint, a make-trouble device by somebody who has nothing to complain about. This meaning originated as a consequence of a labor-union effort to organize the choppers in the Maine woods. Since choppers are well paid, with all fringes; eat and sleep as if in the best hotel; have a five-day week; and get to go home to Canada every Friday, the men were hard put to think of something to set down when the organizers asked them to list their "grievances." One little fellow, eager to please, finally wrote down, "I don't get enough *French toast*." The only reason anybody in a lumber camp doesn't get enough *French toast* is because he doesn't ask for it.

❦ / FRESH HAND AT THE BELLOWS   A sudden increase in wind for sailing, like having a new pumper on the blacksmith's bellows. An interesting term since it shows a land expression going to sea; a good deal of Maine's adaptation is the other way around. Bellows was usually pronounced "bellus" both asea and ashore.

❦ / FRESH-WATER CLAMS   Maine does have a bivalve in inland waters, not eaten by humans but admired by muskrats. Alongshore, an occasional joker will shuck (see *shock*) saltwater clams and then *souse* them in fresh water; it makes them swell so it doesn't take so many to make a quart. A man who will *fresh-water* his *shocked* clams is not the *finest kind*.

❦ / FRESH-WATER LOBSTER   The word crayfish is a no-no in Maine, where to protect the native lobster industry the inferior varieties are legislated into what the State House considers oblivion. But unbeknownst to many Maine people, the state does have small native crayfish in certain inland waters. They don't grow to any size, and because we are not allowed to say *crayfish*, we call them *fresh-water lobsters*.

❦ / FRIG   A word with four-letter nuance almost everywhere except Maine. Here, it means fiddle around, dawdle, fidget, fuss, fondle idly, putter. A Maine lady of unimpeachable gentility once described her late husband as nervous and ill at ease in public, and said he would sit "*frigging* with his necktie." Charlie Thompson, asked where he had been, said, "Up in the pasture *frigging* with the boy's kite."

❦ / FROCK   Usually barn *frock*. A jacket for barn work usually made of the same material as overalls. To *frock* up for chores includes the overalls. Most farm homes had, and some still have, a *frock* hook in the shed so that smelly barn clothes didn't come into the house.

❦ / FROG IT   To cross a swampy place by jumping like a frog from hummock to hummock. More specifically, to walk a canoe through water too shallow to float it with a person aboard. Also, to take a canoe through white water that is either too dangerous or in which the canoeist is timid. A good woodsman will run the rapids; a novice will *frog it*.

❦ / FROM AWAY   From some other place. (See *furriner*.)

❦ / FROM NUTHIN'   Heard in the expression, "Dumb? She don't know *from nothin'*!" This is at least one notch dumber than knowing nothing at all.

❦ / FRONT ROOM   The parlor, living room, or sitting room, because it is usually on the front of the house. Before central heating, Maine life tended to center about the kitchen, and *front rooms* would be closed off all winter. To open the *front room* often meant a wedding or funeral, or at least some special visitors. *Front room* is still the favorite term of many Mainers for the living room.

❧ / FROTH   One who is angry will be said to *froth*, or *froth* up, no doubt as a mad dog. The word is also used in Maine cookery for whisk or beat: "I'll *froth* up some eggs and make an omelet." Also, to baste a roast, from the way the heat *froths* up the sauce.

❧ / FROW, FROE   The tool used to split shakes from a block of wood. Hence, to *frow* something is to cleave it, break it open, even demolish it. Shakes are split; shingles sawn.

❧ / FUB   To bungle, or to accomplish something in a left-handed manner. "He *fubs* everything he touches." "Joe will *fub* around with a motor until he gets it running." "He *fubbed* around all forenoon, and anybody else could have done it in ten minutes."

❧ / FUDDYDUD   Maine preference for fuddy-duddy, but used with more latitude than is found in the dictionaries. A person who is a *fuddydud* is a *niddy-noddy*. To *fuddydud around* suggests namby-pamby, perhaps a ladylike approach to a man's job. It can relate to abstractions; one *fuddyduds* about coming to grips with a problem. In some uses *fuddydud* is much like *fub*.

❧ / FUMMYDIDDLE   Somewhat like *fub* and *fuddydud* but in usage it suggests base intent or incompetence: "He came to fix the pump, and after he *fummydiddled* all morning he soaked me twenty dollars!"

❧ / FUNNY EYE   A twig of a tree bent to form the eye ring in the head of a lobster trap, now available in metal.

It derives from funnel eye, because that part of a lobster trap is the funnel. Sometimes *funny eye* is *funny* hoop. See *hakemouth*.

❧ / FURRINER  A somewhat forced Maine-ism for an out-of-stater and also a person from another part of the state if the context suits. Maine speech does not lack in things to call folks *from away*, and *furriner* doesn't come trippingly on the tongue. Aroostookians always use *outsider*, and most down-state Mainers prefer *from away*. *Furriner* tends to be a word out-of-staters THINK Mainers call them, and which they call themselves ingratiatingly.

❧ / FUSH OUT  A strictly *down east* expression meaning to play out, give up, cease and desist. A wind *fushes out* to calm. Exuberance over a new church *fushed out* when the committee got the contractor's estimate.

❧ / FUSS  A baby will fuss, but the word is extended to grown-up fault-finding: "What are you *fussin'* about?" It also means a muddle or mix-up: "They finally straightened the *fuss* out." Undue agitation is meant by "all *fussed* up." It also means to putter, to take pains: "He *fussed* all day with the clock, and got it running again," and, "A job wouldn't take him so long if he didn't *fuss* so over it."

❧ / FUTURES  As in all commodity trading where a price is guaranteed for future delivery. In Maine, a special application to the handling of Aroostook potatoes. There has been so much controversy about *futures* that the mercantile aspects have social, political, and almost religious hues. Most people in *The County* take politics, church, philosophy, liquor, food and women in stride, but if you mention *futures* they go crazy.

# G

❧ / Gad   Maine farm word for the goad or goadstick used in teaming oxen. It is also a verb; to *gad* an ox, or to *gad* somebody figuratively into action. The forked alder stick used to bring trout home from the brook by the gills is also a *gad*: "That's the prettiest *gad* o' trout I ever saw!"

❧ / Gaff   Usually pronounced *garft*. To grab or rescue, deriving from the boathook or the *gaff* used to land or boat bigger fish. When a largish summer lady slipped on a gangplank and needed assistance, Tim Mosely described his alert response this way: "I just *garft* her and steered her into the bo't on her belly." *Gaff* is also used for *guff*: "I don't have to take none of your *gaff*!"

❧ / Gaffle   Unique to Maine, the word is heard in the phrase "to *gaffle* onto," and may bear some relationship to *gaff*. A group of men *gaffle* or *gaffle* onto a heavy object and all lift together. The boss-man will say, "All right, now, all hands *gaffle* on!" An old English meaning of *gaffer* is the boss of a physical work gang, so this may be the derivation. If, on the other hand, *gaffle* comes from *gaff* (above), it is strange that Mainers don't pronounce it garffle.

❧ / Galamander   A wagon with very large wheels, equipped with derrick so huge blocks of granite may be underslung and transported from the quarry. The Rev. W. H. Littlefield, once pastor of Vinalhaven's Union Church, is credited with inventing the device, although smaller vehicles had earlier used somewhat the same principle for moving heavy ship timbers. Restored *galamanders* may be seen on exhibition at Vinalhaven and Franklin.

❧ / GALLIVANT  A word not especially Maine, but one Mainers like to toss off for a woman's capricious flitting about, and for ostentatiousness: "She *gallivants* all over town blabbin' everything she hears!" "Traipse" is also used in this same sense, and Mainers attach no meretricious meaning to it.

❧ / GAM  This word means a school of whales; it was given an additional meaning by Maine sea captains who used it to describe a gathering of home folks in foreign ports. In Singapore, Rio, Liverpool, the captains (and families, if present) would visit together and have a talk-fest. One evening during each regatta of the Friendship Sloop Society is devoted to a skipper's *gam*.

❧ / GANG  The number of traps a lobsterman will haul at one time. With several hundred out, he can't get to them all in one day, so he'll divide them into *gangs* and haul a *gang* each morning.

❧ / GANGING  Pronounced *gan-jing* or *gain-jing*. Older and complete dictionaries have this word, but it survives in Maine with no great relationship to their definitions. In earlier times it was that portion of a fishing line to which the hook was attached; the act of attaching such a hook; and a protective winding for the line. Today in Maine it means the twine from which a fishing line is made and one buys *ganging* just as he buys *snoodin'* by the hank. *Ganging* makes a cod line in one size, and in the smaller cunner-size it's great for kite strings. A Christmas package may be wrapped for mailing with *ganging*. The final *g* of *ganging* is always carefully pronounced (see *ceiling*) even though *ganging* is often misspelled (as seldom as Mainers write it) as *gangion* and *gangeon*.

❦ / GANGWAY PENDULUM    Kenneth Roberts used the *gangway pendulum* effectively in his novel *Captain Caution*. Invented by a Maine ship captain turned privateer in the War of 1812, it was a plumb line suspended from a tripod on the open deck of his vessel. By watching the swinging plumb bob, he could tell when his ship was on an even keel, level with the horizon. By touching off his guns at that precise instant, he gained point-blank accuracy. The British, who didn't have this sophistication, fired when ready, and usually over-shot or under-shot, according to the roll of their ships. The advantage this gave the Americans in that war is explained in *Captain Caution*. On modern warships the same principle is used; electronic firing circuits will not close until the ship is level.

❦ / GARAGE    When automobiles began to appear, Mainers reserved *garage* for the mechanics' shops where repairs were made (cahs were pahked in the bahn!). In those days *garage* was pronounced garr-ridge, to rhyme with carriage. In the early 1920s the ladies and girls affected a new hair-do which was inelegantly dubbed the "cootie garage." Puffs of hair over each ear suggested a stabling place for the troublesome cooties (lice) of the trenches in World War I. Radio was blossoming, and Maine speech began to be nationalized by it. The fad of cootie garages thus taught Maine people to say *g'rarj*.

❦ / GARSTLEY    Ghastly. After a bout with the flu, a man will look *garstley*.

❦ / GATE    A control point on a private timberland road; and also a Canadian-U.S. border checkpoint which leads into the Maine wilderness over a private road, such as those at Estcourt, Daaquam, Ste. Aurélie. *Gate* is rather the name used to locate these places on a map, while in speech Mainers prefer to call them *chains*. (See *chain*).

❧ / GEAR   A favorite word in Maine for the tools and implements of whatever is at hand. The *wangan, turkey*, and *kennebecker*, all of which see, may be spoken of by the woodsman as "my gear." Instead of saying a person "picked up his marbles and went home," to describe leaving in a huff the Mainers may say he "took his *gear* and left." Fishing equipment is *gear*. See *tub* for *tub* of *gear*. Ronnie Fessenden used to dignify his jacknife by calling it his "whittlin' *gear*."

❧ / GELDING TOBACCO   Cut plug, for smoking.

❧ / GET   The catch or take of a fishing vessel; hence, the degree of success attending any venture or effort: "He ran for office and had a fair *get*, but he lost." If you can stand hearing it again, the classic Maine illustration is the story of the man who drowned. When his body was recovered some days later, a delegation approached the widow to say, "We found Kenny, and he's full of eels." She replied, "Bring me the *get*, and set him again."

❧ / GET ALONG   To see eye to eye without friction: "They *get along* just fine." Also, to make do: "I *get along* fine without coffee if I can just have my tea." And, to set out: "It's four o'clock, I better *get along* home."

❧ / GETCHELL BIRCH   Maine term for the short-lived gray birch; pronounced *gitch'l*. It has no commercial value, as do white and yellow birches, but it makes a fair firewood. As it doesn't grow large, it is usually cut in *sled length* (which see).

❧ / GET YOUR BAIT BACK   To catch just enough fish to match your bait expense; to break even. The expression is transferred variously. A boy who is wayward or subnormal may be compared: "Eyah, the lad's a problem—Henry didn't *get his bait back* on him." The expression is often used for a very small baby: "Weighed four pounds—hardly more'n *got his bait back*."

❧ / GILLS   Hanging by the *gills;* it describes a fish caught up in a gill net. The mesh of the seine is the right size to hold a fish after it has thrust its head in. Anybody hanging by the *gills* has had some kind of a *come-uppance.*

❧ / GINGERBREAD   The dictionaries recognize this as "something showy but unsubstantial and inartistic." In Maine it means specifically an ornamentation of the finish woodwork of a home's exterior. A sort of scrimshaw by the carpenter. It will be seen in gables, over doors and windows, and many times along the eaves. It is always interesting, usually artistic, and fairly substantial. *Gingerbread* differs from town to town depending on the skill of local carpenters. Friendship is a good place to see typical Maine *gingerbread.*

❧ / GIRLIN'   Said of a boy conducting a courtship: "Jimmie's out *girlin'* tonight." (Woman's Lib please note: Nobody in Maine ever says a girl is out "boyin'.")

❧ / GIVE THE VERY JESSE   To comb somebody out, direct a tirade, cuss thoroughly: "He gave me the *very Jesse!*"

❧ / GLASS KNOTHOLE   A theodolite, transit, and the navigator's sextant. Captains shot the sun through a *glass knothole.*

❦ / GLASSYASS   Sometimes given the sound of *glarssy-arse*. It is a variant for *flatarse* to describe an absolute calm at sea, but perhaps even a little flatter than *flatarse*.

❦ / GLIN, GLINN   A certain glint of light on the horizon, usually seen in cold weather, a portent of storm: "See a sea *glin*, catch a wet skin."

❦ / GLORYHOLE   In early days, a ship's stronghold or treasure room; later merely living quarters for cooks and stewards. (Mainers like to pronounce steward stoo-ert.) Nowadays, any catch-all that may be in constant disorder. A Fibber McGee closet. (If you don't remember Fibber McGee's closet, its contents fell into the room every time he opened the door.)

❦ / GO COOK   *Go*, in this sense, means to sign on as a crew member of a vessel, or simply to sail as a *hand*. One who *goes cook* signs on as cook for the voyage. (See *go two*.)

❦ / GOATFISH   The hake; from the hake's somewhat goatlike chin whiskers.

❦ / GOBBET   A word older than Maine (confer Friar John of the funnels and *gobbets* in *Gargantua* by Rabelais), and meaning a chunk of meat. Mainers have seemingly settled on the size of it, generally about like a fist. They have also developed "gobbin" and "gubbin"; to break off into chunks (*junks*) or *gobbets*. An old recipe calls for "a *gobbet* the size of a duck's egg."

❦ / GO-DEVIL   A word applied to many vehicles and contrivances used in Maine. A box-sleigh or pung body mounted forward on logging sleds to give a mite of comfort while teaming was a *go-devil*. The swing-dingle (see *dingle*) is often called a *go-devil*. The pole drag of the Indians—poles dragging like unattached thills behind a single horse—has been used for bringing game out of the woods, and is a *go-devil*. Early homemade farm tractors, often from parts of several automobiles, were called *go-devils*, sometimes doodlebugs. The pump-lever handcar used by railroad section men is a *go-devil*. Children make *go-devils* for sliding—a small seat erected on a barrel stave. Hence, about any device one may ride on or move a load with, but of some irregular sort. People who object to snowmobiles have been heard to call them "snow-devils."

❧ / GODFREY  A favorite Maine term for the Almighty which is not considered offensive. This nicety runs through Maine speech even though the state is far from averse to profanity. Harry Shorey, editor of the Bridgton *News*, whimsically uses *darn* in his paper for a water *dam*, and a lady in Millinocket once said, "I like to speak of Ambajejus Lake because it sounds like swearing and isn't." *By Godfrey* and *Godfrey Mighty!* are the commonest ways to use *Godfrey*. *Godfrey*, dad-blamed, ding-busted, goldarned, and a few other easements balance off the Mainer's more vivid profanity, and are as artful in their own way as the completely opposite ability to swear in the middle of a word: "Don't be so omni-goddam-nicient!" and, "I ain't under no obli-goddam-gations to nobody!" A pleasant emphasis is often given to *Godfrey* by adding Jeezum! A minister who heard his stingiest communicant had actually dropped five dollars in the collection plate is said to have exclaimed, "*Godfrey Jeezum!*"

❧ / GOIN'  Travel conditions. Heavy snow makes for bad *goin'*, but after the mud dries out in the spring you'll have nice *goin'* for a time. A good *goin'* snow was one that packed down just right for sledding.

❧ / GOIN'-HOME-ACRYIN'  From the way an unhappy child will run home to mummy in tears; a comeuppance. If a boy sarses another boy and gets his nose punched, that's his *goin'-home-acryin'*. R.P.T. (Alphabet) Coffin liked this expression and used it frequently in his books. It is not reserved for children; an older person who gets hoist on his own foolishness will get his *goin'-home-acryin'*.

❧ / GOING OUT OF STYLE    It suggests excessive enthusiasm about using something up before it ceases to be popular: "The way he spends money, you'd think it was *going out of style*." Or, "He eats ice cream 'sif 'twas *goin' out of style*."

❧ / GOLDEN ROAD    A new term in Maine lore, this is the private highway of the Great Northern Paper Company into their land holdings north of Moosehead Lake. Called *Golden Road* because of its expense, it replaces the Penobscot River as a means of transporting pulpwood from woods to mill. (Great Northern made its last river drive in 1971.) It is a gravel road, unpaved, but otherwise one of the finest engineered highways in the state. Canadian woodsmen give it the name *le grand chemin*, but Mainers seem settled on *Golden Road*. Officially, it is West Branch Logging Road.

❧ / GONE ASTERN    The seafaring term for something *abaft the aft* (see *abaft*), or left behind, is applied to an enterprise or endeavor that is losing money. A business that drops below last year's earnings has *gone astern*.

❧ / GONER    Something past repairing: "My motor's a *goner*; crankshaft snapped." More poignantly: "He's a *goner*; Doc gives him three months."

❧ / GOOSE    Used in Maine as elsewhere for an intimacy of sorts, it has other meanings in the senses of sudden impetus, special persuasion, and exhortation into activity. "*Goose* your engine and you'll back off that shoal." When a truck is stuck in the mud and everybody is ready to push, the cry will be, "Now *goose* her!"—this means for the driver to rev the engine. A man who is reluctant to join a cause may be *goosed* by forthright persuasion.

❧ / GOOSE AND GOD   This improbable combination shows up in the Mainer's oft-used expression for complete ignorance: "He don't know no more than a goose knows God."

❧ / GOOSE GREENS   Also called *shore greens*. A short, smoothed-stemmed plant found along the Maine shore. Some would liefer have them than dandelions and *fiddleheads*.

❧ / GOOSE-RUN   Sometimes duck-run. A hunting hiatus incidental to other cruising. In the old days when so much of Maine's 'longshore business moved by boats, the arrival of the mail at an island might be delayed because the captain encountered a raft of birds he couldn't resist going after. In gunning season, passengers were sometimes forewarned that sea-ducks might delay arrival. Arriving late, a salesman might apologize by saying he was held up by a dam' *goose-run*. A lobsterman may say, as he leaves his harbor, "I may be late comin' in, if I make a *goose-run*." The term is transferred to almost any situation which gets delayed: "We meant to start out right after breakfast, but the women had to make some kind of a dam' *goose-run*, and we didn't get away 'til most noon."

❧ / GORBY   Also *gorbie* or *gorby-bird*. The handsome Canada jay of Audubon, also called moosebird and whiskeyjack. A deep woods relative of the blue jay, it seldom appears near villages, but is most friendly around woods *camps*. It'll come to take crumbs from one's hands in mere minutes. Woodsmen consider the *gorby* a lucky bird, as seamen do the albatross. In Maine legend they have led lost hunters back to *camp*.

❧ / GORE   A triangular or irregular area of land left over after surveyors have run their straight lines, and in Maine a word for certain townships thus shaped. Stanley B. Attwood (*The Length and Breadth of Maine*) says a *gore* may result from inaccuracies. Most original *gores* have been absorbed into adjacent townships, as Prout's *Gore* became a part of Freeport. Misery *Gore* in Somerset County and Coburn *Gore* in Franklin County have remained separate townships. *Gore* is thus another of the Maine terms that mean *place*, others being station, location, *landing*, village, etc.

❧ / GORM   Pronounced gawm. A favorite Maine word of delightfully obscure origin meaning to behave in a stupid, awkward manner. It is also a noun: a clumsy oaf. And an adjective: *gormy* and *gorming*. The word and its derivatives are heard in several English dialects and also in Tennessee, but not with the nuances of Maine. In England, they have the word *gormless*, which means nothing to a Mainer. *Gorm* and its derivatives have two meanings: one, "to behave in a stupid manner, to stare or gape"; the other, "to smudge or smear, especially with something sticky or greasy." Mainers use *gorm* both ways. A boy with two left hands is a *gorm;* but a recipe for red-flannel hash says to "mix it loose but not *gormy*." A mother may call at her son, "Get your big *gormin'* hands out o' that cookie jar!" A man who bungles a job has *gormed it*. Anybody who stumbles over his own feet is *gormy*. The illustrative colloquy runs thus:

"Ain't he the boy broke your plow, smashed your cart, lost the 40-quart can down the well, and got your Edie in a family way?"

"Ayeh."

"*Gormy* cuss, ain't he?"

❧ / Go two   Referring to the number of men on a work boat of any kind: some *go two*, some go three. (See *go cook*.)

❧ / Granny   When the simple reef or square knot is improperly bent, it becomes a *granny*. This defeats the simplicity of undoing it. To make a *granny* is to pull a boo-boo; to do something *barse-ackwards*.

❧ / Grass about the bows   A way to describe a man who has started to grow a beard. The term has been revived in some degree by the "hippy" look.

❧ / Grease   Included here because in Maine it is always pronounced like the country Greece. The southerly "greaze" is not heard; nor is *slick* used in Maine for slippery or greasy. Woods cooks call lard and other shortenings *grease*. Launchways were *greased* to help a vessel slide into the water; hence, "to have your skids *greased*" is to be hurried along. (In lumbering parlance the skids would be iced.)

❧ / Great ponds   The basic common and statutory law in Maine relating to public rights to "the great waters of the state" is known as The *Great Ponds* Law. This involves the ocean and its tributaries and all inland lakes over ten acres. Court interpretations have been numerous. If one becomes personally concerned over his access to and privileges on the *Great Ponds*, he will want to consult an attorney. Much of the original intent of the *Great Ponds* Law to keep certain resources common has become vaporish over the years.

❧ / Green geese   Goslings under four months; high on the list of delicacies.

❦ / GREENING   Going *greening* is to gather dandelions, *fiddleheads, goose greens* for table. Also, trees leaving out in the spring are said to be *greenin'*, or *greenin'* out.

❦ / GREEN TO GREEN   This means everything's fine; clear sailing. It comes from the rules of navigation and the helmsman's jingle:

> *Green to green* and red to red,
> Perfect safety, go ahead, etc.

Reference is to port and starboard lamps, and meeting a vessel at sea: "If things look *green to green*, we'll go to the fair tomorrow."

❦ / GREENVILLE READING   Before Loring Air Force Base at Limestone was made a weather station, Maine's temperature was officially reported out of Greenville, an exposed community at the down-state end of Moosehead Lake. Greenville was frequently the coldest place in the United States. The way to take a *Greenville reading* is to dig down in the snow and see how far the mercury hangs below the bottom of the thermometer. The rest of Maine always seemed a little warmer to folks after the radio brought them the *Greenville reading*.

❦ / GRINDING SHEEP   Springtime chore of Maine farmers whose land is extremely rocky. Two farmers will *change work*, and while one turns the crank, the other holds a sheep's nose to the grindstone. Unless brought to a point, a sheep's nose can't thrust between rocks to graze. Sarcastic term for poor soil. A farmer who has to *grind sheep* is not prosperous.

❦ / GROANER   A foghorn with a prolonged moan and only one tone. A two-toned horn, listed on charts as a diaphone, is called a grunter.

❦ / GROG   The usual rum and water associated with marine affairs, but in Maine a general term for "any given kind." A *grog*-shop is seldom a tavern in Maine, but means the state liquor store; sometimes "Dr. *Grog's*" and (from the uniform color of paint formerly used) "Dr. Green's."

❦ / GROPIE   The sculpin, mostly along the York County shore.

❦ / GROUT   Broken pieces of granite from quarry operations, favored for breakwaters and jetties and to fill a crib wharf. *Grout* is also a thin concrete, mostly gravel, used in construction where strength is not essential.

❦ / GROW ON BUSHES   Something money does not do. Used for anything not in large supply: "Girls like Louise don't *grow on every bush*."

❦ / GUESS   No Mainer, yet, has ever "reckoned" when he means *guess*, as in "I reckon so!" Grocery and lumberyard bills are reckoned in Maine, and a reckoning is a statement of account (the German *Rechnung* and the French *l'addition*) and the settlement of an account or a difference: "Joe and Jim had a spat, but came to a reckoning." Accordingly, for opinion purposes a Mainer *guesses*, and this runs the gamut of surmise, presume, suppose, estimate, think, expect, anticipate, consider, and reckon. Calculate or "cal'late" is attributed to Mainers much more often than they use it, and some days you won't hear it at all.

❦ / GUFF   See *gaff*.

❦ / GULL   From the way a gull gulps food, to gobble down supper posthaste and to over-indulge: "He *gulls* enough at one sittin' to last me a month!"

❧ / GUM, GUMMER, GUMMING   Relating to the gathering of spruce gum in the Maine woods to be sold to a processing firm at Five Islands. Some choppers didn't bother, but others would collect the resinous globules from felled trees and bring out bagsful in the spring. There was a mite of tarnish to being a *gummer;* less enterprising choppers made fun of them mildly. *Gum* is also used to describe toothless eating: "Until my new choppers come, I'm *gummin'* it."

❧ / GUN   The Maine word for hunt. Hunting season is *gunning* season. A hunter is a *gunner. Gun* is used for hunting when no gun is involved: "He's been *gunnin'* around looking for clocks in antique shops." Anybody foolishly inviting a comeuppance is said to be *gunning* around for trouble. In sports, a *gunner* is an athlete more interested in personal glory than in team play: "He *guns* for every basket when he ought to pass off."

❧ / GUNDALOW   Pronounced gun-low. A river and harbor craft developed from a flat-bottomed, square-ended scow, propelled by sweeps or sails and sometimes poled. It evolved into a definite type of spoon-bowed, round-stern vessel decked completely over and capable of about thirty-five tons of cargo. It was used in sheltered waters to carry lumber and hay, mostly. The word is still heard when somebody compares an odd-looking mahogany job to a *gundalow,* and even for a person of work-a-day nature.

❧ / GUNKHOLE   A small, out-of-the-way harbor or inlet, larger than an *eel rut.* Yachtsmen exploring the Maine coast delight in finding cozy and charming *gunkholes.*

❧ / GUNWALES   Pronounced *gunn'ls.* A wale is a strake or a plank on a ship's hull, and the topmost wale was the one on which guns were placed. The *gunn'ls* are thus the limit of capacity, and when a man has tippled until he is "loaded to the *gunn'ls*" he is *rap full*, for sure.

❧ / GURNET   A word of unknown origin, it means a thoroughfare in salt water. Older Mainers pronounced it *GURN-n't*, accenting the first syllable, but today it is usually *gur-NETT*. *The Gurnet* connects Harpswell Sound with the Atlantic Ocean, and adjacent land in both Brunswick and Harpswell is called *The Gurnet*. The Casco Bay Steamship Lines formerly had a vessel named *Gurnet*, and it was used mostly to carry shore-dinner customers to the old Gurnet House at Brunswick.

❧ / GURRY   Fish cleanings, particularly as they adhere to boats, gear, and clothing: "I won't step inside, I'm all covered with *gurry*." To be "all *gurried* up" is to be in a mess, whether from fish gurry or something else.

❧ / GURRYBUTT   A bowl, pail, tub, etc., used as a receptacle for clam and lobster shells at table.

❧ / GUT BUCKET   A bait boat. Hence, any untidy craft, and a home, shop, baithouse, shed that needs a house-cleaning.

❧ / GUZZLE HOLE   A basin or inlet with some kind of population, thus better than an *eel rut* and larger than a *gunkhole*. A *guzzle hole* should have at least one store where visiting boats can find something to guzzle.

# H

/\.\/\.\/\.\

**❀ / Hack** Maine contraction of *hackmatack* when cut for pulpwood and lumber. In the Maritimes *hack* is called juniper, and in some places along the Maine coast sawmills and lumber dealers also say juniper, but in general Mainers use juniper for the low-bush pasture yew that yields berries to flavor medicines and gin. Westerly, *hack* is the tamarack. It's the deciduous conifer celebrated in Longfellow's account of the building of Hiawatha's canoe. *Hackmatack* lumber resists weather and makes good porch floors. In Maine shipbuilding lore, there is frequent mention of *hackmatack* knees. The main root of the *hack* grows at right angles to the trunk, and woodsmen dug out this natural joint, or bracket, to sell to shipyards, where it was used as a support for deck timbers. Each stump and trunk thus provided yielded two knees when rip-sawn down the middle.

**❀ / Hail** The name of a vessel's home port, from which she *hails*. The *hail* is properly painted or carved on the stern or transom along with the name, thus: *Miss Gussie—Portland.* Also, *hail* is to speak to a passing boat to exchange greetings or messages, and sometimes more: "*Hail* her, and ask if they can let us have some matches!" *Hail* is also the term for the estimated *get* of a fishing vessel, the approximate tonnage being brought into port; the skipper will radio his *hail* in the hold, average size of the fish, and estimated time of arrival at dockside.

❧ / HAILING DISTANCE   As explained under *hail*, vessels are not "called at," but are *hailed*. Thus the distance the voice (and also mechanical signals) could reach would be *hailing distance*. It denotes some proximity, whether from ship to ship or from ship to shore. The term as transferred means near enough: "He was in *hailing distance* of getting married one time, but the girl called it off."

❧ / HAIR   The smallest unit of human pain, as in the expression, "He fell thirty feet off the roof and never hurt a *hair*." A man who is caught up in a lie and brazens it out with nonchalance is said "to never turn a *hair*."

❧ / HAIRED UP   Angry, upset, *feather white*, all of a dither. Perhaps a mite stronger than *feather white*. From the bristling of a wary or threatening dog: "I never saw anybody so *haired up* as he was."

❧ / HAIRPIN   Mainer's word for a crook; a liar and a cheat is a *hairpin*. To be "crooked as a corkscrew" and "crooked as a ram's horn" convey the same idea of morality askew: "He's so crooked they won't dig a hole when he dies—they'll just screw him in the ground." (Crooked, of course, is crook-id; a *hairpin* is crook-id.)

❧ / HAIR POUNDER   From the slapping of reins on flanks, the woodsman's term for a teamster.

❧ / HAKEMOUTH   Instead of shaping their trap heads in a circle (see *funny-eye*), some lobstermen prefer a flattened shape that suggests the mouth of a hake. More than one lobsterman given to this has been nicknamed *Hakemouth*.

❧ / HALF-SEAS OVER   The point of no return in the terrible ordeal of becoming intoxicated; somewhat advanced of *feeling no pain*, but not "over the bay."

❦ / HALIBUT  Entered here only to give the correct Maine pronunciation. Give it the long haul—*haulibut*. Never as in Prince Hal.

❦ / HAND  A workman, but a term that had its special nuance when it originated at sea. Those who did not *go cook*, bos'n, master, mate, etc., went as *hands*. Thus fore-masthand and doryhand. The early requirement of an ordinary seaman was, ". . . able to *hand*, reef and steer." Today this ability is used for somebody just getting by and not likely to set the world afire, since the ordinary *hand* aboard ship was on the low rung of the status ladder. Use of *hand* and *hands* for inland employes stems from the sea usage. (See *Hannah Cook*.)

❦ / HANDLE  Said of a new baby boy: "Mother put a *handle* to this one!"

❦ / HANDLINE  A deep-sea fishing line constantly at-tended by a man on deck or in a dory. In contrast, various trawl and set lines are left alone for a time to be attended later. *Handlines* are often called cod lines, not so much from the variety of fish being sought but from the size of the *ganging*. Going *handlining* is to go for groundfish with such a line. A *handliner* is a fisherman who does *handlining*.

❦ / HAND-SCYTHE  The word *hand* here is redundant to many ears, since a scythe is hand-swung anyway. How-ever, Mainers use the unnecessary *hand* with numerous tools; in finishing granite in the quarries the men used hand-sets, hand hammers, hand tracers, hand points, and others. Besides, the blade in the cutter-bar of a mowing machine is also called a scythe, so there is such a thing as a machine-scythe, too. (See *hound-dog*.)

❦ / HANDSHAKER  A genial sort who doesn't have much to follow up his first manual approach. After you've shook, that's about all. Politicians are wonderful *handshak-ers*. The expression is often used thus: "He's a great *hand-shaker*, but . . . "

❧ / HAND SHARK   A farmer's utility hand sled. Used about as a *moose sled* in the woods, it replaced the summertime wheelbarrow. *Moose sleds* often had wooden runners, but *hand sharks* were generally ironed.

❧ / HANDY   Talented: "He's *handy* with tools," or, "Jimmie's *handy* at arithmetic." Also, ready and able: "He's *handy* with his fists," or, "She's *handy* with a sharp word."

❧ / HANG   The ax of primitive man was never really sophisticated until Maine *choppers* went to work. The blade was improved by Maine forgers, and the double-bitted ax created. Meantime, the handle got much thought from woodsmen. The European versions of the chopping ax were fitted with heavy, unyielding handles that jounced a *chopper* with every blow, and these were soon discarded for more willowy and whipping handles made from native American woods. It is of great importance in this connection to bear in mind the extreme care and attention the Maine *choppers* lavished on their axes in the days before crosscut saws, when trees were truly chopped down. They did not buy axes that were already fitted with handles, but each man shaved and shaped the handle he could work with best, and fitting it to his ax was called *hanging*. A well-hung ax for one man might not suit another. The Maine *chopper* devised the curved ax handle for the *pole-ax*; until his time, ax handles had been straight. Today, anywhere in Maine, if one man handles another man's ax, he will test it for the *hang*, a custom that gives us the expression to "get the *hang*" of anything. In coastal boat-building, *hang* is the word for attaching strakes or planks to a boat's frame. No other word, such as fasten or secure, is used for this: "I got four more planks to *hang*, and I can 'close the *shutter*.' " (*See shutter.*)

**&#x2767; / HANG TOUGH**   To endure and sweat out at all costs and against all odds. The term arose in the woods and is used for sticking things out when a man yearns to leave camp and assuage things in town. Overcoming his desires, he *hangs tough*. If he doesn't *hang tough*, he might go to the foreman and complain of a toothache. (See *dentist*.)

**&#x2767; / HANG UP YOUR BOOTS**   To die, or, less deperately, to come to the end of your working days. A river driver who died on the job would be buried near the scene of the tragedy, the blacksmith would fashion an iron cross to mark the grave, and the poor devil's calked river boots would be hung on the cross.

**&#x2767; / HANNAH COOK**   John Bartlett says "doesn't amount to a *Hannah Cook*" is a saying common in Maine and on Cape Cod. Of his three proffered derivations, his third is correct: it comes from seafaring and has to do with signing on as a member of a ship's crew. (See *hand*.) A man who signed on as a hand or cook didn't have status as one or the other and could be worked in the galley or before the mast as the captain wished. The hand or cook was nondescript, got smaller wages, and became the *Hannah Cook* of the adage.

**&#x2767; / HARBOR MASTER**   Like the *fence viewer*, the *harbor master* is a minor town official in Maine, but unlike the *fence viewer* he has held over into the present. All coastal towns with any harbor activity have one. He assigns moorings and is expected to keep the peace if need be. Yachtsmen penetrating a strange harbor do well to make themselves known to the local *harbor master*; aside from the courtesy of this, he may make suggestions of value.

**&#x2767; / HARDSCRABBLE**   A word used generally elsewhere in the same meaning; Mainers liked it for that section of town where farmers had to *grind sheep*. Many towns had a

*Hardscrabble* Road which led out to "the *hardscrabble*," and it is possibly amusing that newer residents in those sections find the term objectionable. *Hardscrabble* Road in Freeport has been decently changed to Bailey Avenue.

❧ / HARD UP  To be up against it, but not quite a pauper. When you get so *hard up* you have to *call on* (for town aid), you no longer have your head above water. It also means a last-ditch conjecture: "I'd have to be awful *hard up* to make a pass at her!"

❧ / HARDWARE  Heavy trolling gear in fresh-water fishing. Look at a Davis Spinner in a tackle shop; that's *hardware*.

❧ / HARK  Means to be quiet; children are told to "*Hark* your noise!" Also, to listen: "Nobody *harks* to me."

❧ / HARNESS CASK  An oaken tub with brass hoops used for overnight soaking or freshening of salted meats. Both mariners and woodsmen always maintained most of the meat they got was "salt-horse," so the word *harness* is apt.

❧ / HATCH COVERS UPSIDE DOWN  It is poor seamanship to leave hatch covers wrong-side up; thus the light superstition about this is comparable to leaving a hat on a bed, etc. Don't do it.

❧ / HAUL  Throughout Maine, *haul* is a preferred word in contexts where others might say drag, pull, lift, carry, and so on. Interestingly, Vermont farmers always "draw out" their winter wood, but Mainers *haul* it. Although, of course, *yard* is a substitute word for *hauling* wood, and sometimes Maine farmers like the word "start": "Tomorrow, I'll *start* my cordwood." A log jam *hauls* when it is broken and begins to move. Lobstermen *haul* their traps (preferably on "good *haulin'* days"), and when so doing are gone to *haul* or out to *haul*. The question, "What did he *haul?*" covers the area he *hauled* in, the number of traps handled, and the poundage of lobsters brought ashore. Anchors, lines, sails, are *hauled*. Boats taken from the water for winter storage are *hauled*. Children are *hauled* to school, not bused. Groceries are *hauled* home. Water is *hauled* from a well by pail, and then *hauled* into the house: "I'm sick and tired of *hauling* water!" was always a starting point for the promotion of new-fangled plumbing. A dentist *hauls* teeth. Manure is *hauled* out to be spread. The RFD man *hauls* the mail. Variations of *haul* are many, even to, "That Shrine time must have been a pip, Ned didn't *haul* home till three in the morning!"

❦ / HAUL AROUND   See *back in*. A wind that *hauls around* usually brings good weather.

❦ / HAUL-OFF   A line with pulleys from shore or wharf to a permanent mooring below low-water mark—not unlike a woman's clothesline from porch to a tree. Its purpose is to keep a small boat afloat and within reach at any point of the tide. Sometimes called an off-haul or an outhaul.

❦ / HAWSEPIPE, HAWSEHOLE   The hole in the bow of a vessel through which the anchor chain or hawser passes. In the old days a sailing master who began his career as a foremast hand was said to have "come in through the *hawsepipe*"; when heard today the expression means a self-made man in any profession. Pronounce with an *s*—hoss.

❦ / HAYBURNER   A horse; today it's "gas guzzler" for an automobile.

❦ / HAYWIRE   The baling wire on hay was handy around the farm for all sorts of repairs. Flimsy, patched-up

H / 127

makeshifts led to *haywire* for something not in the best shape. People, objects, and situations can go *haywire*.

❦ / Head  This word for a toilet aboard ship comes from the use of the forward part of a vessel, or knight *head*, as a latrine by crew members. Today the *head* may be aft, and lobstermen have facetiously borrowed the word from yachtsmen with reference to a bucket. A heading is a compass point toward which a vessel is making passage, and this gives us such phrases as *head* for, *head* out, *head* home, and *head* in: "I told him where to *head in!*" means some exceptionally good advice was imparted.

❦ / Head in a bucket  This means about the same as being led around by the nose. Hogs are not easy to lead, but can be directed into a pen or freight car by clapping a pail over their heads. They try to back out of the pail, and by adroitly maneuvering the pail a farmer can make them go anywhere. Anybody with his *head in a bucket* is being manipulated.

❦ / Heap  To "fall in a *heap*" is to be much flatter than the word *heap* normally means. It suggests tumbling from a ladder and making like a pancake. A wrecked automobile, approaching total demolition, will be said to be "all piled up in a *heap*."

❦ / Heated term  Men who know what it is to work out of doors in a rigorous Maine winter appreciate the arrival of the *heated term*—summer.

❦ / Heater piece  The common household flatiron, made hot on the top of a stove, was triangular in shape and was called a *heater*. A *heater piece* is thus a triangular plot of land; specifically, the grassy place at a road intersection left untraveled by wagons that always cut the corners.

*Heater piece* is reserved for these small plots; a larger field or meadow piece with triangular shape is usually called a triangle piece or a triangle field, (An amusing booboo appeared in a WPA-sponsored book about Maine which was published during the FDR days. It said the *heater piece* in Scarborough was so called because the highway crews heated their snow removal equipment there! The book did not explain why Scarborough warmed its snowplows.)

❧ / HEAVE    With many Mainers, this word replaces toss and throw in all meanings: "*Heave* me that hammer!" or, "She *hove* him over (jilted him)."

❧ / HEAVE A PROJECT    Occasionally heard in the sense of cast a spell, but not with any suggestion of witchcraft: "She *hove* me a *project* and I can't get her off my mind!" To make an impression on somebody.

❧ / HEEL    To tip or slant; at sea a vessel *heels* from the pressure of the wind, whereas she lists to one side or the other from unequal weight below decks. Both *heel* and list are used in Maine for anything aslant, from a toppling shed to a person in his cups.

❧ / HEEL TAP    Often just *heel*, the end slice of a loaf of home-baked bread. "I *hosey* the *heel tap*!" is the cry of the alert child who first notices that Mother is starting a new loaf. Luther Rodick, consoling his dying wife by the bedside, said, "I've tried to make you a good husband, Nellie—I always ate the *heel tap* so's you wouldn't have to." "Yes," she said, "and I always wanted it."

❧ / HEIRSHIP PROPERTY    Real estate on which the title is clouded by the claims of heirs. Out-of-staters seeking their dream-place have often found it, only to be told by the real estate agent that they can't buy it—it's *heirship property*. (When misunderstood as "airship," an explanation

H / 129

follows.) Many old home places in Maine, the old folks gone and the family scattered, are in this situation; many times a distant cousin, out of pure cussidness, will refuse to sign off. (See *warrantee.*)

❧ / HEIST  A hoist, pulley, cable (see *hoist* for a Maine variation). *Heist* is simply the way Mainers like to pronounce *hoist*. Besides a lift, the word can mean a jolt: "She tripped on the top step and gave herself a helluva *heist*!"

❧ / HELL RIPPER  A real hurricane that rips hell out of everything.

❧ / HELL TO BREAKFAST  One of numerous Maine terms for the general surroundings in all directions. "All over hell's kitchen" is another. So is "to hell and gone." "All over Christ's Kingdom" is not meant to be more profane than "from Dan to Beersheba," which is about what it means.

❧ / HELL TO PAY  Used thus and in full; *hell to pay and no pitch hot. Pay*, in this sense, is the word for running hot tar or pitch into a vessel's seams, and has no connection with money. Men who payed deck seams knew that *paying all hell* would be quite some job. The same allusion is found in the alternate expression, "enough to pay hell a mile." This *pay* is sometimes changed to patch, probably because tar and miles are now associated with highway work. *Hell to pay and no pitch hot* means contretemps; an unenviable situation; a *jeezley* foul-up.

❧ / HEN FRIGATE  A vessel on which the captain's wife and family accompanied him at sea. Marty Gregson had his wife, his mother-in-law, and ten daughters as his immediate family, and he once called his house a "goddam *hen frigate*."

❧ / Hen's wing   A bird plucked for Sunday dinner would yield two wing tips that made excellent household brushes on the old farms. In certain expressions *wing* is equivalent to brush: "*Wing* the crumbs off the table while I'm bringing the pie."

❧ / Herb, a big   A big wheel, an important man, a VIP. And not exactly in jest; *a big Herb* will really be somebody.

❧ / Herm up   To cloud up and become overcast, but there is a difference in usage with *herm up* and *smear in*. *Smear in* requires the high clouds known as *mare's tails and mackerel sky.*

❧ / Herring-choker   Specifically, a New Brunswicker, but loosely construed in old Maine usage to any native of the Maritime Provinces. The saying was that the people ate so many herring they couldn't take their shirts off because of the bones sticking from their shoulders. See *Bluenose, Pea-Eye,* and *Canuck.* As with some such terms, time has tempered original dubious inferences, and Maritimers today do not mind their nicknames as much as they used to.

❧ / Het   Past participle of heat for many Mainers. Usually with "up": "After she *het* some water up, she popped in the lobsters." (A comparable oddity is *sot,* which see.)

❧ / High and dry   Too far aground to be lifted by the tide. Hence, to be powerless and deserted: "He was *high and dry* with a flat tire and no jack."

❧ / High check rein   It was considered stylish to drive a horse that held his head high, and the *check rein* was that part of the harness that kept him from lowering his head.

To carry the check rein high was a *ritchbitch* practice simple farmers did not affect. *High check reins* were uppity. Hence, any ostentatious display or snobbish comportment is *high check rein* stuff.

❦ / HIGHLANDER   The Maine tide-water man's disdainful term for anybody who lives farther from the ocean than he does. In general, farmers and woodsmen.

❦ / HIGHLINER   Originally, the first vessel of a fishing fleet to reach port with a completely filled hold; up to the *highline* of the hold with fish. *Highline* boats were called "killers" because they often over-supplied the market and killed the price to following boats. Because the crew shared profits, men liked to sail on the *highline* money-makers. The term has since come to mean the man in any harbor who consistently makes the best catches. To be *highline* in your own harbor is a status matter. *Highliners* are always said to be *lucky* (see *lucky*).

❦ / HIGH-WATER MARK   The line along the shore made by the high or full tide. On beaches it is a drift of rockweed, derelict lobster gear, and plastic bottles. The opposite is low-water mark, the point of lowest drain of tide. Some colonial deeds gave riparian ownership to low-water mark, but nearly all Maine property ownership ends at the *high water mark*. Clam flats, thus, are common property (see *Great Ponds*). *High-water* pants have legs that are too short.

❦ / HIGHWAY PATROL   In Maine, this does not mean the state constabulary as it does in other places. In Maine it is the road repair gang, seen moving very slowly except when going home to dinner.

❦ / HIND SIDE TO   Back to the front, in reverse. The Maine euphemism for this is *barse-ackwards*.

❧ / Hitch   Originally, the distance covered by a sailing vessel in a single tack. Transferred as a length of time, it becomes a *hitch* in the navy or a *hitch* as a woods cook. Incidentally, in waterfront language, *hitch* is never a verb; a farmer will *hitch* a horse, a sailor will make him *fast*. *Hitch* is also the nub or crux of a problem: "The *hitch* is, we don't have the money!"

❧ / Hod   The clam *hod* or *rocker* is also used as a measure. Harold Jameson reported he dug fifteen *hods* of potatoes. Holding about a half-bushel, the *hod* is a slatted container into which clams are thrown as they are dug, and then transported. The slatted sides are to permit passage of water when *soused, doused*, etc. (See *rocker*.)

❧ / Hog on ice   The full expression is *independent as a hog on ice*. Some think this refers to a butchered pig in refrigeration, but it really comes from the helplessness of a hog on a frozen pond. Pigs can't walk on ice, and if they try it, there is no relationship to anything intelligent. That's pretty independent.

❧ / Hogback   Sometimes horseback; a long knoll or ridge of land, not too high, common in the Maine landscape from glacial action.

❧ / Hogging   Humping up in the middle. An elderly vessel with a humped rail line amidships, looking as if it might break in two and suggesting the shape of a barnyard hog, is *hogging*.

❧ / Hogsets   About as close as type will come to giving the Maine coast pronunciation of hogsheads. The hogshead and other sizes of casks have always been important in Maine not only as containers for many cargoes, but as units of measurement. Containing two liquid barrels, the *hogset* is by no means limited to holding molasses, rum, vinegar. It equals $7\frac{1}{2}$ bushels of herring. It was also used on the farm for watering tubs, mixing vats for hogfeed, rain barrels, and laying down the October essence of the Maine apple.

❧ / Hog wild  In a rampant, berserk manner, from the way a pig charges around when so inclined. A team *sluiced* on a *skid road* goes *hog wild.* Anybody ravin' and rantin' and chargin' about is *hog wild.*

❧ / Hoist  Used as elsewhere in the correct sense of moving upwards, but interestingly used all along the Maine coast for exactly the opposite: a man will stand on a float and call to someone up on the pier, "*Hoist* down them bait tubs!"

❧ / Hold  The cargo space of a vessel, in which sense it is pronounced as spelled, but more often as hole. *Hold,* to grasp or take *hold,* is usually pronounced holt, or more likely hoult. A swept *hold* is emptiness; thus a man invited to dinner will say, "I got a swept *hole* and can eat a raw dog!"

❧ / Holden  An ancient past participle heard in formal contexts: "Regular stated meeting of Ladies Aid was *holden* . . ."

❧ / Hold turn  The turn of a line on capstan or winch that is held taut; if the *hold turn* is slacked off the line slips on the niggerhead. Thus to *hold turn* is to hang onto what you've got: "Had a chance to sell the woodlot, but decided to *hold turn.*" (See *round turn.*)

❧ / Hole in the snow  Worthless; not worth a *hole in the snow.* (It is a certain kind of a hole, however.)

❧ / Holiday   A skip in painting, a spot missed by the brush.

❧ / Holystone   Soft sandstone slab for scrubbing a vessel's decks; the *holy* came from association with Sunday, the traditional day for neatin' up—probably for devotional services on deck. "Six days shalt thou labor and do all that thou art able, and on the seventh *holystone* the deck and scrape the cable."

❧ / Homeward bound stitches   Temporary sailmaking at sea, intended to last until coming into port where better repairs can be made. The term is now used to describe any hasty and disinterested effort, as when a child neglects his chores and makes *homeward bound stitches* so he can sooner run off to play.

❧ / Honeypot   Seems to be a Maine-ism for a quagmire; a spring mudhole in the highway.

❧ / Hooker   Originally a Dutch fishing boat with sturdy lines; hence, any good workboat, and a stiff slug of something good for what ails you.

❧ / Hook, line, and sinker   All the way; as when a ravenous fish takes in all he can get. A gullible person will swallow a tall story *hook, line, and sinker*. A gentleman too soon brought to wedlock by a designing lady is caught *hook, line, and sinker*.

❧ / Hornswoggle   The standard dictionaries define this as to cheat, hoax, swindle, and bamboozle. But Mainers use it in quite another sense to indicate amazement. Usually, a happy surprise. When a good friend you haven't seen in years walks into your yard, you may grab his hand and exclaim, "Well, I'll be *hornswoggled*—look who's here!"

❧ / Horse-ail   In all Maine usage, horse can be hoss. *Horse-ail* is an indisposition peculiar to horses, and the word survives for a minor and undiagnosed affliction for humans: "Guess I've got the *horse-ail*. I been snifflin' and sneezin' all mornin'!" *Spanish mildew* (which see) suggests malingering; *horse-ail* is likely to be a mild but real disturbance.

❧ / Horse corn   The standard Maine term for yellow corn, as distinguished from sweet corn. The tendency to suppose this derives from feeding it to horses is probably unjustified; *horse* also means coarse, rough, vulgar.

❧ / Horse high   One of the three primary requisites of a good Maine pasture fence: *Horse high*, bull strong, and hog tight.

❧ / Horse Mackerel   Also horsefish, the bluefin tuna. The *horse* in this instance means large or coarse, as in horseplay, horseradish, horse-laughter, etc. Genteel efforts to persuade Maine fishermen to stop saying horsefish because it downgrades the sporty tuna which attracts summer trade have not perceptibly prevailed.

❧ / Hosey   To claim something up for grabs. When Father starts to carve the turkey, one child may cry, "I *hosey* the wishbone!" Mainers generally recognize that the first to cry *hoseys* has established a claim.

❧ / Hosspipe   See *hawsepipe*. While this word has no connection with a horse or hoss, Mainers invariably give it an equine and extreme sibilancy. To say anything like hawzepipe is ridiculous.

❧ / Hot supper   An exciting occasion, and seldom used for the excellent meal from which it derives. A *hot supper* is the finest kind; hence, "That was some *hot supper* of a town meetin'!"

❧ / HOUND-DOG   The tautology is good Maine (see *hand-scythe.*) Rarely does a Mainer say merely *hound.* A *hound-dog* mile, used to measure a walking trail in the woods, is the distance a *hound-dog* chases a rabbit before he (the *hound-dog*) drops dead.

❧ / HOUSE   The word for the enclosed area about the wheel on a lobster or other boat. On a pleasure boat the area will be entirely closed in or at least open only toward the stern. Lobstermen leave the *house* open on the hauling side (some work to port, others to starboard) and toward the stern. A boat without a *house* may gain the same protection from sea and weather with a *sprayhood;* if not, there is an open cockpit. Ashore, *house* is interchangeable with *place* to designate a family dwelling: the Jones *house* (place). This means the Jones family has lived there long enough to be fairly permanently associated—it will remain the Jones *house* for a generation or so after the Joneses are all gone and the property has had several new owners. This traditional Maine custom bothers people like the Gotrocks who buy an old farm and wonder why it doesn't immediately become "the Gotrocks place," even if they hang out a sign. (If they hang out a sign on the Jones *place* which says "Windemereholm," that bothers Mainers just as much.)

❧ / HOVEL   A shelter for lumbercamp horses; hence, a roof over your head. When the great "King" LaCroix went from Eagle Lake down to Philadelphia to buy locomotives from the Pennsylvania Railroad for his tramway operation, he got off the train and asked a taxi driver to take him to "the best *hovel* in town." The taxi man thought he said "hotel," which is what LaCroix meant but not what he said.

❧ / HULLAHWEE TRIBE   An honorary tribe of Maine Indians composed entirely of out-of-state sports. When they come out of the woods onto a road, they look up and down and say, "Where the *Hullahwee?*"

❦ / Humdurgan   A stone lashed to a crotch of a tree limb and used for a rough anchor. The difference between *killick* and *humdurgan* is academic. Some think *killick* was originally a stone placed ashore with a line out to hold a boat in, and a *humdurgan* had the refinement of the crotched stick to make it serviceable in deeper water. In general Maine usage today, the terms are interchangeable.

❦ / Hump   To move right along: "Now, let's get *humpin'* here!" Children are told to *hump* right along, not to dilly-dally. A possible synonym is *hyper*, which see.

❦ / Hung down   Said of a trawl, lobster pot, and anchor which has caught somehow on the ocean floor. Since in this situation it hardly seems "hung up," it is *hung down*.

❦ / Hung drive   A river drive that isn't smoothly following schedule; hence, any project that doesn't come off, or takes longer than it should. If a man and a woman have been keeping company for years but there are no wedding bells, it may be a *hung drive*.

❦ / Huntin' in close   Or gunnin' close. Shooting too near a camp, endangering woodchoppers and others. One year Nellie Bubier of Rangeley went to visit a daughter in Floridy, and a policeman came to shoot a rattlesnake under the steps of the house next door. When the policeman's revolver went off, Nellie jumped and said, "Jeezus-to-mighty! They sure *hunt in close* down here!"

❦ / Hurth   A hearth. Maine masons use *hurth* and harth about fifty-fifty not only for that part of an open fireplace, but for the little shelf on a stove. People who are not masons seem to run toward harth.

❧ / Husband  A ship's *husband* was the man sailing aboard her who was in charge of the business affairs. He kept the manifest, dealt with customs officers, and represented the owners at all times. He was often a part-owner. His job was not unlike that of the *pen-pusher* in a lumber camp, and something of the same joshing attitude went with both titles. These were what we now call "company men." (See *ship's wife.*)

❧ / Hyper  This good prefix is used in Maine as a self-sufficient verb: "He was *hypering* along like a gale o' wind!" To move with great speed. In the story, *The Fastest Hound Dog in the State of Maine*, the Bangor & Aroostook train was just *a-hyperin'*.

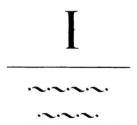

# I

❧ / ICE CREAM SHOT   An easy hunting shot. In the days when ice cream was brought to sporting camps in large wooden tubs, packed with ice and salt, the tubs were returned to town for credit. The choreboy would dump the salt brine from them in a certain place behind camp to attract deer, whose delight in finding salt is well known. Then, in hunting season, a sport who had not shot his deer but had come to the end of his outing would be given an *ice cream shot* on his last day. No need for a paying guest to go home empty-handed! "Salting" or baiting game was and is illegal, but the ice cream water had to be dumped somewhere. The term is used to describe any easy shot, as when a buck stands side to about 20 yards away, whether salted or not. It is also applied to easy scores in athletics, as an unguarded basket or a football play that lets a backfield man score standing up.

❧ / IMPLY   In Maine usage, *imply* carries little sense of implication, but means something more definite. "He *implied* that he would come" usually means that he definitely said that he would come. For the usual meanings of *imply*, Mainers like the word insinuate. "He insinuated that he would come" means that he indicated he would, but didn't actually say so.

❦ / IN   One goes *in* the woods, and one comes *out* of the woods, although members of the *Hullahwee Tribe* (which see) have been known to do the opposite.

❦ / IN COMPANY   Cozy Maine sea-captains' term for crossing the ocean accompanied by several other Maine vessels. Logs told of whole companies of down-Maine ships within sight of each other during the long weeks of the Indian Ocean. (See *gam* for another term covering this aspect of back-home folksiness abroad.)

❦ / IN-OR-OUT   Its freshness long gone through daily repetition, this is still the Mainer's best description of a dog: "*In-or-out*, he's always on the wrong side of the door."

❦ / IRISH   Mainers took part in the general laughter of the times about the Irish. *Irish* draperies are cobwebs, perhaps a bit of one-upmanship with "lace-curtain" *Irish*. "*Irish horse*" is—or was—salted beef. An "*Irish* hurricane" is a *flat-arse calm*. "*Irish* pennants" are loose strands on the ends of lines.

❦ / IRISH MOSS   In this term, the word *Irish* casts no aspersions. *Irish moss* is carrageen, a marine plant harvested along the Maine coast. Nova Scotia, Prince Edward Island, and New Brunswick also produce it commercially. After processing, it is used as a stabilizer in food. Early coastal housewives knew it could be boiled to make a pudding of the blancmange type, and along in the 1930s the dairy industry began using it to smooth out ice cream and give it that quality which lets it hold its shape even after it has melted. Today *Irish moss* is included under one name or another in almost all processed and pre-packaged foods where it suits. Along the Maine coast the *Irish* is usually dropped, and a man who *mosses* is a *mosser*, etc. The plant is pulled or raked at low tide periods, and in warmer weather *mossers* will wade and dive for it. It is brown when harvested, but is bleached white in processing.

🌺 / Iron sick   Used to describe a wooden boat in which the metal fastenings are loose because of age and rust. Sometimes "nail sick."

🌺 / Irregardless   Possibly for emphasis, and possibly because he likes the extra syllable, a Mainer is likely to say *irregardless* when regardless would suffice: "I'm going to go, *irregardless!*"

🌺 / Island cranberries   The very special, superior cranberries found on coastal islands by the happy people able to get to them. When asked by a *summer complaint* if Maine people pick *island cranberries*, Eleanor Mayo once answered, "Pick 'em! We FIGHT over 'em!" Mainers familiar with *island cranberries* will tell you the Cape Cod version isn't worth a trip to the store.

🌺 / Italian sandwich   Originated as such by an Italian-American restaurateur in Portland, *Italian sandwich* is the Maine term for the submarine, grinder, etc.

# J

## ΛΛΛΛ

❦ / JACK (1)   To shine a light into the eyes of game at night, with special Maine reference to deer. It is illegal, except for locating treed raccoons. A deer, entranced, will stand gazing at the light until shot. *Jacking* carries stiff penalties, and to deter it the Maine legislature enacted a law forbidding shining night lights at any game, in season or out, and whether hunting or not. The law is so worded that carrying a flashlight to an outhouse seems to be a criminal act. Any many-celled flashlight is called a "jacklight" in Maine, whether used for *jacking* or not. One who *jacks* is a *jacker*.

❦ / JACK (2)   Dough or batter, as in *flapjack*, yellowjack, *blackjack*.

❦ / JACKASS BRIG   A cross 'twixt a brig and schooner, square-rigged forward. Also called a hermaphrodite *brig*, except that Maine people pronounce that "morphodite." The *jackass brig* could be worked with fewer hands, and this economy made them popular. In time, *jackass brig* has become *jackass rig*, and this term is used today for anything not conforming to type, or something mixed up and offbeat.

❦ / JAG   Since a cord of firewood is a precise quantity (128 cubic feet) about which seller and buyer might dispute, Maine farmers took to selling wood by the load. There was now a set price for whatever the wagon would hold. A wagon so fully loaded with fitted wood that one more stick would slide off was called a *jag* of wood. Accordingly, a gentleman carrying about all the spirits he can manage is said to have a *jag* on or to be on a *jag*.

❧ / JAM   A log *jam*. In river driving, logs got hung up (see *jillpoke*) until thousands were *jammed* together, a situation extremely dangerous to the men.

❧ / JEEZER   A chap, fellow, guy, joker, etc. Used chiefly in Aroostook County, it has the muted tone of blasphemy, but there is none in its usage. A quotation from the Fort Fairfield *Review* of February 23, 1972: ". . . the poor *jeezer* hardly got a word in edgewise."

❧ / JEEZLY   Jeez is a euphemistic interjection, but *jeezly* is a long accepted Maine adjective and adverb without relevancy to Jeez or Jesus: "Don't be so *jeezly* hard to get along with!" Small biscuits can be *jeezly* biscuits and *jeezly* small biscuits. "I never saw such *jeezly* poor fishing!"

❧ / JEEZ-ZUZ!   As an expletive, the extra fillip given the basic word constitutes emphasis for dismay, astonishment, incredulity, amazement, and advanced reactions.

❧ / JESUS TO JESUS AND EIGHT HANDS AROUND!   An exclamation of complete astonishment and utter disbelief; sometimes sheer exuberance. Probably an enthusiastic imitation of a square-dance call, although some say it was the way woodsmen described a very big tree—earth to heaven and eight reaches in circumference.

❧ / JIB   The triangular sail forward on a vessel and hence, the dominant feature of a person. The "cut of one's *jib*" means his foremost appearance; at first sight. Usually heard in the negative: "I didn't like the cut of his *jib*."

❧ / Jigger  A four-wheeled wagon peculiar to the Bangor waterfront in the old days and said to have been designed there. Low-slung, it would probably be a dray in other places. *Jigger* is also the term for a small, triangular sail at the stern of small craft, now seen mostly on lobster boats as a "steadier." On the five- and six-masted schooners (and also on the famous seven-masted *Thomas W. Lawson*) the fifth mast was called the *jigger*-mast, but this lore is largely lost and even old-timers have varying recollections. (The masts on the *Lawson* are sometimes given as fore, main, mizzen, spanker, *jigger*, driver, and pusher.)

❧ / Jillpoke  A long log on a river drive which gets one end stuck somehow and swings to start a *jam*. Thus, an awkward person likely to do something foolish or start trouble. A real *gormy* person is a *jillpoke*.

❧ / Jizzicked  Anything so far gone that repairs are pointless: "That washing machine is so *jizzicked* you might's well buy a new one."

❧ / Jog  Several Maine meanings. When fishermen suspend operations in rough weather, particularly trawling, they are said to be *jogging*. Lobstermen *jog* from hauling one trap to the next. A mother-vessel with dories scattered at *hand lining* will *jog* back and forth until time to pick up the dories. A *jog* is also an irregularly shaped field or piece of timberland, which probably explains *jog* of pie: a piece of pie, not too large, not too small, "just a *jog*." Mainers also use *jog* for reminding: to *jog* a memory.

❧ / John D  Maine woods term for kerosene oil, after Mr. Rockefeller. "Put the *John D* to her!" means to kindle a fire. Maine guides early invented "kerodust," a bottle of sawdust impregnated with *John D.* A tablespoon of it will start a fire in a rainstorm.

❦ / JOHNNYWOOD BOATS, JOHNNY BOATS    Small boats that specialized in bringing firewood for Maine's lime kilns. The name derives from the St. John River, where most of these boats were built. It took 30 cords of wood to fire a single burning of lime, so *Johnnywood boats* were numerous in and out of Rockport, Rockland, and Thomaston. *Johnnywood boats* were also known as kiln-wooders, kiln-coasters, and lime-wooders.

❦ / JOHN R. BRADEN    A sure thing, a winner, *John R. Braden* was an incredible harness-racing horse in post-World War I days, who held and broke most records. He had his personal bank account and was once honored guest at a testimonial banquet in Presque Isle. He is buried and memorialized at Northern Maine Fair grounds. Hence, to have anything verging on a *John R. Braden* is to be well fixed. A popular song all Mainers sang in the 1920s had this couplet:

> John R. Braden, you're a winner
> Just as sure as I'm a sinner . . .

❦ / JOHN THE BAPTISTS    Small bits of yeast-bread dough snitched before the batch is put in pans for baking, and fried as a breakfast hotbread. Bacon or pork fat gives them a crisp outside. Well buttered, they are delicious with jam, molasses, maple syrup, and honey.

❦ / JOKER    Another word like *jeezer, cuss, party, bugger*, etc., which Mainers like to toss off for person.

❦ / JONAH    Derived from poor Jonah in the Bible, the word means a hard-luck artist, and both at sea and in the woods certain crew members had reputations for enticing dire consequences. Such were termed the *jonah* of the crew. Specifically, in Maine cookery a *jonah* is a *cry-baby* cookie filled with red pepper or something other than sweets. When it was mixed with the good cookies at table, the one who got it became the *jonah* and was expected to pay a forfeit. (See the C. A. Stephens short story, *How Hannibal Hamlin Got the Jonah*.)

❦ / JUG  The Maine word for a bottle as acquired at the state liquor store.

❦ / JUMPER (1)  In Maine, this is usually "jumping Frenchman." The term for a person whose startle response is more exaggerated and dramatic than usual. For some time medical authorities erroneously believed it was peculiar to Canadian-Frenchmen working in the Maine woods. In recent years a Portland neurologist, Dr. E. Charles Kunkle, has spent much time studying these people, and he now says he believes it seemed indigenous to Maine only because it was first noticed here and gained attention through lumber-camp horseplay. It has always seemed great fun to jump a *jumper*. Any sudden noise or outcry will send him into an uncontrolled reaction, sometimes severe enough to injure himself or others. Stories of Maine *jumpers* are a dime a dozen. When Dr. Kunkle began his studies, the personnel manager of one Maine paper mill gave him the names of fifteen *jumpers* in one crew! Holman Day, Maine bard of camp and fireside, has a rhyme about a *jumper* who, every night when a passing train whistled outside his house, would belt his wife again.

❦ / JUMPER (2)  Apart from "jumping Frenchmen," *jumper* is a small child's sled, perhaps because he jumps on it to ride. Sometimes a barrel stave rigged with a small seat for coasting. A *jumper* is also a frock for shop work or chores. In the woods, the front sled of a double logging rig

J / 149

is the *jumper*, and if used alone for work is called a one-sled. Two such sleds in tandem thus become a two-sled, and early logging roads improved enough to accommodate the double loads were called two-sled roads. This didn't mean they were "two sleds wide," but only that they were used by two-sleds.

❧ / JUNK   The Maine way to pronounce chunk. A *junk* of wood for the stove, meat for a pot-roast, pie for a dinner pail. A fairish-sized piece; a hunk. Wood which has been sawn to stove-length but not yet split (*fitted*) is *junked*. The parent word, chunk, is almost never used in Maine.

❧ / JURY RIG   Temporary repairs to a vessel or her rigging, made at sea to bring her into port after storm or other damage, were *jury-rigged*. It is make-do until better can be had. Ashore, it means any bailing-wire job; and *jury-rigged* is, of course, the seafaring origin of the inaccuracy "jerry-rigged."

❧ / JUSTICE   Of the peace. Unlike some states where the "JP" has status and judicial duties, Maine relegates him to a minor officer. He never presides in court, and frequently isn't even an attorney. There is no reason to address him as Judge. He makes jurats, signs depositions, can marry people, and in emergencies can act for other lawful officers in their absence, but in Maine jurisprudence he is a notch below the Notary Public.

# K

⁓⁓⁓⁓
⁓⁓⁓

❧ / Kaybecker For Québecker, used in the Maine woods for Canadian workers from *La Belle Province*. It is considered kinder than, and has somewhat supplanted, the old *Canuck*. The common United States pronunciation of Kwee-beck is, of course, linguistically wrong.

❧ / Kay-Eye See *KI*.

❧ / Keelson In general usage *keelson* is pronounced with the long *ee* sound, but sometimes kel-son; indeed, kel-son is given as an alternate spelling. In Maine, keelson is pronounced kill-s'n. The related word, keelhaul—to haul a person by a rope from one side of a ship to the other under the keel for punishment—is not used literally in Maine today, but always refers to some similar terrible fate: "Pneumonia keelhauled the poor *joker*. He came out of the hospital and didn't weigh 90 pounds soaking wet."

❧ / Keep The Maine term for the operation of the public school system; school *keeps*. School does not *keep* during vacation. The word is important in a derived Maine expression to show intense happiness and indifference to consequences: "He was so full of Nell's lobster stew he didn't care if school *keeps* or not!" One time a summercater walked down on Sim Coombs's wharf and said to Sim,

"Folks around here don't seem too friendly!" Sim said, "Oh, them kind'll all be gone soon's school *keeps*."

🌿 / Keeper   A lobsterman's *counter*, but more often applied to fresh-water sport-fish. A salmon under 14 inches cannot be lawfully kept, but if longer than 14 inches he is a *keeper*. A *keeper* is also an apple or vegetable that keeps well in winter storage; the Northern Spy is a good *keeper*.

🌿 / Kee-reist!   Like *Jeez-zuz!*—an extreme accent. There is the old Maine story of the superintendent of schools who was examining the pupils at end-of-term, and whenever a good little boy or girl gave a proper answer he would exclaim, "Kee-RECK!" When the naughty little boy gave him a naughty answer, he let go, "Kee-REIST!"

🌿 / Kench   Also *kinch*. Bins in which fish are salted. *Kenching* is the art of laying fish and salt alternately to get just the right corn or brine; a good *kencher* doesn't waste salt, but gets on enough.

🌿 / Kennebecker   A Maine woodsman's knapsack or packsack, and now including the packbasket.

🌿 / Kennebec turkey   A *bloater*.

🌿 / Kental   Maine pronunciation and often spelling of *quintal*, which see.

🌿 / Kerf   The educated forester's uppity word for what every Maine chopper and sawyer calls the *scarf*. It is the cut or groove made by the ax to direct the falling tree in the right direction; and it is also the cut made by a saw in the log at the mill. The standard 54-inch circular saw of the old Maine sawmills took out a ¼-inch *kerf/scarf*, and the various log rules that estimated MBF (1000 board feet) in a log made allowance for this.

❦ / KETTLEBOTTOM   Maine term for what geologists usually call a kettle hole. Glacial ice got covered with gravel moraine, and when the ice melted in after times, part of the surface caved in to make a crater. *Kettlebottoms* are numerous in Maine's gravel areas; one of the larger ones is in the town of Bowdoin and is near enough to a good road to be easily visited. It's on the old Abel Grover *place*, just north of Purinton's Corner.

❦ / KI   Localism for Katahdin Iron Works, a township in Piscataquis County where ore smelting was once done. The works are still there, and the area is a state park.

❦ / KIB   An invention of Maine woodsmen to keep black flies at bay while sleeping. A box-like frame was covered with netting to permit breathing, and one side was open for the communicant to stick in his head. The loose end of the netting about the neck was tucked under the blanket or jacket collar. The *kib* amounted to a screened-in porch just big enough for one man's head. The only drawback was that it sometimes got pretty warm in there.

❦ / KIDS   Pens on the deck of a fishing boat for holding the catch as it comes aboard. Each man hove into his own *kid*, and later would call out his tally to the skipper as he moved them into the main *kid*. To *kid* somebody in the sense of misusing him and putting him on seems not to have been traced to this origin by the dictionary makers.

❦ / KILL-DEVIL   Ah, that demon rum! A spot of *kill-devil* kills the bedevilment of aches and pains that flesh is heir to.

❦ / KILLICK   Most authorities say "origin unknown." A *killick* is a small anchor, usually homemade and sometimes from a rock. See *humdurgan*. To put down a *killick* means to settle in, almost to take root. A selectman said, "We watch these newcomers to town, and if they look's-if they're going to drop their *killicks*, we charge 'em back to the place they came from." This means that if they look as if they might go on welfare, their residence is carefully established in town of origin before the time limit that would make them "settled" and the responsibility of the new town.

❧ / KILLIG POLE    About the same as the *Samson pole*, which see. The *killig pole* is usually precautionary and the *Samson pole* is rigged after the tree has "leaned toward *sawyers*." (See *sawyers*.) Both are leverage devices in lumbering; when heavier duty comes along, the word *Samson* naturally applies.

❧ / KIN TO KAINT    From can see to can't see; dawn to dusk. In outdoor work the weather is a factor, and in shipyards, on farms, and in the woods it was the custom to work *stiddy* in pleasant weather from *kin to kaint*.

❧ / KINDERGARTEN    Sometimes nursery; a place in fresh-water streams where smaller fish grow up and later migrate into a pond. True sportsmen keep away, as the fish are small and easy to catch, but when other places aren't yielding, a *kindergarten* will provide panfish for breakfast.

❧ / KING SPOKE    The uppermost spoke in the ship's steering wheel when the rudder is full amidships. The *king spoke* is marked, usually with a Turk's head knot. *King spoke* has the same conversational value as king pin (from bowling)—a big shot or something crucial and important.

❧ / KITE    To fly around, and thus in Maine speech something of a synonym for *gallivant* and traipse. There may be a spicy context, such as a female who *kites* around up to no good, but there needn't be: "The cow *kited* over the fence and took off."

❧ / KITTY-CORNER   Maine preference for what others designate as quarter-corner or cater-corner. Obliquely across: The church sits *kitty-corner* to the post office.

❧ / KNEE-HIGH TO A SCUPPER   Since a scupper is flush with the deck, this is about as short as anybody can be. *Knee-high* to a grasshopper and *knee-high* to Mother's ap'n-hem are variants. Used to describe a short person, it is more often self-reminiscent: "I warn't more'n *knee-high to a scupper* when my Old Man first took me seinin'."

❧ / KNITTING   Odd jobs of a fill-in kind; *knitting* was woman's work she could pick up and lay down between other duties. Sharpening fence stakes can be *knitting* work between maple season and plowing. The making of nets, bait bags, and lobster-pot heads is also *knitting* in this sense of an odd-moment task, but see *mash, mash board,* and *mash needle* for coastal terminology.

❧ / KNITTLES   The short lines on each side of a sail which, when tied together at the foot of the canvas, will reduce the surface exposed to the wind. Reef points.

❧ / KRAWM   For crum; a lot of rubbish. *Culch* does not suggest the uselessness and offensiveness of *krawm*. *Culch* may have value; *krawm* is to be hove out. The word is used to downgrade excellence: after a bountiful meal of delicious goodies opulently served, a sated guest may say, "There! That's about all of that *krawm* I can take!"

# L

/\\.\\/\\/\\.\\

❦ / Laborin' oar The oar that does more of the work, usually the one to leeward. Anybody willing to do just a mite more than is expected of him is compared to a *laborin' oar*.

❦ / Lackin' Deficient, especially in wit and judgment: "She was *lackin'* when she married that no-good!"

❦ / Ladder A word that shows how Acadian French has touched the Maine vocabulary. Tourists to *The Valley* who use an overnight room think it quaint when a boy carries their baggage up the *ladder* which is, of course, a staircase. Early Acadian settlers had rude cabins with lofts that were reached by a ladder—*échelle*. When homes were sophisticated and stairways built, the people had either forgotten or did not know the parent French word for them—*escalier*. They continued to call staircases *ladders—des échelles*.

❦ / Lamb Out-of-season venison. *Lamb* actually is the word for a yearling deer. A gentleman who poaches a deer will package the meat neatly and put it in his freezer marked *Lamb*. (See *bullbeef*; sometimes venison is served as such.)

❦ / Lanch And, of course, *larnch*. Launch is always given the *lanch* and *larnch* sounds now, but in the days of naphtha launches there was a disposition to make an exception, and they were given a decided *lawnch*.

❦ / Land-baisted   Maine variant of lambasted.

❦ / Landing   A *landing* place, as a wharf; specifically in Maine the public *landing* maintained with tax funds and called the "town *landing*." A privately owned *landing* will more likely be called a wharf. The term *landing* has been enlarged to mean the area of a community in the vicinity of a *landing* until it is almost synonymous with waterfront. Brunswick has such a *landing* along the river front. *Landing* is also a timberland term for a place to unload and store logs, a *brow*. The combination of the coastal and inland meanings is exemplified at Freeport, where the town has two sections known as Porter's Landing and Mast Landing. Mast Landing was a place to unload ship timbers; Porter's Landing was the scene of maritime activities by the Porter family. Today neither is any sort of a landing in the old sense, but the term now means those sections of town. Some people who live at Porter's Landing are out of sight of the water.

❦ / Land poor   Maine farmers unable to work all the land they own are said to be *land poor*.

❦ / Lapstrake   Often spoken as if lapstreak, this is a term for overlapping planks or strakes on a boat's frame. The Rangeley boat is *lapstraked*. Saltwater folks sometimes called such construction "clinker-built."

❦ / Larboard   If heard at all today, it's a hoity-toity matter, as if somebody said "prithee" or "eftsoons!" Maine ship captains pretty much kicked it out of the language. In the old British marine, *larboard* and starboard had their day, but Mainers found that, bellow as they could on deck, the words sounded too much alike to a man reefing sail in a topmast blow. Distinct, easily understood commands were important as vessels got larger. *Larboard* became the Yankee port.

❧ / LARRIGANS  The old felt boots and rubbers of the Maine woodsman; warm, comfortable footwear for the climate. The rubber bottom (originally detachable for evening wear) on a felt or leather boot gave L. L. Bean his idea for the famous Maine Hunting Shoe.

❧ / LARRUPING  Although Maine people use *larrup around* for reckless speed, etc., they are more likely to use *larruping* for a spanking or even a downright *thrashin'*: "Marty gave Joe a helluva *larrupin'!*"

❧ / LASH  The seaman's term for making anything secure with a rope. Beckets were on sea chests not only as handles, but for *lashing* the chests to secure them in heavy weather. The word is used generally for any kind of tightening up: a load of loose hay may be *lashed* to the rack with a line, or the cellar door *lashed* by simply closing it and shooting a bolt.

❧ / LAUNDRESS  One of many friendly Maine terms for the wife. Since she manipulates the washing, a gentleman introduces her with, "Want you to meet my *laundress!*"

❧ / LAW  With reference to hunting and fishing, the Maine *law* is either on or off. Instead of "open season," the *law* is off. When the season closes, the *law* goes on. When moose were well-nigh extinct in Maine, the state "put on" a *law*; now that moose have increased, there is agitation to "take the *law* off."

❧ / LAY AWAY  Kindly term for destroying an animal: "We had to *lay* old Tige *away*."

❧ / Lay by   As a verb, to put money away for a rainy day, or to store up any asset: "He's got quite a wad *laid by,*" or, "They've *laid by* twenty bushels of potatoes for winter." As a noun, a *lay-by* is a turn-out on a log-haul where one vehicle *lays by* until another passes. The original state highway from Eustis to Coburn Gore, completed in 1928, was described as "a one-lane gravel road with *lay-bys.*"

❧ / Lay up   Usually *laid up;* ill, probably sick abed: "Ben's been *laid up* with pneumonia."

❧ / Lazaret   The *lazaret* aboard ship was a storage cuddy toward the stern. Ashore, it's any kind of a catch-all, a *glory hole.* Real salty old Mainers used to call Henry Ford's rumble seats *lazarets,* and the word has been applied to the luggage trunks on newer automobiles.

❧ / Lazy dog   A *lazy dog* is the opposite of a downhill *cant.* It is easy to roll a log downhill, but if the tree lay so the logs had to be rolled uphill onto the sled *bunks,* the men had a *lazy dog.* The explanation of this seems to be nothing more than a pun. A slope up, a slow pup, a *lazy dog.*

❧ / Lead   The leaden weight on the line dropped overboard to learn the depth of water, and in usage the whole thing, line and *lead* together. Thus, "to heave the *lead*" is to plumb the depths, to find out how things stand. The *lead* weight had a cupped bottom to bring up samples of bottom ground when it was used in fishing. (See *butter.*) Fathometers using radar echoes are now in vogue, but "to sound somebody out" (like *heaving the lead*) is still in the language, it means an inquiry to ascertain his opinion.

❧ / Leave   To pass an object at sea and *leave* it astern. Old logs had such sentences as, "Sighted brig A.M., by noon *left* her wide to starboard." Boating instructions may be,

"Come up the gut and *leave* Poopadoo Island on your left hand." (Mainers do NOT always use port and starboard!)

❧ / LEE Opposite of windward, and much used in Maine speech. The old seafaring admonition that a bucket must always be emptied to *lee* has application in several advisory contexts, and is a measure of sanity: "He's fool enough to try to spit to wind'ard!" A *lee* shore will be on a vessel's *lee*, one toward which the wind is blowing, and a bad place to *beach up*: "If she don't stop spending so much money, that marriage will wind up on a *lee* shore!"

❧ / LEEWARD *Lee*, alone, is always pronounced as spelled, but *leeward* is always loo-ward. Opposite of windward, in which the second *w* is dropped: wind'ard. Geographical dictionaries notwithstanding, the *Leeward* Islands were always the Loo-ards to Mainers, many of whom knew them well.

❧ / LENGTH AND BREADTH The right phrase for describing Maine totally. *The Length and Breadth of Maine* is the title of Stanley B. Attwood's excellent compendium of facts about the state: geography, derivations, flora and fauna, and much historical data. Mr. Attwood found the phrase in common use before he wrote his book. "In the *length and breadth* of Maine," the tourist pamphlets say, "you will find no poisonous snakes." Candidates for governor and senator like to toss off, "As I've traveled the length and breadth of Maine . . ." Senator Fred Hale used to vary this cliché by saying, "From Kittery to Fort Kent, from Eastport to the Magalloway . . ." He meant the *length and breadth* of Maine.

❧ / LET UP Rain *lets up*. "If this weather'll *let up*, I'll plant my beans." Similarly, one who has been hammering a pet project will *let up* on it and talk about something else for a change.

L / 161

❦ / LIARS' BENCH   A settee before the village store, inside by the stove, or at the post office, where gentlemen exchange veracities. (See *deacon seat.*)

❦ / LIBERRY   At least 999 out of 1000 times, the library.

❦ / LICENSE TO STEAL   A Mainer's traditional gauge of the second best unit of prosperity: "I'd rather have his luck than a *license to steal.*" Or, "With looks like hers, who needs a *license to steal?*"

❦ / LIEF   Dictionaries say this is archaic in general English, but it is alive and bright in Maine: "I'd as *lief* eat fish any day as have a steak." The comparative is frequently heard: "I'd *liefer* go than stay home alone."

❦ / LIGHT 'N' FLUFFY   Highest praise for hot biscuits. When they come out'*n* the oven *light 'n' fluffy*, the world is bright.

❦ / LIGHTNING STRIKE   A forest fire started by lightning, and also the browned-out area that remains an eyesore for years to come. A *lightning strike* will be used as a landmark: "Fish down the lake to the *lightning strike*, but you won't likely hook anything beyond that."

❦ / LIGHT OUT   The numerous standard dictionary meanings of *light*, both as to illumination and heft, do not seem to cover precisely the Mainer's meaning of *light out* for a "quick start." Sometimes *light out* doesn't suggest speed and is merely a synonym for start, go, proceed: "After supper we *lit out* for town." More often it does suggest speed: "He *lit out* like *salts through a goose!*"—i.e., he took off.

❧ / LIKE A TRAIN OF CARS  "Going to beat the cars" is a variant of this. Using a railroad train as a unit of speed, and also suggesting some clatter and excitement. However, a boat may be described as coming up the harbor *like a train of cars*. Moving right along.

❧ / LIKE EATIN' PIE  Easy and pleasurable to do, in any context: "I thought we'd have trouble haulin' that bo't, but it was just *like eatin' pie!*" What's nicer than *eatin' pie?*

❧ / LIKE MAD  No doubt from "like a madman," this means in an utmost fashion. Driving *like mad, working like mad*, eating *like mad*, running *like mad*.

❧ / LILY IRON  The harpoon with detachable head, used for whales, swordfish, and horsefish. To put the *lily iron* to somebody is to deflate him, and perhaps even to beat him up.

❧ / LIMB OUT  To cut the limbs and top from a tree that has been felled. Accordingly, if somebody gets *limbed out*, he's been trimmed down considerably: "The new schoolteacher *limbed out* that Huxley kid this morning!"

❧ / LINE CAR  Special heated boxcars used by the Bangor & Aroostook railroad for shipping potatoes. (See *potato bug* [2].)

❧ / LINE STORM  Traditionally, a severe weather disturbance along the North Atlantic seaboard on or about the times of the vernal and autumnal equinoxes; an equinoctial storm. *Line*, of course, means equator. Meteorologists now say there is no scientific basis for associating a storm with the sun's crossing the *line*, but *line storms* are entrenched in Maine lore: "Rain? I guess it rained! You'd think we were having the *line storm.*"

❦ / LINE TRAWLER   A fishing trawler using long lines suspended over the sea floor from spaced buoys, and shorter lines running down with baited hooks.

❦ / LINE TREE   A tree growing precisely on the common land line of two owners. When one owner cuts lumber and the other doesn't, the usual practice is to start at one corner and take every second *line tree* as it comes. But regrettable mistakes occur, and many a man has found that his neighbor cut off and left no *line trees* at all. You can go to law about it.

❦ / LINKUMVITTY   Maine shipyard pronunciation of *lignum vitae*, the extremely hard tropical wood preferred for deadeyes, blocks, and certain other fittings aboard ship.

❦ / LITTLE   A rather nice variation occurs in Maine usage: "He hit his thumb with the hammer, and he didn't like it a *little* bit!" Not at all, AT ALL! (Compare the equivalent French *un peu*.)

❦ / LITTLE NO'TH O' NO'TH   Entered here (rather than under *no'th*) since the word *little* has a down-playing effect. Anything a *little no'th o' no'th* is incredible; maybe something from the liar's bench, or a morsel of fresh gossip.

❦ / LIVE   Alive (*'live*). In sawmills, a log being made into boards is first slabbed until square, so all the boards from one log will be the same width. But sometimes, to get full advantage of very good lumber, boards are ripped out without prior slabbing, so they come off the saw carriage with bark on both edges. Such boards are said to be sawn *'live* or *'live* edge. Boatbuilders like *'live* boards. (Not the same as wainy; see *wain*.)

❦ / LIVER-FISH   Hatchery fish stocked by the Fish & Game wardens, as differentiated from native spawned fish.

Newly-released trout need a certain time to clear their systems of the odd flavor that comes from hatchery food that is largely beef liver.

❧ / LIVE SHORT   To be cheated a mite in life; it happens to people who don't live in Maine: "It took a month back in Rockport to show us we'd *lived short* all those years in Connecticut."

❧ / LIVE STORM   A gale with rain or snow, as distinguished from a *dry gale*.

❧ / LIVID   A state of being which, in Maine, is not especially related to color. It signifies agitation: "Talk about being *exercised*—he was *livid!*" (Give it the sound of *livvid*.)

❧ / LOBSTER LAKE   A Maine lake (3R14 and XR14, *WELS* (see WELS) that looks on the map very like a lobster. As happens so often with Maine geographical terms, reference to it means a region as well as the specific lake; the Lobster *operation* is a widespread pulpwood cutting.

❧ / LOCK DAM   In Maine lumbering, a dam which holds back water completely and has no spillway. The purpose is to divert water elsewhere for better driving conditions or for hydroelectric uses. The most famous *Lock Dam* in Maine is that at Chamberlain Lake, which turns Allagash River waters down the East Branch of the Penobscot.

❧ / LODGED   A tree that, in being felled, falls against another standing tree and is hung up. The situation is often fraught with some danger to the chopper, and vexes him. Any untoward happenstance may produce a Maine simile based on this. Also, grass or grain which has been trampled or laid down by a storm is said to be *lodged*, and is difficult to mow with a scythe: "Persnickety as *lodged* oats."

❧ / Log   The maritime uses of *log* and its derivatives are general; Maine's timberland meanings are more indigenous. *Log* is the term for lumbering; *to log* off an area: "After Paul Bunyan *logged* off Maine, he went to Minnesota." A *logging* operation is a woodland harvest, whether for pulpwood or lumber. A *chopper* may be called a *logger*. A lumber camp is often a *logging* camp. Roads for transporting to the mill are *logging* roads and *log*-hauls. The old *Lombard* steam tractor was a *log*-hauler. *Logging* sled means any heavy winter rigging suitable for hauling *logs*, even if

used for other purposes. There is also the Maine expression, "to sit like a bump on a *log*"; it means to be inactive while others are busy. "Everybody got up and said his piece, but Charley just sat there like a bump on a *log*." "Now we're *loggin'*!" means we have everything under control and going well.

❧ / Logan   A small cove or inlet in fresh water, usually off a pond, and often where a stream comes into a pond. The word suggests sluggish or still water, not too deep, and often a *logan* makes good trout fishing. Presumably the Maine term derives from the Scottish *lochan*, a small loch or lake, but some have wondered if it comes from the Gaelic *bogan*.

❧ / Log-haul   A wilderness roadway built for hauling logs either to a river or all the way to a mill. After the *Lombard* (which see) was perfected, log-hauls were engineered for trains of sleds, and were as well graded as railway lines. Since vestiges of such *log-hauls* are frequent in the Maine wilderness, references to them will be heard often. A logging road is not necessarily a *log-haul*, and the *tote-road* should never be confused with either. (See tote.)

❧ / Log mark   As cattle were later branded on the Plains, Maine timber was marked to identify ownership when several operators drove a river simultaneously. The marks were registered, and in the beginning were straight lines that could be cut with an ax: / /, X, +, etc. Later, embossing heads were put on axes, and today a squirt from a paint gun is used. In present-day speech, to have one's mark on something is reminiscent of this way of proving ownership. "She's sure got him *marked* for wedding bells!"

❧ / LOG RULE   Nothing to do with logarithms, this is a yardstick-like rule marked off so that it will compute the board feet a *sawyer* should get from a log. It is used by *scalers*. The first such rule is said to be the *Bangor Rule*, figured out in Maine for old-growth stumpage, and in popular speech it has become a gauge of probity: if a man goes by the Bangor Rule in his daily affairs, he will be just and upright and can be trusted. A rule similar to the *Bangor Rule* (sometimes called *scale*) is the *International Rule*, now used more generally on second-growth timber, and in some states it has been legislated as the legal gauge. To "go by the rule" has a definite Maine connotation in many expressions which are not related to the more highly publicized, but no more esteemed, Golden Rule.

❧ / LOG WATCH   Even though river-driving has waned, the *log watch* will remain for some time as a wilderness bogeyman. It was his job to patrol the river banks and make sure nobody stole marked wood from the drives. Since unmarked wood was up for salvage, there were frequent disputes between him and farmers along the stream who were "catching" firewood. It wasn't any fun to catch five cords of wood and then find the *log watch* had thrown it back in the river. Children very often grew up thinking the *log watch* was something like a wicked ogre; "The *log watch*'ll get you if you don' watch out!"

❧ / LOMBARD   Mainers often use *lombard* for something huge and spectacular, as if it were a synonym for *rauncher, baister, lunker.* A person who is big, strong, and able may be called a "reg'lar *lombard* of a man." The Lombard family made lumbering equipment in Waterville, and around the turn of the century came up with a steam tractor that greatly changed the harvesting of Maine timberlands. A restored *Lombard* may be seen at the Lumberman's Museum in Patten. The *Lombard* moved west as lumbering did, and was the prototype of the British army tank used in World War I. In the 1920s the steam drive was changed to an internal combustion engine. In Maine usage, *Lombard* is pronouned *lum-b'd.*

❦ / LONG DRINK    Of water. Used to describe a tall person, and usually a female: "Migod, but she's a *long drink* of water!"

❦ / LONG-HANDLED    To describe underwear; long-sleeved and long-legged.

❦ / LONG-JAWED    Almost anything extended and drawn out; lantern-jawed. Nautically, it's a rope with its twist undone. A tiresome speech is *long-jawed,* and it's a *long-jawed* walk to round up a stray cow.

❦ / LONG-LEGGED    A vessel with a deep bottom disproportionate to beam. Also a house on spiles or high foundation, and hence anything tall. The girl compared to a *long drink* of water may be amended to a *long-legged drink* of water.

❦ / LONG NECK    The true Maine clam, also called the soft shell. (See *clam.*)

❦ / LONG-TRAIL    A one-time Indian route, with side trails, running from Micmac and Malacite country in New Brunswick as far south as Chesapeake Bay. In its day it was as definite a thoroughfare as Routes 1 and 95. The section through Maine has been fairly well re-found by Indian and outdoor buffs. Down east Indians, recruited by General Washington to fight in the Revolution, started for Boston over the *Long Trail*, but turned to the sea near present Machias and finished the journey by ship. Early English-speaking settlers of Aroostook County arrived there over the *Long Trail*. To "take the *Long Trail*" in early Maine days meant to go to Boston on foot.

❦ / LOOCIVEE   Mainer's approximation of the *loup cervier* of the French-Canadian woodsmen; the Canada lynx. Through mis-identification and in error, *loocivee* is sometimes applied to the bobcat.

❦ / LOOKINEST   The superlative of looking, coined by Mainers for oddest, most peculiar, most amusing, and usually the most utterly ridiculous spectacle. The tourist in vacation garb doesn't realize that a lobsterman's reaction is often, "That's the *lookinest* thing we've seen all season!"

❦ / LOOM (1)   A coastal term of precise meaning much abused by headline writers who give us, "Trouble *Looms* in Steel Mills." A *loom* is like a mirage on the desert; light rays are refracted by atmospheric conditions until a headland viewed from a ship's deck appears to be elevated above the water. This illusion is the *loom* of the land; land *looms* and it is not necessary to add "up." As one sails the coast of Maine, the various islands will *loom* one by one. After a voyage, the first sighting of land is a landfall, and depending on atmospherics it may or may not *loom*.

❦ / LOOM (2)   Loam. Mainers spell it *loam* but pronounce it *loom*. "Bring a lo'd a *loom* to smooth up my lawn when you get to it."

❦ / LOOWARD   More accurately, *loo'ard*. Entered here under its pronunciation. (See *lee* and *leeward*.)

❦ / Lower than whale dung   Lowest of the low in character references; and also used to describe a downcast mood. (See *whale manure*.)

❦ / Lucky   Amongst Maine fishermen the word means more than chance. It implies proficiency, know-how, know-where, know-when, and skill at handling gear. A *lucky* fisherman brings in good catches. Highliners are *lucky* (see *highliner*.)

❦ / Luff and bear away   This sailing term for maneuvering downwind is used ashore to tell a child underfoot to get out of the way.

❦ / Lug   Used indiscriminately with *tote* and *haul* whenever it means a fairly heavy load. Water is *lugged* in pails, but also may be *hauled* in pails. *Lug* suggests overburden. Horses that strain are *lugging*; so is an automobile that slows and knocks on hills. A woman carrying a small child is said to be *lugging* it in her arms. The bag boy *lugs* your groceries to the automobile, and when you get home you *lug* them in the house. Even when it comes to *carry* or portage, Mainers may prefer to say, "We *lugged* the canoe." A *lug* is a stupid, oafish person; a *gorm*: "Don't ask him to the party, he's an awful *lug!*" To *lug* a shore is to sail close in; hug. To *lug* right along is to make good speed; at sea it means to carry more sail than is prudent, but ashore it will be heard thus: "We got held up in traffic at Bangor, but after that we *lugged* right along." It is possible this last usage confuses the nautical "logging" with lugging, as "logging right along" is a seafaring way of making good time. It is also possible that the highlanders' expression "Now we're logging!" may derive from seafaring instead of lumbering, but few highlanders will suppose so.

❦ / Lug a jug   With an invitation to a picnic, it means to bring your own bottle. Coastal vessels needing rock ballast to keep stable are said to *lug a jug*.

❧ / LULLY    A soggy, boggy mess. Bog mud, or the wet area around a barnyard manure pile. A quagmire or morass. This also includes mental situations: "He waded around in the *lully* of his own foolish argument." A child will make a *lully* if he stirs up his breakfast oatmeal, milk, and molasses.

❧ / LUMBERJACK    Not Maine; see *chopper*.

❧ / LUMPER    Originally used to designate a laborer who helped load or unload vessels, it now generally refers to a man engaged in any unskilled work. "We could do with a *lumper* to clean up the mess around this place."

❧ / LUNCHGROUND    A wilderness picnic area designated by a forestry warden where fires may be made without permit. Some have been in use a long time and have special names: Canoe Pool Lunchground, Fontinales Lunchground, etc. Mainers would not use *lunchground* for a highway rest area or just any picnic spot.

❧ / LUNKER    A big deer will be termed a *rauncher*, but a big game fish is a *lunker*. *Baister* means about the same.

❧ / LUTE    Perhaps *loot*. A scoop used with a horse for excavating. It has two handles like a wheelbarrow, and when the handles are held down it digs. It then rides with the dirt flat on the ground, and dumps itself when the handles are lifted. Seems to be a word unique to Maine. It is also a verb: *to lute* a cellar hole. When similar tools became available for attaching to farm tractors, the manufacturers offered them as *scoops*, but Maine farmers continued to call them *lutes*.

❧ / L-Y    The correct Maine pronunciation of alewife, the lesser herring known in the Maritimes as the *gaspereau*. The plural of *L-Y* is *L-wise*.

# M

❧ / Mackerel sky   When the sky is said to *smear in*, the high wispiness comes in two recognizable Maine terms; *mares'-tails* and *mackerel sky*. The suggestion of a horse's tail is obvious; the mottled pattern of the patchy kind suggests the back markings of a mackerel. In Maine lore the combination of these two shapes of clouds is more than a portent; it's an absolute certainty: "*Mares'-tails* and *mackerel sky*, never twenty-four hours dry."

❧ / Mackinaw   Most lumbering terms originated in Maine and were picked up by westerners; this is one Maine borrowed from the Great Lakes country. The heavy outgarment with abbreviated lower line was ideal for lumbering and other outdoor winter work. "Holy Old *Mackinaw!*" became such a favorite mild, Maine-woods expletive that Stewart Holbrook used it as the title of his history of lumbering. In use, *mackinaws* absorb occupational tang until a "boiled *mackinaw*" suggests unpalatable and tough food.

❧ / Madawaska French   A combination of English and French developed in Maine's St. John River valley after English-speaking settlers mingled with the Acadians already there. In its own way, it is not unlike the pidgin English developed in the Orient. *Madawaska* is an Indian name for a region now divided between Maine and New Brunswick, and it is the name of Maine's northernmost town. *Madawaska French* is sometimes called Fort Kent English. It has served well for cross-language communications in the region, but the French Academy has not (up to a late hour) sanctioned it as pure. A sample is a sign posted on a wilderness road across a dam:

AVIS!
Vitess sure set ecluse pas
plus que 15 miles a leure!

❦ / MAGALLOWAY SALMON    A chub or dace that grows to some size in Magalloway River and Parmacheene Lake. It will hit a salmon or trout fly and for a moment the angler thinks he's having fun. Decidedly a trash fish. Anglers who first heard the term from Magalloway guides took it to other places, and today a big chub about anywhere in Maine is a *Magalloway salmon*.

❦ / MAGGOT PIE    In Hancock and Washington Counties, a blueberry pie. Inspectors from the Maine Department of Agriculture keep an eye on the incidence of infestation by the blueberry maggot, but the indelicate suggestion persists that if the crop is unfit for sale, it can be baked off for local consumption.

❦ / MAIN, THE    The mainland. Early European fishermen found the offshore islands of Maine, and beyond them *the main*, which explains the state's name. James Rosier, official scribe for the George Waymouth expedition of 1605, says as much: "Our captaine discovered up a great river trending alongst into the maine about forty miles." The final *e* on both *captaine* and *maine* is merely olde English orthography. The mainland is still called *the main* by people on Vinalhaven, Matinicus, Criehaven, and Monhegan, who say, "I'm going to *the main* tomorrow." (There is an identical situation in South America, where the term Spanish Main originally meant the mainland of that continent.)

❧ / MAINEIAC   The homonymic implications of this word do not offend Maine people, and they do not take umbrage when it is applied to them. *Maineiac* is more used by out-of-staters than by bona fide residents of the Pine Tree Precinct, but the latter are capable of tossing it off to describe themselves when it suits, and with more than a little pride. The word *Mainer* has been preferred throughout this treasury of Maine-isms, but not for esoteric reasons; nobody seemed sure about the orthographic variations of *Maineiac*, *Mainiac*, *Maine-iac*, etc. In well-handled Maine speech, the identification of *Maineiac* is largely avoided by the custom of giving Maine, always, a direction; thus, when a Mainer might say, "Yes, I'm a *Maineiac*," he is far more likely to phrase it indigenously, "I come from up-Maine." Or down-Maine, as the case may be.

❧ / MAINE WHERRY   A boat for sailing and rowing which originated at Ash Point near Rockland and was used for tub trawling, handlining, and lobstering.

❧ / MAKE   Weather *makes* in various Maine expressions: "Looks like it's *making up* to snow." A stiff sou-westerly may *make up* such seas that lobstermen will stay ashore.

❧ / MAKE OUT   To do all right; to succeed. "How'd you *make out?*" after a meal means, "Did you get enough to eat?" *Making out* with a lady involves seduction.

❧ / MALAGA ISLANDITE   About the turn of the century unpleasant conditions among the residents of Malaga Island in eastern Casco Bay forced the state welfare authorities to resettle them by families in numerous Maine communities. It was a social-betterment project well ahead of its time. Historically, Malaga Island had been a dumping place for odd people brought to Maine from the waterfronts of the world, with consequent confusion. The families thus settled became known in each community as *Malaga Island-*

*ites;* most of them assimilated well, and if the term is heard today it is a reaching-back by others to explain their origins.

❧ / MARCH OF SOLDIERS  Another term for *wild geese* (which see), in respect to sparks in a fireplace.

❧ / MARE'S-NEST  Also, "hooraw's-nest." Any wild jumble of unrelated things; a mess of *culch*. A *mare's-nest*, actually, is a bunching up of debris in a stream where a fallen log catches what comes down. Sticks and leaves and stuff. The suggestion that a mare constructs a nest is certainly no more far-fetched than that a hooraw does. To clean out a *mare's-nest* is to tidy up something unkempt and disorderly, such as a boy's room.

❧ / MARES'-TAILS  See *mackerel sky*. The high cirrus clouds thus described look (as Polonius might say) very like a *mare's-tail*.

❧ / MARKS AND DEEPS  Divisions on the line of a sounding lead so the man casting can read the depth. The Plimsoll symbols on a vessel's hull, showing her load depth, are called *marks*, and a person "down to his *marks*" has had all he should take at this time, thank you. Creature *marks* were notches cut in the ears of cattle to identify ownership; precursors of branding *marks;* all Maine farmers had their *marks*.

❧ / MARLINSPIKE  The Maine uses of *marlin* and *marlinspike* are the same as elsewhere, but this makes a good place to explain that to old-time coastal Maine any metal nail from a carpet-tack to a 60-penny spike was a *spike*. The only nails that ever went to sea were treenails, which were spelled and pronounced "trunnels." The *marlinspike* is a pointed tool used to separate rope strands.

❧ / MAROONED   Used now and then in Maine for quarantined: "The whole family is *marooned* with mumps." It makes sense if you reflect on it.

❧ / MASH   Mesh. The word is pronounced thus by highlanders who mean a screen or sieve for sifting gravel or some screen wire for a window, and by coastal people who refer to the opening in a net and derivatives therefrom: the finished net, bait bags, trap heads, etc.

❧ / MASHIN'   As indicated under *mash* (above), *mashin'* is the inclusive term for fishermen's netting; the making of it, the size of the apertures, the twine used (see *snoodin'*), and all related thereto. A *mash* board is the smooth wedge used in knitting or *mashin'* to regulate the size of the holes between strands. The *mash needle* is the shuttle used. Almost all Maine lobstermen know how to make their own *mash* for bait bags and trap heads, but some evade the tedium by saying their hands are *gormy* and they hire it done. The set-up for *mashin'* is a cup-hook screwed into a windowsill to hold the work, and the person *mashin'* sits in a rocker in hopes something like a dog fight may occur outside to give him something to watch. The only substitute word for *mashin'* is knitting.

❧ / MASONIC TEMPERATURE   The freezing point, from the 32° F.

❧ / MASSACHUSETTS DRIVER   The worst kind, and worse on Maine roads. Elizabeth Coatsworth did them full justice in one of her splendid essays. They pass on outside curves, etc. Jim Durgin said, "I don't dare ride with my wife; she's worse than a *Massachusetts driver!*"

❧ / MASTER   A title traditionally reserved for the captain of a merchant ship; a master mariner. He is top dog in the merchant marine. Deriving from this shipboard meaning, Mainers have made the word into an adjective denoting excellence and large size: "This is a *master* dining room!" Or, "Joe caught a *master* big horsefish."

**❧ / MAST PAINT**  Pea soup. As with red for barns, blue for tipcarts, and green for blinds, Mainers liked to paint their masts a certain yellow.

**❧ / MAST PINE**  A richly historical Maine term. It means a native eastern white pine suitable for a ship's mast, and also one that will yield smaller spars and timbers. About the time Maine began to exploit its rich forest resource, England was developing her navy and merchant marine, and was in great need of good ship timbers. Agents of the crown *cruised* Maine and struck the "broad arrow of the king" into trees thus reserved. Then the fun began, because Mainers were 3000 miles from Whitehall and they could sell trees in lots of places. Until the time of the Revolution, Maine and New Hampshire loggers had a running controversy with the crown agents over whatever became of His Majesty's tree, anyway? *Mast pine* is still used in Maine for a fine, straight, tall white pine, but seldom is one found that measures up to the admiralty requirements when George III was king. (The "broad arrow" is still used in England as a mark for crown property.)

**❧ / MATT**  And often *Matt Peasley*. A sea lawyer, and by extension somebody inclined to *snedricks* (which see). The term is fairly new, dating from 1920 when Peter B. Kyne introduced the "Cappy Ricks Stories." Fictional Cappy Ricks was a retired Pacific Coast shipping line owner whose daughter had married one *Matt Peasley* from Rockland, Maine. Cappy and *Matt* had a running tilt over seafaring, and *Matt* always came out on top. This delineation of a Maine coastal character pleased folks along the coast, and the stories were popular with Mainers. A man who was adept at one-upmanship was often compared to *Matt Peasley*.

❧ / MAVERICK  Mainers put this word in the language, but the derivation is out of the Massachusetts Bay Colony. The dictionaries are quite wrong when they ascribe the term to a Texan. Sam Maverick was already settled on an island in the harbor when the Puritans came in 1630 to establish Boston. The Puritans had been granted totalitarian authority, but were required nevertheless to respect the rights of prior settlers. Thus Sam Maverick became the only Bostonian permitted to vote without church affiliation. As the free-thinker, or the odd-ball, he was the "stray." Later, when Mainers were required to swear allegiance to Massachusetts to protect their land titles (see *oath, the*), they recalled the situation of Maverick, which was not unlike their own, and a word was born. Use of *maverick* for an unmarked log in a Maine river drive preceded the meaning of an unbranded calf on the western plains by many years. Sam Maverick is mentioned often in early Boston records, and was never in Texas.

❧ / MEASLY  Small, but Mainers are more likely to express the idea with *jeezly*, which see.

❧ / MEATMAN  The *camp hunter* (which see) who procured fresh meat for table in the early Maine lumber camps. Before refrigeration and conservation laws, this was the only way to do it. He brought in moose, caribou, deer, bear, and also rabbits and partridges. Through the ice or with an *otter* (which see) he would take trouts. When Maine enacted legislation forbidding the serving of game at lumber and sporting camp tables, a number of these *meatmen*, now out of work, became game wardens.

❧ / MELK  Milk. "When I make my biscuits, I use a whole cup of *melk*." The transition from *i* to *e* is progressive from west to east, until in far-down Washington County milk rhymes with elk. There seems to be no other *i* word (for example, *built*, silk, spilled) in which Mainers make this change.

❦ / MERRYMEETING BAY   Maine's best known waterfowl area, some of it now a refuge, which frequently occasions questions as to what makes the meeting so merry. No answer: but the five rivers that meet there are the Androscoggin, Kennebec, Muddy, Abagadusset, and Cathance.

❦ / MESS   A special Maine meaning is the use of this word for the tangle that must be unscrambled after a hearty northeast storm has raised havoc with lobster traps. When the sea calms enough, the men go out to see how much of a *mess* there is. Also used for something to eat sufficient for a family meal: for example, a *mess* of clams or dandelion greens.

❦ / METHODIST HELL   The peak of theological heat. Steve Mitchell sold parlor heaters with the absolute guarantee they would heat any room hotter than a *Methodist Hell*. An old-time bunkhouse would get that hot just before bedtime, and it's a good description of a Grange anteroom when the Outer Gatekeeper has neglected to shut the damper during closed session. It should be borne in mind that the rigors of the Maine winter have never caused Mainers to be fearful of a cozy seat near a perpetual fire.

❦ / MIDDLESEX   Average, ordinary. A *middlesex* kind of dog is half conjecture and half something else. A *middlesex* day is seasonable, but nothing to cheer about. A *middlesex* person is acceptable, but not the *finest kind*.

❦ / MILITARY ROAD   Specifically, the 40-mile stretch of highway from Macwahoc to Houlton, laid out to move troops to the Aroostook War in 1836. It is still there, but new Route 95 has absorbed much of its traffic. A famous Maine roadway often referred to.

❧ / MILLIONIST   What else? A millionaire.

❧ / MIND   Heard often as a holdover of Scottish influences, it means remember. "Do you *mind* the time we all went to Boston?" *Mind* as for obey ("*Mind*, now!") is interestingly used in Maine in reverse: "I yell at that boy all day, and he don't pay me the least *never-mind!*"

❧ / MINISTER APPLE   An early fall apple rightly named the Strawberry St. Lawrence. The comparison to a cleric was explained by Rod Bailey this way: "It looks good, but that's about it."

❧ / MINISTERIAL LOT   See *church lot.*

❧ / MISDOUBT   An emphasized doubt. To *misdoubt* means to doubt very much. (See *mistrust*, below.) "I *misdoubt* he'll be too happy in that new job."

❧ / MISTER   A word almost never heard in Maine in the normal relationship of people-to-people. A gentleman who answers his telephone by saying, "Mr. Jones speaking!" probably moved here recently *from away.* True, it has its formal uses, and is recognized as such when it appears: "Now I want to introduce our speaker—Mr. Jones!" Mr. Jones, the speaker, is elevated momentarily; tomorrow he will be Joe Jones all over town, as always. Mainers are naturally first-name people. *Mister* was reserved in olden times for shipboard status, and it is still used to address presiding officers in legislature and town meeting: "Mr. Moderator!" The term will be used facetiously, as when two old cronies chance to meet in the liquor store and one of them says, "Why, *Mister* Jones! Fancy meeting you here!" Sports are called *mister* by their guides and waitresses; *summer complaints* who keep getting *mister* year after year know they haven't made the grade yet. In fact, when one good Mainer calls another one *mister*, it is usually in anger and disrespect: "Let me tell you something, *Mister* Man—I think you're a goddam *hairpin!*" Similarly, *sir* is not good Maine, as in *yes sir* and *no sir*.

❧ / MISTRUST   The dictionaries say that *mistrust* in the sense of suspect or surmise is rare, but it will be heard every day in Maine speech. "I *mistrusted* you might come today!" means a premonition is fulfilled. The word is also used for an error in identification: "He *mistrusted* I was you." Misdoubt and *mistrust* have some interchangeable nuances, but not always. One will misdoubt the future in the negative; i.e., that something will not happen. To *mistrust* the future suggests the likelihood it will happen. Mainers almost never use *mistrust* for distrust; more likely they would just say "I don't trust him."

❧ / MITTEN MONEY   Any kind of a tip, and sometimes a bribe: "I hear he gets more *mitten money* than salary out of that job." The term comes from an extra charge added to a regular pilot's fee during the winter months, when the added difficulties of navigation and the hardships of the season make it seem only fair.

❧ / MODERATE   When pronounced modd-r't, it means slow and deliberate, as a person who isn't going to set the world on fire: a *moderate* man never gets too much excited about anything. When pronounced modd-der-eight, it means the weather is going to warm and *soften*, or that somebody is going to preside as moderator at town meeting.

❧ / MONEY CAT   A calico cat whose fur shows at least three or four colors. Mainers have always believed this oddity of color happens only in the female, and that if anybody ever finds it on a tomcat the thing will be "worth money."

❦ / Monkey's fist   A knot made into the end of a heaving line. The knot gives some heft for tossing, and a good *monkey's fist* will have a stone or a piece of metal in it.

❦ / Moon dog   Essentially the same as a sun dog; the nightime version is properly a paraselene, and sometimes called a "mock moon." Both sun and *moon dogs* are caused by moisture in the atmosphere and foretell a storm.

❦ / Moosebird   The Canada jay. (See *gorby*.)

❦ / Moose fritters   Known only in the Maine woods story of the hunter who agreed to cook for his party. He said he'd cook so long as nobody complained about the food. After he tired of cooking, he began serving poor meals to encourage complaints, and his companions pretended they liked everything so none of them would have to take over. In a supreme effort, he scraped up moose droppings in the woods and fried them for breakfast. "What's this?" they asked. "Moose fritters," he said. "My, my," they said, "unusual, but goo-ood!"

❦ / Moose sled   A wide-runnered hand sled presumably first designed for transporting moose meat into camp. It is a utility sled used in lumber and sporting camps for odd chores, replaced in summer by a wheelbarrow. The *hand shark* is a similar sled.

❦ / Morey   Worth having more of: "That's a real *morey* cake—don't mind if I do!"

❦ / Mortifyin' weather   Unseasonably warm weather that mortifies the flesh, as when a February thaw catches everybody with his *long-handled* underwear still on. To be mortified, in Maine parlance, suggests discomfort, but also carries a sense of embarrassment: "Gawd! I don't know when I was so mortified! I slapped her on the tail, thinking she was Martha, and when she turned around—'twarn't Martha at all!"

❧ / Moses boat   A small, flat-bottomed boat built in Maine in great numbers and used considerably as harbor craft. They caught on in the West Indies and became a favorite lighter for rum and molasses handling. Their shape resembled (some said) the cradle in which Pharaoh's daughter found the infant Moses. (Or, as some others say, the cradle in which she told people she found him!)

❧ / Moss   See *Irish moss*. In the woods, swamp or sphagnum moss was used to chink log buildings. To *moss* a camp is to chink it between the logs. As soon as enough logs were at hand to start a *camp*, a *mossing* crew would be sent into the swamp to gather chinking.

❧ / Mountain, the   In Maine this has one meaning — Mount Katahdin, at 5267 feet the state's highest peak. Otherwise, numerous places have hills they refer to as *the mountain*: one goes over *the mountain* to arrive at Kennebago Lake, or over *the mountain* on Great Sebascodegan Island. Since skiing became important to Maine, those who attend the slopes and lifts are said to "work on *the mountain.*"

❧ / Move a stove   A fictitious chore pleasantly presumed. If somebody asks you to "help me *move a stove*," he is asking you to socialize to the extent of at least one glass. It is equivalent to "Would you like to see my cellar?" If you step in and find the *jeezer* really does have a stove to move, you've been had.

❧ / Move no better'n a toad in a tar bucket   Self-explanatory, deriving from the moderate movements of any toad, and the Mainer's familiarity with the pail of sticky tar used to *pay* seams. The expression is used for somebody who doesn't step around very fast at his job.

✤ / Mud pattens  Slats or small boards fastened to the feet in the manner of snowshoes to facilitate walking on mud, as on a clam flat. *Pattens* derived easily from *battens*.

✤ / Mud season  Since paved roads, this term has lost some of its pithiness. *Mud season* was Maine's fifth season (the others are Fall, Winter, Spring, and July). When the frost was leaving the ground, teaming was suspended, the dooryard was a *lully*, and Mother made everybody take off boots on the doorstep. (See *flatform.*)

✤ / Mug up  Maine coastal perennial for the coffee break. Probably a *mug up* may be had in a lunch room or drug store, but the term means first of all the snack at any time of day when you stop by a fishing-village home in passing. *Mug up* suggests friendly hospitality to be shirked neither in the offering nor the accepting.

✤ / Mull  The word most often used in Maine for *thick o' fog*; a *fog mull*. It suspends all harborfront activity and must be waited out. A simple fog will sometimes *scale off*, but a *fog mull* needs a change in weather.

✤ / Muscovado  Occasionally mentioned in reminiscence by older folks with long memories, *muscovado* is the brown-sugar precipitate inside a barrel of West Indies molasses. It probably still could be had by children growing up to spread on their home-made bread except for two things: 1. Mommies don't bake bread any more, and 2. Daddies don't bring home barrels of molasses.

✤ / Mustard plaster  For the Maine version, see *blister plaster*.

✤ / Muzzle-loader  From the firearm; a lumber-camp bunk that was loaded from the end. Multiple bunks were constructed side by side with no room between, and a man got into bed by climbing in at the foot.

❧ / MY This use of the pronoun could have been entered just as well under his, your, her, their. The habit of Maine people to presume possessiveness about wild deer running in the woods amuses folks *from away* no end. "Got *your* deer yet?" "I'm all done for the season. Got *my* deer the first day." "Joe got *his* deer Tuesday up at The Forks." "She's quite a hunter—gets *her* deer every year."

# N

/.V.V.V.V.\

❦ / NAILS  Hard as *nails* means physical stamina, but it can also mean tough in spirit, disposition, and manners: "She's a doll of a child, but that red-headed brother of hers is hard as *nails*." Being "mad enough to chew *nails*" is to be pretty well fed up with something or other. Also, it can be used to describe physical appearance: "She's homely enough to bite a *nail* in two."

❦ / NANNY–PLUM TEA  A home remedy for measles whose efficacy was happily exploded long since: sheep droppings (*nanny plums*) steeped in rain water. (If you think this sounds severe, try the Maine remedy for a tapeworm: one tablespoon gunpowder dissolved in a cup of hot gin.)

❦ / NARSTY  Nasty, but with a difference: inclement weather will give us a *narsty* day; Jim has a *narsty* session with the tax collector; Mary has a *narsty* cold in her head. And not used over-much in the normal meaning of nasty. (See *nasty-neat*.)

❦ / NASH  Tender, of a sensitive disposition; ladylike and overly soft of temperament, perhaps sissified: "He's so *nash* you can't say 'damn' but he'll cry tears."

❦ / NASTY-NEAT  Neat and clean to the point of offensiveness; cleaner than clean and tidier than tidy. Said of a housewife over-zealous to the point that one is uncomfortable in her perfect parlor.

❦ / NEAR  Reluctant to part with money; saving; not generous. A man who is "*near* with his money" will have the first nickel he ever earned. It can mean stingy and self-centered. Not unlike *tight* in "*tight* as the bark to a tree," but not so extreme sometimes; a person who is cautious and frugal, perhaps merely thrifty, would not be called *tight*, but will be said to be "a mite *near*."

❦ / NECKTIE  Synecdoche in Maine for dress-up men's clothing. In a state given largely to outdoor work, the *other ones* are for special occasions; the term *necktie* means Sunday best in the same sense that black tie on a social invitation means formal wear. Told he was expected to attend open house at the new *liberry*, Tim Barter said, "Gawd, I s'pose that calls for a *necktie!*" It may be said without too much generalization that Maine men are uncomfortable in anything approaching sartorial nicety.

❦ / NEEDLE  The shuttle used for making netting; the *mashin' needle*. It is not truly a needle, as is the sail-maker's *needle*; the latter is a heavy steel needle with a triangular point and flattened eye made for sewing heavy canvas and thrust home with the *palm*, or sail-maker's thimble. Otherwise *needle* is used as elsewhere, but see *gad, brad, plague*.

❦ / NEIGHBOR  The verb: "Folks don't *neighbor* same's they used to." To go *neighborin'* is to make an informal call in the vicinity.

❦ / NEITHER HAY NOR GRASS  Halfway between; half-baked; neither one nor t'other. Title of a John Gould book. Pronounced *nee-ther*.

❦ / NEST  Word that describes the way fishing dories are piled one in another on a vessel's deck, much like a stack of soup plates. On trips to and from the fishing grounds, dories are *nested*.

✿ / NETHER TEAT    Mainer's summation of his circumstances when things are not going well: "sucking the *nether teat*" means second place, at least. A gentleman who is trailing at cribbage will say, "Well, I seem to be sucking the *nether teat* here. How about dealing me a good hand for a change?" Although the word *nether* means "under," and suggests only two of a kind, some explain that *nether teat* derives from the occasion when a sow will have more pigs in her litter than she has spigots to oblige. Often one little piggy (the runt of the litter) is away out behind with no parent stem to tackle, in which situation he is far worse off than a man losing a cribbage game.

✿ / NEW HAMPSHIRE SCREWDRIVER    A carpenter's hammer. The inference is that Maine carpenters take the time to set screws right with the proper tool, whereas in New Hampshire the less careful and less skilled workmen just whack 'em home. *New Hampshire* is changed to New York, Massachusetts, New Brunswick, etc., as the occasion requires.

✿ / NICE    A very special Maine usage is involved here which must be approached in round-about fashion because of the prudery of the editors. Mainers have developed endless similes to describe the lady who values herself too highly; the stuck-up female who is just too-too *nice*. Without exception, "She's so *nice* that she thinks . . ." is followed by something not *nice* enough to be included here. Listen for these very fine poetic figures of speech.

✿ / NICELY    Without complaint; used almost entirely in answer to a greeting:

> "How are you, Ben?"
> "*Nicely*, thank you."

(See *poorly*.)

❧ / Niddy-noddy   Often *niddy-naddy*. The *niddy-noddy* is a device for winding yarn in skeins, so designed that a person using it throws his (or her) hands and arms about a good deal in a manner never used in another way. Hence, a person considered a *niddy-noddy* is erratic, flighty, vacillating, unable to settle down: "Him? Oh, don't pay any attention to him; he's just an old *niddy-noddy*." As with many another doubled-up word, *niddy-noddy* itself somewhat expresses the motion involved.

❧ / Nineteen   Cribbage has always been a favorite Maine card game, particularly in the woods. In this game, it is mathematically impossible to hold a hand that will count a total of nineteen. Hence, if a man holds a hand which has no score whatever in it, he will toss it down and say, "*Nineteen!*" Almost everybody in Maine knows that *nineteen* means nothing at all; accordingly, a duck hunter who didn't bring anything home may report he shot *nineteen*.

❧ / Nippers   The word for the large woolen mittens knitted specifically for fishermen and lobstermen. They are oversize to accommodate the shrinking when wet, and they are always wet in use. Traditionally, *nippers* are white. The reason for the term cannot be traced, but one old-timer suggested they were to keep the cold from "*nippin'* " too much.

❧ / No breakfast, no supper   This happy improvisation refers to vessels hailing from New Brunswick and Nova Scotia: *N.B.* and *N.S.* identifies them respectively on their transoms.

❧ / Noonin'   Taking the noon time dinner break. Anybody who pauses to tackle his dinner before high twelve is said to be "takin' an early *noonin'*."

❧ / Northeast   Correctly, this is pronounced know-theast, with the *th* sound of those, instead of the *th* of thing.

The four quarter-points in boxing the Maine compass are spoken thus: know-theast, sow-theast, sow-west, and norwest. Northing is pronounced knowth-ing, and southing is sow-thing. The dictionary-sanctioned nor-east and nor-easter are absolutely in error, and shouldn't be spoken anywhere. The reasons for these pronunciations go back to the days when vocal commands from a vessel's quarterdeck had to be instantly and unquestionably understood by men working the ship. Nor-east and nor-west sounded too much alike for shipboard clarity. (See *larboard* for another example of sound-alikes.)

❧ / NORTHERN   Familiar name in the upper part of the state for Great Northern Paper Company, the largest single property owner in Maine. A man will tell you he works for *Northern*. Occasionally *The Northern*.

❧ / NOSE BAG   A *chopper's* dinner pail. Quite rightly the teamsters would hang the canvas *nose bags* with oats on the horses' heads while the men took their *noonin'*. "To put on the *nose bag*" is a common Maine expression for pausing to eat, whether from a dinner bucket or at the kitchen table.

❧ / NOTIONAL   Said of an animal given to caprice. A cow that won't eat certain things is said to be *notional* about them. A horse that won't step across a wooden bridge because he doesn't like the noise of his own hoofs is said to be *notional* about bridges. The word is sometimes applied to persons, too, but a *notional* child is more likely than a *notional* adult. An adult would be "opinionated."

❧ / NOVA SCOTIA CAKE   A large vanilla cake that may or may not have ever been baked. In Prohibition days there was some desperate use of vanilla extract to assuage thirsts that couldn't otherwise be controlled. The alcoholic content was around 90 percent, so it had some effect, although a drunk smelled more than delicious. Men buying a bottle of vanilla at the store often felt obliged to explain such a purchase, and the standard remark was, "My wife's going to make a *Nova Scotia cake!*" *Nova Scotia cake* means any absurd excuse.

❦ / Numb   A mild version of dumb, in the sense of somewhat stupid. A *numb*-head doesn't know enough to come in out of the rain. Physical numbness, transferred to intelligence, is suggested by "as *numb* as a pounded thumb." A Mainer might call somebody dumb behind his back, but to his face he'd use *numb*: "You seem a little *numb* about learnin' how to do that!"

# O

⁓⁓⁓⁓·

⁓·⁓⁓·

❧ / OAKUM   Untwisted and tarred hemp used to caulk seams in boats. "To put the *oakum*" to somebody means to close him up, as when a sharp retort leaves him without a reply.

❧ / OATH, THE   This term is wholly historical now, but puzzles some who find references to it in old Maine writings. After Sir Ferdinand Gorges died in the 1600s, Maine land titles needed affirming. The Massachusetts Bay authorities were the ones to do this. Agents sent into Maine required an oath of allegiance to Massachusetts as a requisite of owning land and having the vote. This *oath* was not only political, but involved the bigoted and despotic Puritan religion of The Bay. Mainers were never much for Puritanism, but to get their titles they took the *oath* with a wink and a smile. *The oath* had to do mostly with the York County area, and somewhat in Cumberland County. (See *Maverick*.)

❧ / OCEAN   *Ocean* and *sea* are two words Mainers handle with a difference, and sparingly. *Ocean*-going ships are deep-water ships, and, unless speaking specifically of an *ocean* (Indian *Ocean*), Mainers use terms like outside, across the water, down the bay, and such-like substitutes for the *sea* in the abstract. One does stand on the shore and look off at the *ocean*, but a tourist may hang around Maine all summer and never hear a coastal resident use the word *ocean*. (See *sea*.)

❦ / OFFHAUL    The preferred word for a *haul-off*, unless perhaps it's *outhaul*. The variations in this (see *haul-off*) depend mostly on where you are on the Maine coast.

❦ / OFFING    A point some distance from the shore but within sight of it. As with *loom*, American newspapers like the word without full respect for its meaning: "Labor Unrest In Offing." To have a good *offing* is to be well clear of the land with plenty of room to navigate. It is a term to be used from the deck of a vessel, and has no particular meaning once it comes ashore.

❦ / OFF-ISLANDER    A term used by residents of Maine islands to describe anybody who doesn't live on their particular island. Basically, it is not snobbish; but when picked up by summer people to describe other summer people on the mainland it achieves a disparaging nuance never intended by the originators.

❦ / OIL UP    To put on weather gear, or oilskins. To dress for foul weather. Early rain suits were impregnated with linseed oil, but today neoprene and other treated fabrics are used. Ashore, "oiling up" means to become at least slightly tipsy: "Come Sattee night, he likes to *oil up* some," but there seems no reason to associate this with "ileskins."

❦ / OLD CUFFEY    Heard only in the old expression, "as big as *Old Cuffey!*" "I tell you, he was sittin' there as big as *Old Cuffey* an' as smug as the cat that swallered the canary." Paul (?) Cuffey or Cuffy was a Negro ship captain out of the New Bedford area, who was well-known in Maine ports, and who attained prominence by recruiting Afro-Americans to settle in Sierra Leone (c. 1787). Proposed by Britain, this settlement was to take freed and run-away slaves back to their home continent, and Halifax was the principal embarkation port. Thus the movement from the South to Halifax greatly involved Maine, and Cuffey became a byword. Some references in the New Bedford area indicate he was not really a big man physically, and it's possible his attributed hugeness comes from the Mainer's lefthanded way of calling bald-headed fellows Curly and tall men Shorty. If so, this whimsy has been lost in the mean-time, and *Old Cuffey* now definitely means great size.

❦ / Old Scholar   The seafaring man's affectionate term for God.

❦ / Old seed-folks   The ancestors and original Main-ers; now any old-timers who are native born.

❦ / Old woman   Often said of a man whose methodi-cal methods and tidiness are exemplary: "He's a regular *old woman* when it comes to hanging up his tools." There seems to be no comparable term for a lady thus oriented; *nasty-neat* suggests an overly eager neatness which *old woman* does not. Many men careless about their affairs would like to be more of an *old woman*, but a lady accused of being *nasty-neat* to her face would take offense. In an-other sense, *old woman* is applied to a man who shows a tendency to gossip: "He's as bad as an *old woman* when it comes to bein' a *bahskit!*" (See *basket.*)

❦ / On   Sometimes meaning *of*: "I bought four new tires, and one *on* 'em blew out before I got home!" (See *light 'n' fluffy.*)

❦ / One lunger   The first gasoline engines offered for marine and farm use had one cylinder or lung. (See *breaker.*) The term persists for any contrivance whose ef-ficiency might be better.

❦ / On or about   Used for the estimated time of a vessel's departure. The old sailing cards would announce that a vessel would sail *on or about* May 15. Passengers waited until cargo was stowed, and it was not until the days of the *packet* that more precise schedules were set. Today, the term is used for a random time without thought of its tidewater origin.

❦ / Open and shut   Threatening weather with quick changes from sunshine to clouds. The adage runs: "*Open and shet*; sign o' wet."

❦ / Opening note   If this means the first sound from an orchestra at the beginning of a concert, wilderness resort owners in Maine don't think of it that way. An *opening note* is a note negotiated at the bank to cover the expenses of making a camp open for guests. When guests start paying, or at the end of the season, the *opening note* will be redeemed. The *opening note* covers the payroll for cleaning women, men to ready wharves and boats, *choreboys* to stack wood, etc.

❦ / Operation   Other than surgical, this means a lumbering project from first to last. It covers *cruising*, construction of *camp*, hiring, feeding, bedding, chopping, *hauling*, and, in the old days, *driving*. The new Great Northern cutting along the *Golden Road* is called the "Lobster *Operation*" because it is in the vicinity of Lobster Lake.

❦ / Orts   A good Old English word mostly lost but surviving in Maine. Originally, it meant the leavings of inedible hay in a cow's manger, and farmers cleaned the *orts* from the animals' *cribs* from time to time. Mainers then extended the meaning to other leavings: "Take the *orts* out to the hens" means to carry the table scraps or sink *swill* dish to the barnyard. While *orts* is now used generally in a context that can include *culch*, a distinction is indicated when somebody says, "Tomorrow morning I want you children to pick up the *orts* and *culch* in the dooryard!"

❧ / OTHER ONES   A man's best suit of clothes. Instead of saying he's about to dress up, a Mainer is quite likely to excuse himself while he puts on his *other ones*.

❧ / OTTER   In ocean fishing and minesweeping an *otter* is a vane that keeps towed gear abeam of the vessel, rather than astern. But in Maine the *otter* is also a board similarly vaned which rides abreast of a canoe or rowboat with many baited hooks attached for taking trouts. They are now illegal; but in older times they were the device by which lumber and sporting camps (see *meatman*) took fish in quantity to feed guests and crews at table. To use an *otter* in some situations thus suggests forthright action, perhaps some greediness, and possibly snide and unapproved tactics.

❧ / OUT   See *in*. Seasonal visitors like to say they went *out* into the woods and then came back again into town. That's *barse-ackwards*. *Out* is also where the weather is: "It's rainin' *out*." Outside, out-of-doors. The expression often runs with typical Maine down-play and understatement: when it's −35° somebody will offer, "It's frosty *out*."

❧ / OUT EAST   To Maine's blue-water sailors of the later 1800s *Out East* meant Australian, East Indian, and Chinese ports of call. *Out West* meant any part of present U.S.A. beyond the Mississippi, but not as far as the coast, which in Maine parlance was the Pacific Coast. The West Coast always meant the west coast of South America for cargoes of hides, guano, nitrate, and copper. A good bit of this special nomenclature holds over into present Maine usage.

O / 197

❧ / Outhaul    See *haul-off* and *offhaul*.

❧ / Outlander    Used in Maine with the meaning of the German *Ausländer* but more often embellished into the adjective form, *outlandish*: "He's an *outlandish* man." It is reserved for somebody who has moved in *from away* to make his home, and is not applied to casual or seasonal people. Captain Ray Haskins happened to be born on Deer Isle, Canada, within sight of Lubec where he lived all the rest of his life. This unfortunate happenstance prevented absolute assimilation, and he always said, "After all, I'm an *outlandish* man!"

❧ / Outlet    The place where a stream forms to flow out of a lake. Moosehead Lake has an East *Outlet* and a West *Outlet*, the two streams joining later to form the Kennebec River. *Outlet* is used like *branch* and *landing* to encompass an area around the actual *outlet*.

❧ / Out straight    Anybody bustling about, full of business, too active to do anything else, is right *out straight*. The phrase comes from teaming oxen; as they lean into their yoke and strain every muscle the chain connecting them to the load is right *out straight*.

❧ / Out West    See *out East* for Maine distinctions in this connection. *Out West* is used in Maine with the same generalization implied by down South and up North when used in New York or Georgia. Following the Civil War, a good part of Maine's young manhood was drained into the prairie and mountain states to prospect, work, and homestead. Almost every family had somebody *out West*. In some places "going West" has the meaning of dying, but this is not common in Maine speech; to Mainers, going West was a term for making a career in a new place, equal to going to *sea*.

❧ / OVERHAULS   The aspirate is clearly heard in this Maine rendition of overalls; probably because one *hauls* (see *haul*) them on over his other clothing.

❧ / OVER IN YOUR BOOK   Getting along toward the last chapter in your life's story; the sere and yellow leaf: "When he got *over in his book*, he went soft as a custard."

❧ / OVERSHOE   The mythical Maine town of East *Overshoe* has its counterpart in almost all *Heimat* geography. That's where the *numb* ones come from. Beyond East *Overshoe* is beyond the beyond. In a state given to *larrigans*, brogans, *calk-boots*, and hip rubbers, *overshoes* have a hoity-toity tone. A stewed *overshoe* is a sub-par meal.

❧ / OWLIN' 'ROUND   Night roving, but not always the kind with dalliance in mind; a gentleman who can't sleep and gets up to make a glass of warm milk is *owlin' 'round*, too.

❧ / OX ROAD   An early highway leading from the docks in Portland into the White Mountains region of New Hampshire. The term figures in the town histories of all the communities that grew up along the *Ox Road*. When the Canadian National Railways built the Grand Trunk Line from Portland to Montréal, it followed the route of the old road. In the Bethel and Norway-Paris section of Maine, aerial photographs of present forest growth reveal in the tree cover the location of some of the route.

❧ / OX-SLING   An ox cannot stand on three legs to have his shoes attached, as a horse can, so it was necessary to *sling* him. A belly-band drawn up by a winch and gantry lifted him clear of the floor, and he hung there while all four feet were attended. (That means eight operations, since an ox is cloven-hoofed and each shoe is made in two pieces.)

O / 199

Sometimes a fractious horse (see *twister*) would prove so difficult he would require use of the *ox sling*, and when this was done it was no compliment to the intelligence of the horse. The *ox-sling* figures in many Maine expressions. To have somebody in a sling indicates an effort is being made to bring him around to a different way of thinking. The delightful metaphor, "to have one's arse in a sling," implies self-inflicted embarrassment, or to have worked yourself into a situation where you are helpless.

# P

/\.\/\.\/\.\/\.

❧ / PACK AND BACK   One of several woods terms to describe the carrying of two packsacks at once, which is done by alternating them on the trail. Carrying one ahead and then returning for the other, a man would tote the second on ahead of the first, and so repeat until he arrived in camp with both. Experienced woodsmen long ago proved it is faster and easier than making two trips, because you rest while you're back-tracking. In prohibition days, this was the customary way to bring booze down from Canada for guests at sporting camps. One story is that Joel Bubier once tried three packs of booze, but somewhere along the trail to King & Bartlett Township he lost track of one. A search was instituted after he gave up looking, but nobody ever came right out and said he found that third pack. *Pack and back* is often called "walk and hide."

❧ / PACKET   Originally, *packets* were the fast-sailing vessels of the latter clipper days which carried *packets* of government mail. The term then came to mean a vessel making scheduled trips rather than one which sailed *on or about* (which see), and one where passengers and mail were equally important as cargo.

❧ / PACKET RAT   Used in disdain by his betters for a crewman on a *packet*, *packet rat* is still so used for somebody who falls short in the social graces, etc. Steamboaters and blue-water sailors considered themselves the betters of *packet* people.

✤ / PADDLE-BOAT   A small version of the Rangeley boat made for small ponds in the Franklin County region. It could hold two, had no oarlocks, and was handled by a single paddle. A few survive in the area.

✤ / PALAVER   From the Latin for a parable, it came into Maine notice from Portuguese sailors in their meaning of "word." *Palaver* became a conversation between two who didn't know each other's tongue well, and it had much the meaning of "talkee" in pidgin English. Now Mainers use *palaver* for excessive tongue-wagging, large talk that means little, and particularly unctuous and unwarranted flattery. A lawyer who pounds the table and belabors extraneous arguments is said to *palaver*.

✤ / PALM   The sail-maker's device held in the palm of the hand and used to force his needle through sailcloth. It suggests forceful measures to Mainers, and to *palm* anybody is to push him a mite, even to bulldozing. Palm is pronounced "parm" in Maine.

✤ / PAPER THE WALL   To spout in a flux of words. John Coffin, brother of the poet, was a witness in court one time, and in describing the excessive verbiage of a door-to-door salesman he said, "He plahstered it all over the wall!" The lawyer asked, "He did what?" John said, "He *papered* the room with it!" The lawyer said, "The room? What room?" There was no room, of course, and after this good Maine expression was explained to the lawyer the trial continued.

✤ / PARCELING   To prevent fraying ends a rope is wound with tape or strips of canvas, tarred, and wound with cord. This whole process is *parceling*. A knot in the end will also prevent fraying, but the line will not then pass through a fairlead. *Parceling* was done neatly and with care, so in modern Maine speech to *parcel* something is to take pains and do it right; never a make-shift.

❧ / PARTED HER FASTS    A vessel gone astray from wharf or mooring has *parted her fasts*, *fasts* being the lines that secure her. Accordingly, an overloaded clothesline that snaps off has *parted her fasts*, and the term suits any similar situation. Lem Spofford had a pair of pants that gave him zipper trouble, and he said, "She *parts her fasts* by herself."

❧ / PARTY    When U.S. Postal Regulations forbade second-class newspapers the privilege of mailing copies containing advertising about "gambling," it turned out that the simple game of Beano was included in the ban. Maine newspapers accordingly advertised a *party*, which was mailable and which everybody knew was Beano. *Party* is also a word of mock elegance equivalent to *joker*, *jeezer*, chap, fellow, etc.: "This *party* stopped me and tried to sell me a monkey!"

❧ / PATENT    Used by Mainers to describe something new and different, and particularly a manufactured innovation that is replacing the homemade item. Old wood-burning lime kilns gave way to the *patent* kind that burned coal. *Patent* doesn't necessarily apply to things on which somebody holds a *patent*. Flint Johnson has a special way to erect a wall tent, which he calls his *patent* way.

❧ / PA'TRIDGE    There are no native partridges in Maine, but the two grouses are called *pa'tridges*: the ruffed grouse and the spruce grouse. Up to late hour, no Mainer has ever called a grouse a grouse.

❧ / PAY    See *Hell to pay*. Deck seams are *payed*; not the same word as to *pay* a debt.

❦ / Pea–Eye  This could just as well be entered as *P–I*; it derives from the initials of Prince Edward Island and it is the general term in the Maine woods for a *chopper* who originated in the Maritime Provinces, as distinguished from the French-speaking *Canuck*. An exception was the Newfoundlander, who was a *Newfie*. Along the coast, a *Newfie* was also a *Newfie;* only the Prince Edward Islander was a *P-I*. The New Brunswicker was a *Herring-choker;* and the Nova Scotian was a *Bluenose*.

❦ / Peaked  Pronounced pee-kid. Spindly, wan, not tip-top; usually the aftermath of illness.
  "You look a little pee-kid."
  "Ayeh, feel's if I was drug through a knothole—had the flu!"

❦ / Peapod  A double-ended rowing and less often a sailing boat that originated in the Jonesport area. Still used and still being built. Fishermen acknowledge them an excellent rough-weather small boat, and summer yachtsmen like them for tenders. The dory-ish shape does suggest a pod of green peas. The Maine way to handle them is to stand up, facing forward, pushing (see *push rowin'*) the oars in wooden tholepins rather than metal oarlocks.

❦ / Pearl diver  Clearly stemming from voyages that took Maine men to pearl-diving areas, this is the term for the dishwasher. It now incudes restaurant workers and kitchen help in the woods who dive into dishpans. (See *pot-walloper*.)

❦ / Peavey  A tool for canting logs that is essentially a *canthook*, but with differences. Joseph Peavey was a blacksmith who made tools, and he saw two shortcomings of the already well-used *canthook*. One was its lack of a pike point such as river drivers had on their picaroons. The other was the flopping manner of the way the hinged *dog* was attached to the shaft. In 1858 he made his first *peavey*, which is a *canthook* with a pike and a *dog* that doesn't flop laterally but is always in line with the shaft. His improved tool immediately had acceptance world-wide. The old Peavey factory in Brewer was identified for years by a sign that said P          V. In general usage the words *canthook* and *peavey* are synonyms today, but amongst the men who used them in the glory-days of lumbering the difference was important. Tourists should visit the Peavey family lot in the cemetery at Bangor to see the carved peaveys on the monument.

❧ / PEN-PUSHER   Used generally for somebody who works at a desk, usually in a humdrum job, in Maine this means specifically the company clerk in a lumber camp. He does the paper work, and is liaison between the main office and the *entrepreneur de bois*. The most celebrated Maine *pen-pusher* was the indefatigable Johnny Inkslinger who handled the immense affairs of Paul Bunyan. One winter he saved seven barrels of ink by leaving the dots off his i's and the crosses off his t's.

❧ / PERAMBULATE   This improbable Maine elegance for a simple walk is thus explained: Maine law requires town officials to "*perambulate* the town bounds" regularly in company with the officials of adjoining towns. The purpose is to establish lines, set markers, and review the common boundary from time to time. With congenial officials, the occasion makes a pleasant outing. The word *perambulate* in the statute is thus well known to small-town citizens, and they like it as a high–sounding substitute for going afoot: "Well, I guess I'll *perambulate* down to the *store* and see what's goin' on."

❧ / PERSNICKETY   Petulant and hard to get along with. A *persnickety* person is fussy, opinionated, difficult, erratic, sometimes sulky and surly, and in general the opposite of what a proper person should be. A child who for no reason won't eat his porridge may be said to be *persnickety* about eating porridge. Occasionally *persnickety* is applied to extreme social nicety: "No, don't invite her; she's too *persnickety* to come down off her high horse and associate with us!"

❦ / PERTETTER    Potato, as nearly as type can approximate the Aroostook County pronunciation. (In Maine French, *pomme de terre* will be readily understood, but *patate* is more likely. French fries are *patates frites*.)

❦ / PERTETTER HOUSE    The farm winter storage building to house an Aroostook *pertetter* crop. Along with that of the silo and the corn crib, its architecture is strictly an American contribution. Built usually on a side-hill, it has one end and both sides underground; the front only is exposed. *Pertetters* are brought in through the gable on the upper level and taken out on the lower. Fairly impervious to northern Maine frost, they have heaters if needed.

❦ / PERUVIAN BARK    Cinchona, from which quinine is extracted. Malaria came early to Maine when the state put to sea, and a touch of quinine became many a mariner's constant companion. Taken often with a spot of wine, it was always called *Peruvian bark*, and Mainers were well aware of its Andean origin.

❦ / PETITION    A wall between two rooms, and a paper drawn up and signed by a number of people.

❦ / PICK    For *pick* up, the Maine word for gathering potatoes after the mechanical digger has left them lying in rows. Men go to Aroostook in the fall to *pick* potatoes. Maine people also *pick* apples (although they *rake* and *plum* blueberries!) but as used in the Aroostook fields *pick* hardly has that same sense of "pluck."

❦ / PICKING THE REAR   This suggestive Maine-ism refers only to cleaning up the stray logs after a river drive. After the main drive has passed down, eddies and *logans* are *picked* and the stragglers thrown back into the channel. Since the term is regularly applied to the boss of the crew rather than to the men in general, the term has a bounce when strangers first hear it:

"Where's Arthur Bessey?"
"He's over on the South Branch *picking his rear*."

❦ / PICKPOLE   The three words *pickpole*, pikepole and picaroon cover the various kinds of lance–like poles used in handling floating logs in a drive. (See *peavey*.) The sharp spike often had a twisted point like a screw thread, and when jammed into a log it would hold so the driver could draw the log towards him. A quick counterclockwise twist of the shaft easily disengaged this screw when desired. The poles used were long enough so the tool became a balancing aid if the river driver walked on floating logs, and such poles are seen at sportsmen's shows where present-day entertainers "birl" on logs in tanks to see which of two can roll the other one off. Birling was never a Maine term, but if two river drivers put on such an act for fun in the old days, turning and twisting the log with their calk-boots to entertain other woodsmen, they called it log-rolling and let it go at that.

❦ / PICUL   A word that came home to Maine during the trading *out East*. It is a measure of about 1⅓ hundred-weight used mainly for manifesting cargo of pepper. Usually heard only from oldsters, it survives in Maine as an indefinite amount, although quite a good bit. Peter Piper might have picked a *picul* of pickled peppers.

❦ / PICKWANCY   Another mock elegance Mainers like to toss off; from, of course, the French *piquant*. It works in both directions; a mince pie will have *pickwancy;* so will a sour owl.

🌺 / PIECEN OUT   To round out the sum total: "He ate enough for a horse, and then *piecened out* with two slabs of pie!"

🌺 / PIEPLANT   The rhubarb. To Mainers, the rhubarb is the first vernal showing of new pie material. When apples and pumpkins are gone, the mincemeat is down, and everybody is tired of the interim custards, rhubarb looks good. Mainers call rhubarb *pieplant* sometimes, otherwise they call it rue-bub.

🌺 / PIG   The Children of Israel were not the only ones to know about the hazards of pork in the way of food poisoning. Pork never worked out as a seafaring food, and it was always a bad omen even to say *pig* aboard a Maine ship. If the word had to come up, they'd use some such equivalent as, "You know, that little grunting thing with the curly tail." Even today, many a fisherman refuses to carry roast pork sandwiches.

🌺 / PIGGIN   Originally a *piggin* was a small wooden pail with one longer stave for a handle. It came to mean a quantity or amount, and now it means a dipperful or a ladleful. A *piggin* of blueberries might be just enough for one pie.

🌺 / PILGRIM   A lovely Pine Tree State term (borrowed from Chaucer) for a tourist:

Whan priketh all the Mayne in hir corages,
Than longen folk to goon on pilgrimages!

🌺 / PINK   For some reason, the color of "stink" in Maine. Nobody in Maine has ever truly been in a blue

funk, but almost every day somebody goes into a "*pink
stink.*" Stink seems to involve perturbation, where a funk
prefers dismay or doldrums.

❧ / Pinky   A distinctive small schooner with sharp or
"pinked" stern. Designed in Massachusetts, they had a
vogue in Nova Scotia and were common along the Maine
coast in short-haul trading. An occasional *pinky* is seen
today in the summer fleet, preserved by someone who cares.
A woman compared to a *pinky* will not be too heavy in the
stern, perhaps *slab-sided*.

❧ / Pint   In Maine towns near the Québec border,
*pint* is a good word to know. It means a quart, and is pronounced "pant." Canadian French couldn't use the metric
system of France, but had to adapt to the imperial gallon.
Somehow the 40-ounce Canadian quart came to be *une
pinte*, and when tourists buy liquid goods this knowledge is
useful. (An American *pint* logically becomes a French
*demi-pinte*.)

❧ / Pipe staves   The making of *pipe staves* was
Maine's very first forest-based industry. A *pipe* is a particular size barrel. Oak staves for making pipes or wine casks
were shipped in the early 1600s from Pipestave Landing on
the Piscataqua River. Through the great age of Maine's seafaring, barrels, casks, hogsheads and all manner of tubs were
needed in great quantities, and cooperages flourished. The
development of the Aroostook potato fields called for more
barrels. *Pipes* varied in size, but those for wine would hold
at least 100 gallons.

❧ / Piss-cutter   A word not tossed off in genteel
company, but very much used throughout Maine as a term
for somebody putting on a bit of a show of excellence. The
term is easily explained. *Cutter* derives from "crittur,"
which in turn derives from creature, the Maine term for an

animal for slaughtering. (However, see *creatures*, as derived from the French.) Gentleman hogs, allowed to grow elderly and then altered, had a fine appearance and that's about all. The pork from them gave off a suggestion of urine when laid in a frying pan. In short, a *piss-cutter* was a good-looker who couldn't live up to his guarantee. A young man who is all dressed up to go and make an impression on his girl-friend may elicit from his rougher cronies, "Boy-o-boy! Ain't you the *piss-cutter!*"

❦ / Pistol   A Maine lobster which has lost a claw, regrettably—or more regrettably—both claws.

❦ / Pitch   Of water; word to describe the amount of flow in a stream, both for river driving and canoeing and also for angling. A good *pitch* is better for driving logs and shooting rapids in a canoe, but trout and salmon fishermen like a lower *pitch*. When there is very little *pitch* the canoeists have to *frog it* (see *frog*) and this maneuver is known as "coming down with your canoe under your arm."

❦ / Pitchpole   A term to describe how a boat tumbles stern and bow in a breaking sea, and now heard ashore for a somersault. A youngster turning head over heels downhill is said to be "going *pitchpole* down;" sometimes "down *pitchpole*."

❦ / Pitman   The wooden driving rods on mowing machines and the driving bars off a walking-beam on a riverboat are known across the land as *pitmans* or pitman-rods. The word comes from the Maine days of pit-sawn lumber. A board was ripped off a log by two *sawyers* who worked an up-and-down saw in a frame—one stood above and the other stood below in a pit. (A model of a pit-saw operation may be seen at the Lumberman's Museum in Patten.) When sawmills operated by a water-wheel were installed, the rod below that took the place of the man in the pit was called the *pitman*.

❧ / PLACE  Term for land and buildings, as in "the Jones *place*," or "the *place* down the road." Practically synonymous with house as used in this sense. Somebody *from away* named Smith may have bought the Jones property twenty years ago and all the Joneses who once lived there may be dead and buried, but to folks in town it's still "the old Jones *place*."

❧ / PLAGUE  Pronounce "pleg"; to tease, even to the point of downright meanness: "Here, you bully—stop *plaguing* those little children!"

❧ / PLANTERS  This was the official word to describe the first organized English settlers in Maine, those at Popham in 1607. Possibly this term was meant to disarm French suspicions. The French were well established with good fisheries stations, and were not likely to regard *planters* as competition. That the English intended all the while to do more fishing than planting is perhaps best shown by the type of soil they selected at Popham Beach. There has never been high international demand for hardhack, bayberry, sweet fern, and wild cucumbers, which have always been the mainstay of Popham horticulture. Anyway, the people who signed up agreed to come to Maine and be *planters*.

❧ / PLAT  Maine way to pronounce plait; to braid, whether for *platting* the hair or *platting* rugs and plate mats for the giftie shoppe tradie.

❧ / PLEASURIN'  Workaday seaman's and fisherman's word for yachting, or sailing as a pastime. Used now for a picnic or holiday; any diversion from haulin' and fishin': "We'll go *pleasurin'* on Sunday."

❦ / PLUG   This word has some special Maine uses. A *bung* (see *bung*). The wooden pegs that immobilize lobster claws are *plugs*. The wooden pegs to let out rain water in small rowboats are *plugs*. And *plugging* is the term for fresh–water fishing without a rod, as in hand lining at sea.

❦ / PLUMB   Deriving from the *plumb*-bob or the *plumb* of the sounding line, this word has become a synonym for entirely: "I was *plumb* wore out!" This meaning is not inconsistent with dictionary definitions.

❦ / PLUMBER   Maine frivolity for the urologist.

❦ / PLUMMIN'   Berrying, and in particular going after the Maine wild blueberry which more'n–likely comes plumsize. *Rakin'* is the term for gathering blueberries commercially; *plummin'* is done by housewives, children, and *summercaters* by hand.

❦ / PLUNDER   A noun; the esoteric woods term for whatever is in the packsack or *kennebecker*. To describe taking off down the trail, Gerald Averill wrote, "I horsed my *plunder* on my back and lit out."

❦ / POD AUGER   A tool much used alongshore and in the Maine woods for making holes in logs and timbers used for wharves, pilings, bridges, cabins, and particularly booms. Many antique buffs think any of the T-handled bits and augers are *pod augers*. They are not; the *pod auger* had a spoonlike point, without worm, and its handle was a double crank. The hole was bored by a sort of *niddy-noddy* arm action, so the workman seemed to be throwing himself around a good deal. In Maine, *pod-auger* days is equivalent to The Good Old Days; Holman Day celebrated them in his rhyme "Pod–Auger Days."

❧ / POGY   Dictionaries give this as a variant of porgy; Mainers always omit the "r." The *pogy* is the menhaden, an inferior fish yielding an oil once important in making paint. Pogy-oil paint was an excellent preservative, but until suitable driers were developed it required about fifty-five years to dry.

❧ / POISON   A word that appears in northwestern Maine geography, such as *Poison* Pond at Eustis. It's really the French word *poisson*, a fish.

❧ / POKE   The stomach; no doubt deriving from the meaning of a bag or sack. Seldom used in an uplifting way, it usually has reference to unpleasant thoughts: "I got my *poke* full of him!" and, "Her food gives me a pain in the *poke*."

❧ / POLACK FIDDLE   The bucksaw. Before chainsaws, the crosscut saw was handled by two men and was mostly for felling trees. The bucksaw was a one-man tool, and preferred for *bucking* the down trees into four-foot lengths for pulpwood, or into sawlog lengths where the diameter wasn't too great. Polish woodsmen, who came to Maine in great numbers, were experts with these musical instruments. (In Maine woods lingo, *Polack* was pronounced Pole-lock.)

❧ / POLE-AX   Maine for the single-bitted ax and the swinging of it: "He went down as if he was *pole-axed*." The word is used as if Maine woodsmen were still talking in medieval terms about war-axes. Giving a lady instructions about smashing the champagne on a boat about to be launched, a gentleman said, "Just *pole-ax* her!"

❧ / POLLOCK   Pronounced paul-l'k; the lesser cousin of the cod known elsewhere as bluefish and marketed as Boston bluefish. The flesh is softer than cod and haddock, but when properly cured makes excellent salt fish. Deep-sea *pollock* will run cod size, but harbor *pollock* will run with the tinker and spike mackerel and be about that size. They make good sport for *summercaters* with spinning reels.

❧ / POND   The Maine generalization for any inland body of water; Moosehead Lake is 48 miles long but fishermen who set out will say they are going "out on the *pond*." In the Great *Ponds* Law, public access is assured to any *pond* over ten acres in size, whereas in most states the word *pond* would be reserved for bodies smaller than that. Some real estate agents have been caught up in this; they advertise property "on the *pond*," "with view of *pond*," and "with access to *pond*," and out-of-state prospects assume this means something less than a lake. It needn't; it might mean Sebago. *Pond* fishing is done from a boat and is the term to distinguish it from stream fishing. (Maine has eight Long Lakes and thirty Long *Ponds*; some of the long *ponds* are bigger than some of the long lakes!)

❧ / POND WATER   Fresh water dipped from a lake or stream to be used in camp for washing dishes and for ablutions. From most wilderness watersheds it is potable and is often used for drinking. Otherwise, a camp will have drinking water in a jug, and use *pond water* for all else. If an inland Mainer wants loosening material in a cocktail, he will probably ask for *pond water*, not *branch water*. (See *sluice*.)

❧ / POOL   As applied to inland fishing, *pool* has two meanings. It will be the still water below a falls or rips in a stream, or it will be a deeper hole in a lake, perhaps over a springhole. (See *rain barrel*.) When President Eisenhower came to Maine to go fishing, it was announced that he would fish in a *pool*. Some of the Washington newspaper people who came with him thought that a place like a Hollywood swimming pool had been set up for his pleasure.

But he fished the famous *pool* below the rips at Little Boy Falls on the Magalloway River.

❧ / POOR IN   And *poor out.* Two terms now archaic in public welfare, but formerly very important in town meeting affairs. The welfare recipients who were lodged at the town farm (the early version of our nursing home) were called the *poor in,* and those who got aid but were not in the poorhouse were the *poor out.* The *poor out* were usually able to contribute somewhat to their total support; hence, to be a *poor out* was slightly complimentary, as the term favored one who was doing his best to keep his head above water.

❧ / POORLY   This word goes with *nicely* as to the state of one's health. If you cannot claim to be doing *nicely,* your answer will be *poorly.* The words are also used like this: "Lem's been *poorly* all winter, but he's *nicely* now."

❧ / POOR MAN'S FERTILIZER   See *robin snow.*

❧ / POPPLE   Maine pronunciation of poplar, a common tree and before newer papermaking methods the favorite wood for top-grade printing papers. Each season the *popple* sheds a pollen which forms a yellow scum on inland waters and for a few days slows down the trout fishing. "*Popple*-fishing" means dry times, a hard chance, the German's *Saurgurkenzeit.*

❧ / PORCH   Porch, piazza, verandah: one man's *porch* is another man's piazza, but Maine verandahs are almost entirely on summer people's cottages. Some Mainers feel a *porch* is a covered or screened-in piazza, but others call their open piazza the *porch.*

❧ / PORKPICK   Mainer's woodland condescension for the porcupine, from the French *porcpique,* but reserved mainly for *porkpick* stew. The porcupine is edible and can be made delicious by French-Canadian *choppers* who board themselves. Another Maine variant for porcupine is quill-pig.

❧ / PORTLANDITIS   A chronic disease attributed by non-Portlanders to residents of the Forest City, deriving from their self-acknowledged superior culture and nicety (see *nice*). There is no known cure.

❧ / POSTED   Private land is *posted* against trespassing, and in a state where fish and game are the property of the state rather than the land owner, the term is loaded with meaning. One who *posts* his land is no friend of the sportsman. Fish & Game regulations are also *posted;* certain waters are *posted* for fly-fishing only. Highways are *posted* in the spring of the year, while frost is coming out, against over-loads or heavy trucking. Mainers do not *post* a letter; they mail it. To *post* one's wife is to notify the public that you are no longer responsible for her debts, almost always a preliminary to a divorce. The *posting* notice in the weekly newspaper may not have too much legal standing, but at going rates Maine editors still print them:

Notice!
On and after this date I will not be responsible
for debts contracted by other than myself.

❧ / POT   Synonym for *trap* in lobstering; also eel-pot, cunner-pot, etc. In spite of Maine reluctance to use *pot* for a chamber vessel, the word is found in one of the commonest Maine expressions to measure poverty: to be so poor you don't have a *pot* under your bed is to be very poor indeed.

❧ / POTATO BUG   (1) The Colorado beetle, which could lay waste a Maine potato field, long since controlled by insecticides. In Aroostook County, to compare a man to a *potato bug* in this sense is to put him far down on the list of desirables. However, (2) the *potato bug* was the man who rode on freight trains and stoked the small stoves in the *line cars* (which see). He lived in carbon monoxide and always had a cough and a pasty look, but he got some chance to recover on the return trip to Aroostook.

❧ / POT HEAD   The netting (*mash*) installed in a lobster trap to guide the delectables toward the bait and destiny. It also prevents their escape. The standard Maine trap has three such heads; two "side-heads" and the main passageway to the bait chamber. (See *hake-mouth* and *funny eye.*) Inland, a *pot head* is a citizen whose general intelligence suggests a chamber mug. A squash head.

❧ / POTHELLION   An old coastal term for a kind of fish hash, sometimes called "dog-on-the-shore," but this coastal meaning has long been superseded by the woods meaning of an adjustable stew. Starting with scraps of salt pork to sauté brown-sugared venison cubes, the *pothellion* mulls along for a day or two as the cook improvises with whatever meat and vegetables are at hand. Rabbit, *pa'tridge*, squirrel, perhaps porcupine, and almost anything except fish may be considered. The most important "secret" about making a *pothellion* is to start it with enough water to carry it through; adding water half-way along *drownds* it as you couldn't believe. Traditionally, a *pothellion* is topped off with dumplings (see *doughboy*).

❧ / POTWALLOPER   The early British meaning of a householder entitled to vote (see the dictionaries) doesn't apply in Maine, where the *potwalloper* is the drudge who washes pots and pans in lumber and sporting camps, and by extension in restaurants. The seafaring equivalent is a *pearl diver*.

❧ / POUND   The *pound* in standard usage was an enclosure to impound stray domestic animals until claimed by an owner, and in early days all Maine towns had a *pound* and an official "pound-keeper." As a well-known word with a precise meaning, it was the natural one for lobster dealers to assign to the enclosures they built for storing quantities of lobsters to await shipment and to hold for advantageous prices. The term "lobster pound" has been abused considerably by restaurants and wayside snack bars which use it as if any place or any thing containing lobsters is a *pound*. A true *pound* will be a sizeable cove closed off with a barrier that holds the lobsters in captivity but permits free passage of sea water. General misuse notwithstanding, the Maine lobstering fraternity is clear on its meaning of *trap* and *pot*, *pound*, *car*, and *crate*. Incidentally, on the maps of the U. S. Coast and Geodetic Survey, *pounds* are shown as "lobster ponds."

❧ / Pound sand  Another measurement of degree of intelligence: "He don't have brains enough to *pound sand* in a rat hole!" The futility and wasted effort of such endeavor make it an ideal profession for idiots. The term is also used for wasted time that might have been profitably engaged: "The lumber didn't come, so the carpenters *pounded sand* all afternoon."

❧ / Pow-duh  Heard pleasantly in the evaluating metaphor, "He ain't worth the *powduh* to blow him to hell!" Sometimes this is refined to "Kingdom come!" The powder in context is dynamite. River drivers who used dynamite liberally to loosen log jams always called it powder. When farmers used *powder* to blast field rocks they always called it blasting *powder*, in full, inasmuch as they were not using dynamite. See *dynamite*.

❧ / Preachin'  The question, "Where're you *preachin'*?" expresses astonishment at seeing somebody all dressed up. Something of the same Maine sartorial deference toward the church is found in *stiff as a church*, which see.

✤ / PRETTY    Pretty, but a hard-worked qualifying word in almost any Maine sentence: *pretty* good, *pretty* fair, *pretty* awful, *pretty* nigh, *pretty* far-fetched, etc. The word sometimes bats lefthanded in compliments: *pretty* good can be restrained praise. "That's a *pretty* good pie!" usually means it's far better than average. Now and then *pretty* and *some* (see *some*) can be interchanged: "It's *some* hot today!" means it's *pretty* hot.

✤ / PRIVILEGED    Under international rules of the sea, the vessel which has the right of way is *privileged*. (The one which does not is the "burdened" vessel.) One would expect Mainers to use these seafaring terms for highway traffic, and they do: in Maine the vehicle within a rotary is *privileged*; the one about to enter is burdened. Instead of saying, "I had the right of way," a truck driver may insist he was *privileged*.

✤ / PRUNE    Often used elsewhere with the comparison of "wrinkled," the *prune* is a favorite Maine term to describe dry wit: "He's dry as a *prune*." Prunes, as a mild cathartic, were in lumber camp and seafaring diets, and the long time between tree and stewpot often made them very dry indeed.

✤ / PUCKERBRUSH    Small, thick undergrowth difficult to pass through; bushes. Also the Mainer's general term for the wilderness and back country: "Nellie's been in the *puckerbrush* all summer cooking at a boy's camp."

✤ / PUDDING    Always reserved in Maine for the light desserts that are "fun to eat." The frilly and fluffy ones like blancmange, but also tapioca, rice, Indian-meal, etc. Steamed *puddings* are included, and *pudding sauce* is the sweet topping. (See *sauce* in this respect.) Mainers are not familiar with the use of *pudding* for a meat dish.

❦ / PULPHOOK   A hand tool like a freight hook used for handling four-foot wood. Mainers have developed two styles. One is a J-hook, and the other a small version of the fireman's snag-ax. When used on hardwood *bolts*, the same hook or a similar tool is called a birchhook.

❦ / PULPIT   The stand forward of the bow on a fishing vessel from which the harpoonist makes his throw. Often the *pulpit* is merely called the stand. Those who may surmise the fishermen borrowed this term from the church may be quite wrong. Rostrum, the prow of a ship, came to mean a speaker's platform because ancient heroes like Odysseus stood there to make harangue to the troops, and in the development of the word *pulpit* as a clerical platform there could well have been a similar snitching from the sea.

❦ / PUMMY   Maine farmer's pronunciation of pomace, the residue from the press-cloths in squeezing cider. Since the root of the word is the French *pomme*, *pummy* with the "u" sound is more correct than the Southern sound of "pommy," which is used incorrectly for cane and sorghum residue. *Pummy* is often fed to cattle, but if it has started to ferment, bossy may get giddy.

❦ / PUMPLE STONES   Rounded beach stones used to anchor rockweed *banking* (winter insulation about the foundation of a house). *Pumple stones* are also used to border front walks and driveways and flower beds. There was a time a front walk of crushed clam shells and *pumple stones* was much admired, particularly if the *pumple stones* were neatly whitewashed. Often *pumple* gets the sound of *popple*.

❦ / PUMP SHIP   See *water the horse*.

❦ / PUNCHED   Before returning an over-sized or egg-bearing female lobster to the ocean (a conservation practice required by Maine law) the lobsterman *punches* the creature. It is a simple operation, done with a jacknife, and consists of removing a small V from the tail flap. Since *punched* lobsters come again to the traps, a fisherman may see a certain lobster he has *punched* a dozen times in one season, and they get to be old friends. Hence, somebody or something which recurs unnecessarily may be likened to a *punched* lobster.

❧ / PUNCHEON  In addition to a cask larger than a barrel, *puncheon* is the term for certain lumber used by early Maine carpenters for flooring. Today, an old home with an authentic *puncheon* floor lists a little higher in the real estate advertisements; but sometimes simple plank floors are so-called.

❧ / PUNG  A box sleigh, horse drawn, and not a word limited to Maine. But the "set-over *pung*" originated in Maine for use on winter logging roads. The *whiffletree* was off center, so the runners ran in the same grooves as the logging sleds but the single horse could walk in the path made by one of the team horses. It was an odd-looking contraption, but it worked fine, and anything a mite *wee-waw* is often compared to a set-over *pung*.

❧ / PUNKIN PINE  A term now used indifferently for the eastern white pine (*pinus Strobus*), but originally it meant the clear lumber from the old-growth pines of Maine whose age had mellowed the resinous content until the grain suggested the meat of a pumpkin. Pine varies greatly in texture and heft, depending on the soil and exposure where it grows, and not all pine boards have the quality that *punkin pine* conveys. Very little true *punkin pine* is available today, but all cabinet makers and home-workshop buffs try to find some.

❧ / PURCHASE  Originally, a tackle or windlass that held fast something being moved mechanically; hence an advantage in a kinetic situation. In helping to lift (see *gaf-*

*fle*), a man may call out, "Wait a minute! I need a better *purchase!*" He means a grip, or a "holt"; perhaps a better placing of his feet. Things like grain bags and oil drums have no handles, so it is difficult to get a good *purchase* on them. (See *bait*, as to a mechanical *purchase*.) *Purchase* is also one of the many Maine terms for a geographical division, because it is a section of land *purchased* from the state. Abbott's *Purchase* includes Temple, Avon, Phillips, Carthage, Weld, Berlin, Roxbury, and Byron. Bingham's Kennebec *Purchase* was also called the Million Acres *Purchase*.

❧ / Push   The lumber camp foreman, and some of those boys really knew how to *push* the work.

❧ / Push rowin'   Rowing facing forward. Maine lobstermen prefer this and often call it rowin' "Maltese fashion." It violates more stylish rules of handling oars, and they say in the British and U. S. Navies it is positively forbidden. The Maine fishermen who are looking for pot buoys and trawl buoys excuse their lack of conformity by explaining that it's easier to see out of the front of your head.

❧ / Put away   Sometimes the same as *laying away* an animal, but usually reserved for committing somebody to an institution: "Maud waited hand and foot on poor old Leslie, but finally had to have him *put away*," i.e., into the mental hospital.

❧ / Putty   For putter: "Rainy day, so I *puttied* with the catches on the kitchen cupboards." To make odd repairs. Putty itself has no relationship to this usage, although one may occasionally *putty* around by puttying some glass. To *putty* around is to dawdle, and to be busy with unimportant things.

# Q

❦ / QUAHOG  See *clam*. *Quahog* is pronounced Co-hog.

❦ / QUARTERDECK  The after deck and traditionally the domain of a ship's officers, where an ordinary *hand* will not step unless bid. Thus the term *quarterdeck hand* is used for an ordinary person who is uppity and snobbish, at least putting on airs.

❦ / QUERRY  Approximate sound of quarry when spoken by a Mainer. Maine is dotted with quarries, most of them now abandoned, and more than a few towns have *querry* ro'ds which lead to or pass by quarries.

❦ / QUICK  Maine cookbooks use *quick* for things boiled rapidly until tender. Use of the word suggests it means easily chewed. Seabirds and game, if naturally tough, will be cooked in wine or marinated to make the meat *quick*.

❦ / QUINTAL  See *cantel* and *kental*. Variations in spelling aren't significant, because the word is generally written *quintal* and pronounced kant'l and kent'l. Once upon a time it was a weight of 100 kilograms, but Maine fishermen changed that to 100 pounds, and it has always been the term for a cwt of groundfish. There is some classical justification for the Mainer's pronunciation, since the word stems from *centum*, and the Latin would use the hard "c." Although still used for a hundredweight in the fisheries, *quintal* is given a highlander meaning of a considerable amount, quite a good deal, without reference to a precise amount: "She'd be a good deal better off if she'd lose about a *cant'l* of that fat she lugs around!"

❦ / QUODDY BOAT    Also a "Lubec carry-away." Passamaquoddy is regularly shortened to Quoddy in Maine affairs. The *Quoddy boat* was a seaworthy double-ender fitted with sail. It was used to carry herring and lobsters to market.

# R

## ⋀⋀⋀

❦  /  RACE   A strong current of water in the sea; a tide *rip* that will bear watching by navigators. Salt-water sailors read a *race* the way inland canoeists read their *rips* and *pitches*.

❦  /  RACER   A fresh-water term for a female salmon whose spawning cycle has gone awry. She thins out, and takes on the appearance of going hungry, as if she spent all her time racing about.

❦  /  RACK   A touchstone word to test the true Maine coastal tongue. It is the way to pronounce wreck. Wreck Island in Muscongus Bay is "*Rack* Island." *Rack* is also the term for a sizeable set of antlers on a Maine deer.

❦  /  RACKETY   Noisy, and also used interchangeably with "rickety" for wobbly, unstable. *Rickety-rackety* indicates both instability and clatter, as a wheel with loose spokes or a shed door that *chowders* in the wind.

❦  /  RAG   A kind of silencer, and the imagery is obscure. Nellie Simmons went out onto Pitcher Island, where she was born, to put flowers on her mother's grave Memorial Day. She hauled her skiff up, walked up the shore, and came face to face with a possessive summer-lady who had recently bought the island and wanted no part of unsolicited visitors. She ordered Nellie off. Nellie continued toward the little island cemetery, but as she passed by she said, "I was born here, we owned this before you did, and when we owned it we were always glad to see people and were nice to them. So why don't you tie a *rag* to your tongue while I go pay my respects to Ma?"

❧ / RAG OUT   Two words; not the French *ragout*. A sailor joining a ship's crew without necessary clothing beyond what he was wearing would be *ragged out* from the vessel's *slop chest* (which see). He would also expect the captain to make a decent deduction from wages for this service. A man who buys a new suit accordingly *rags* himself *out*, and a lady who passes outgrown children's clothing along to a neighbor is "*ragging* the poor little ones *out*."

❧ / RAIL   The *rail* employed in the favorite Maine simile, thin as a *rail*, is the water bird with the long legs.

❧ / RAIN BARREL   That is, "bar'l." The barrel set by a downspout to catch rain water became a figurative place for catching fish. When cod come extra fast, the miracle is described thus: "They came as if we were fishin' in a *rain bar'l!*" When fish school up in a harbor, somebody may say, "We even had 'em in our *rain bar'l!*" The same comparison is found in fresh-water fishing, where the term means a springhole out in a pond. When the pond in general warms up, trout will seek the cooler water of the deep hole, the hole being likened to a *rain barrel*: "We had no luck until we tried the *rain bar'l*, and we got enough for breakfast."

❧ / RAISE A RUCTION   To start a fuss, by one person or by several. Tax bills come out, and everybody *raises a ruction*. *Ruction* usually suggests a big stew over some small matter, or at least a matter that will not be altered much by the *ruction*. Some scholarly authorities think *ruction* may be Maine for insurrection.

❧ / RAKE  The tined picker—"a cross between a rake and a dust pan"—used in the commercial harvesting of wild Maine blueberries. *Picking* is called *raking*. The blueberry *rake* is not the same as the similar implement for gathering cranberries, although they are close cousins. *Rake* is also another word for a clam hoe, and clam diggers are sometimes said to be *raking* instead of digging. The tilt of a ship's masts, giving her a rakish and jaunty appearance, is her *rake*, and in this sense the word gives us a *rakish* person, one who leans forward in his stride, etc.

❧ / RAKIN' DOWN  A term for a bawling out; a reprimand intended to improve a person's looks, manners, dispostition, etc. The expression comes from *raking down* haymows in the old barns of Maine. As loose hay was laid in, the sides of bays and mows built up unevenly. After the rush of haying season a farmer might take his wooden hand rake and *rake down* these sides merely to give them a neat look. Thus a mow that was *raked down* was visibly improved, and to "*rake* somebody *down*" is an advisory combing out with didactic intent: "You should-da heard the *rakin' down* she gave me when my dog chased her cat!"

❧ / RAM-DOWN  A wood-burning stove meant for heating rather than cooking, and originally turned out by Wood & Bishop foundry in Bangor. Although Wood & Bishop long since went out of business, their *ram-down* stoves are still doing splendid service in Maine woods camps. The entire top of the stove lifts, so long *junks* of firewood may be rammed down inside. The front of the *ram-down* had a hearth, and excellent facilities for fireside enjoyment which some felt were meant for a damper, but which woodsmen aways called the "spittin-fittin's."

❧ / RAM PASTURE  The *barroom* or bedroom in a lumber camp, and now used for anything in the dormitory category.

❧ / RANGE   Besides general meanings, this word has some Maine nuances. Buck deer in rutting season are said to *range;* to travel following the does. A dog given to long jaunts from home is *ranging.* In early surveying, checkerboard county highways laid out a mile apart were called *range* roads, and *ranges* were sections of town; e.g., Allen's Range in Freeport. Maine farmers do not use *range* for pasturage, as in the West, but the term is applied to poultry runs; *range* shelters are open-sided protection for birds put out to *range.*

❧ / RANGELEY BOAT   Not all Maine's distinctive boats originated on tidewater. The round-bottom, *lapstraked,* double-ender *Rangeley boat* was designed by Rufus Crosby at Rangeley Village, and in his lifetime he made hundreds of them. Others took up the design and made hundreds more. Acknowledged to be without equal for safety and ease of handling on inland lakes, these boats had small round seats on the thwarts that are unmistakable identification. To accommodate outboard motors, most of the surviving *Rangeley boats* have been squared off at the stern.

❧ / RAP FULL   Filled sails, drawing well, were *rap full.* Hence, wherever in Maine you hear *rap full* it means complete, loaded, satiated: "Can't touch another morsel—I'm *rap full!*"

❧ / RAUNCHER   A large male deer, and in proper usage the word is reserved for that. But by extension it means anything extra-sized, and at sea it can be a big wave that bumps head on. To "take on a *rauncher*" is to tackle a situation you may not be able to handle. *Baister,* whopper, *stretcher,* and *lunker* are not rightly synonyms, but the element of size is common to them; *master* as an emphatic adjective also has this meaning of size in the right context. Certainly a *master* big buck would be a *rauncher.* Woodsmen think that *rauncher* derives from the raunchiness of male deer in the rutting season.

❦ / RAWZBREE    The exact way older Mainers say raspberry. Younger folks seem to have flattened it to razz-bree. (For *rawzbree* shrub, see *shrub*.)

❦ / REALTY ROAD    A certain private wilderness highway constructed by The American Realty Company, running toward the Allagash region. It is listed here because of the Maine pronunciation: ree-al-ty, with accent on the second syllable.

❦ / REDBREAD    The crimson-orange roe in a cooked lobster: more often called coral.

❦ / RED    Sea superstition disfavored *red* for mittens, socks, and mufflers, but everybody seems to have forgotten why. Something of this no doubt survives in the lobster-man's insistence that his *nippers* (mittens) be white. Ashore, *red* was the farmer's favorite color for barns, but it didn't stem from superstition or artistic selection; it was because red ochre was plentiful and therefore cheap. A man could stir his own paint in a barrel with pogy oil and red ochre, and in areas of Maine where yellow ochre was more easily available, the favorite color was yellow.

❦ / RED OAK SHAVINGS    Any of the breakfast corn flakes.

❦ / REEF    Understood by all sailors to mean shortening sail, the word has some transferred uses ashore. Hand-me-down clothing will fit Junior if Mother takes a *reef* in them. A man who has lost weight will take a *reef* in his belt. Or, "If you don't take a *reef* in that girl, she'll sail smack into trouble!"

❧ / REEL   A hammer used by granite quarry workers for shaping paving blocks. The clacking and whacking of the hammers in use gave Mainers a word for sustained hubbub: *reelin'*.

❧ / REG'LAR-BUILT   Built properly, substantially, and usually with good lines that please the eye; originally said of a vessel but now of anything suiting the phrase. Regular is used frequently in other Maine expressions with about the same meaning; a boisterous child is a regular whirlwind, a light lunch may be a regular meal, etc. Regular seems not to be applied to girls. (See *built*. Somehow girls are never *reg'lar-built*.)

❧ / RENSE   Rinse; sometimes almost (but not quite) wrench: "Be with you soon's I *rense* my hands."

❧ / RESERVED LOT   See *church lot*.

❧ / RITCHBITCH   Folksy but deprecating term for the well-heeled summer lady, particularly in the Bar Harbor vicinity, who has a fine summer residence and calls people "my good man." The male of the species is a *ritchbahstid* (see *bahstid*).

❧ / RIDGE RUNNER   A deer *ranging* the beech ridges in the fall, and from that a general term for somebody well versed in the woods. The term is comparable to the French *coureur de bois*. A veteran trapper may be a *ridge runner*, but so is a boy who likes to hunt and fish. (Gerald Averill wrote a fine book about his experiences in the Maine woods and titled it *The Ridge Runner*.) Out of the woods, a *ridge runner* is a gay blade on the prowl, just hitting the high spots, and certainly looking for game.

❧ / RIG   An amusing sort of chap, *cuss*, *joker*, etc: "Oh, that Newt! He's a *rig!*"

❦ / RIGHT AS RAIN *Finest kind.* Everything serene. Bernice Richmond used *Right as Rain* as a book title and explained the meaning beautifully in her preface.

❦ / RIGHTEN UP To put to rights; to police a room or area. A boy *rightens* his closet; a man *rightens* his affairs. There seems no explanation for an occasional Teutonic verb-ending in Maine speech; compare *piecen out.*

❦ / RIMWRACKED Wagon and buggy wheels were made of four parts: hub, spoke, felloe (rim), and tire. The spokes fitted into holes in the felloe, and in time the holes would wear larger and the spokes would wear smaller. A wheel thus worn was literally *wracked* in the *rim.* So, anything old, past its use, misshapen, toppling, etc., is *rimwracked* in Maine parlance until the word is even applied to a hogging boat, or a shed that is frost-hove on its foundation. A person crippled or aged can be *rimwracked.*

❦ / RINGTAIL PEELER Supposedly this was a term for a political follower of Sir Robert Peel, the British prime minister, but there is evidence it appeared in Maine speech before that gentleman achieved prominence and without reference to him. A *ringtail* was a light sail bent on a long sliding spar off a vessel's main boom. It was meant to give a ship extra speed, and along with the *gangway pendulum* (which see) was one of the surprises the Maine privateers had for the British during the unpleasantness of 1812. The privateer *Dash,* built at Freeport in 1813, was designed as a topsail schooner and so rigged. At sea, she demonstrated that she could carry more sail, so she was converted to a hermaphrodite brig and fitted with a *ringtail* which added a full third to the size of her mainsail. Historian Rowe says, " . . . she knew no equal in speed," and her list of prizes is more than proof that she was quite some vessel. It seems that whenever she *peeled* her *ringtail* and took off downwind, the British lost another one. The appearance of such

R / 231

a vessel certainly suggests the jaunty, aggressive, bouncy nature, the verve and élan of one Mainers would consider a *ringtail peeler*: "You have to go some to keep ahead of him; he's a *reg'lar ringtail peeler!*"

❦ / RIP   On both salt and fresh water, the word for agitation and turbulence in a tidal run or a stream. Conflicting tidal currents create a *rip*-tide, and an undertow is a *rip*-current. In the woods, a *rip* is less than a rapids, and more than a riffle. *Rip* is also the Maine contraction of Ripogenus, the dam and the lake: *Rip* Dam and *Rip* Lake.

❦ / RIVER   In Maine, dictionary definitions of river, brook, stream, etc., fall apart under the Fish & Game laws. Stream fishing closes on August 15, but *rivers* may be fished after that. The only way to tell a Maine *river* from a stream is to look in the book and see what-the-hell the Commissioner calls it. Some large streams close and some smaller *rivers* stay open. Otherwise, Maine usage permits considerable leeway with brook, stream, and *river*. Creek is seldom used. For the use of such terms to represent a region, see *branch*.

❦ / RIVER HOG   A river driver.

❦ / ROAD HUNTER   A deer hunter who is scairt to go in the woods, or too lazy to hike, and does his *gunnin'* along the road. Considering the nature of highways in the northern wilderness, there is some humor in the translation of *road hunter* into Madawaska French: *boulevard chasseur*. Most *road hunters* are members of the *Hullahwee Tribe*, which see.

❦ / ROARIN' FORTIES   A generation in the Silly Seventies which thinks the Roaring Twenties were even better than the Foolish Fifties will be delighted to learn that the *roarin' forties* of Maine were the prevailing, strong westerly winds encountered by Maine vessels between 40° and 50° south latitude. Once in a while somebody uses the term for the similar winds in the northern hemisphere, but Mainers called these simply "the brave west winds."

❧ / ROBIN SNOW  A light fall of perhaps an inch or two coming in late spring as an afterthought of winter. It is usually fluffy and wet and makes a beautiful morning, but it soon melts. Considered good for the greening landscape, a *robin snow* is also called the *poor man's fertilizer*.

❧ / ROCK  An offshore island and sometimes a submerged ledge. Halfway *Rock* is an island with lighthouse halfway from Portland Head Light to Seguin. Many Maine islands shown on official charts are locally known as *rocks*: Mosquito Island, Mosquito *Rock*. In the woods, *rocks* are a river hazard to log driving and canoeing, and many streams have sections known as the *rocks*. Considering the total Maine concern with *rocks*, "going on the *rocks*" can mean only what it does: a wreck, a smash-up, a calamity, a business failure.

❧ / ROCKER  Another word for a clam *hod*. When filled with freshly dug clams, it is *soused* in tidewater and *rocked* back and forth to *rense* mud and sand from the clams.

❧ / ROCK MAPLE  The sugar maple, *Acer saccharum*. Native to Maine, it is the same tree the Vermonters think nobody else has, and which Canadians honor on their flag. Tapped for syrup extensively in Maine, particularly in the wilderness of the upper St. John River, it is also an important forest asset going into bowling alleys, furniture, all kinds of turnings, and firewood. Mainers do know it as sugar maple but more readily identify it as *rock maple* to distinguish it from six other maples found in the state.

R / 233

❧ / ROGUE'S YARN   A fine yarn, hardly more than a thread, running through the strands of a rope to identify the manufacturer. Of a different color from the rope, it serves no purpose except to tell who made the cordage.

❧ / ROLLER   And still another term for a clam *hod*. (See *rocker*.)

❧ / ROOM FOR NAME AND HAIL   See *beamy*.

❧ / ROOST   Another Maine obliqueness for the toilet. The *roost* was a spruce pole offering multilateral accommodations for lumber camp crews, and because the clientele was men only, the approach side was often open. Such a pole-backhouse, which was the more formal term for the *roost*, survives occasionally at abandoned logging sites, but here and there a sporting camp will still have an outhouse which is not truly a *roost* but is so labeled out of, perhaps, respect for the traditions. *Roost* appears frequently in upstate remarks as a synonym for a *convenience* of any style.

❧ / ROPE   On the farms and in the woods of Maine ropes tend to be *ropes*. In coastal contexts *rope* is the general term for a piece of cordage that doesn't happen to be doing anything at the moment, but when it is turned to a specific use it ceases to be *rope* and takes on one of any number of names: twine, cordage, *warp*, line, hawser, painter, halyard, sheet, etc. The elderly expression that a sailor must "learn his *ropes*" explains this distinction nicely, because once he has learned them, he finds there aren't very many. Aboard ship, the *handrope* and *footrope* were in the rigging to hang to and stand on while setting sail; the *manrope* was strung in a gangway to cling to in heavy weather; the *bellrope* was on the clapper to strike the *bells*. Otherwise, a true salt seldom touches a *rope* as such. Lobster *pots* are never attached to a *rope;* always a *warp;* if you wish to buy some of that line, ask for *potwarp*. And so on.

❦ / Rose   The sweet perfume of the rose appeals to Mainers for certain comparisons contrary to expectation: "He's one of these people who can fall in the manure pit and come out smellin' like a *rose*."

❦ / Rose bread   Nothing to do with the flower, and no pun intended. Rose is simply Maine conjugation of risen, as in the Easter greeting, "He is rose!" Riz, rose, rosen. *Rose bread* uses yeast, and this term distinguishes it from the numerous favored hot breads which do not. *Raised bread.*

❦ / Route   Maine people usually say *Route* One or devious *route* as in "root," except that in turn they have their own way of saying root. Try saying "He caught his foot on a root." This flattening of the *oo* is also heard in "roof," so that in, "I put a new roof on my bahn," there is an affinity 'twixt put and roof. But in speaking of the R.F.D. *route*, or a paper *route*, Mainers often say "rout."

❦ / Round turn   Two Maine meanings for this. In lumbering, a *round turn* was provided at a dead end logging road, so teams could come about—a rotary. Thus a person who finds a way out of a difficulty has a *round turn*. Otherwise, from seafaring, a *round turn* is a quick loop around the winch and capstan, or a *spile*, to snub a boat's progress. It differs from the *hold turn* (which see) only in the way it is used—the round turn suggests speedy action, perhaps in an emergency, while the *hold turn* would be routine. For a transferred usage, try this: "He was blattin' his foolish mouth off, and I put in my *round turn* and brought him to a screechin' halt!" Or: "If somebody don't get a *round turn* on that boy, he'll wind up in prison!"

❦ / Royal boy   Heard now and then for a Maine State Policeman. The term is borrowed from the Maritime

Provinces where the provincial constabulary is the Royal Canadian Mounted Police.

❧ / RUGGED   Pronounced rug-gid. A favorite word throughout Maine in the usual dictionary meanings but with a great deal of additional verve and color. The physical condition and state of health which makes a man well set up and powerful establishes him as *rug-gid*, but a ten-year-old boy who is *rug-gid* may be merely chubby. A *rug-gid* meal would be ample of meat, potatoes, and pie, with over-indulgence. The word is transferred, as when a man or horse might be considered *rug-gid*, but instead the word is applied to the load: "He carries a real *rug-gid* packsack." A *rug-gid* disposition often means a short fuse on a temper. A *rug-gid* weekend is exhausting. *Rug-gid* weather is not necessarily severe, but mean enough so you don't enjoy it. When used with typical Maine down-play, *rug-gid* has a lovely quality, as when the old town of Flagstaff was flooded out by a dam and the cemetery there was moved over to high ground in Eustis. Parker Dalrymple, then in his eighties, went over to see his great-great-grandmother exhumed, and he took a peek at the old lady. Somebody asked Parker how she looked, and he said, "Not too *rug-gid*."

❧ / RUMINATIN'   The pensive expression on a cow's face while she is chewing her cud suggests this Maine term for solemn and deep meditation. Or, just sittin' and starin'.

❧ / RUM-STICK   A spirit level.

❧ / RUM SWEAT   All good and true Mainers regard a cold in the head, or any other adaptable ailment, as an excuse to force a *rum sweat*. The treatment consists of taking rum both as prescribed and as desired. It doesn't cure anything, but it makes the illness enjoyable. A Medford or New England type rum is suggested if one cannot get Black Diamond from Nova Scotia or "screech" from Newfoundland.

❦ / RUN  Maine has some favorite and perhaps special uses for this word. A hound-dog *runs*, and if his nose is good he *runs* very well, as when he *runs* a rabbit. Spawning *runs* are made by herring, shad, etc.; as, a good *run* of alewives or the alewives are *runnin'*. A dog will have an enclosure which is a *run*, and when he is let out he will take a *run* for himself. Lines *run* in their sheeves; a clothesline *runs* on its pulley. To *run* something into the barn or undercover merely means to put it there: "*Run* the cultivator undercover!" At sea, *running* is to sail before the wind. Children are *run off* to get them out of the way, and Mother doesn't necessarily mean great speed when she *runs* a boy on an errand. (After Judge Louis A. Jack got soundly trounced in his bid for the U. S. Senate, he used to tell about the time he "walked" for office.) To *run* anything into the ground is to bring it to an end, wear it out, overdo, talk too much.

❦ / RUSTICATOR  A *summer complaint*, but the derivation of the word suggests the farm rather than the seashore or the woods. Originally a *rusticator* was a college student, who, because of poor work or behavior, was "sent back into the country" for a time to work out his problems. He'd live with and be tutored by a small-town clergyman for a year, and then rejoin his classes. Mainers now use the word for city folks who come in season to get fresh eggs and milk and to birdwatch.

# S

❧ / SACK   This word is not used much in Maine for a bag, as in a *sack* of candy; the paper *sack* is usually a bag. However, gunny*sack* is used for a burlap grain bag. Mostly, as used in Maine, *sack* is a verb interchangeable with *tote, lug, carry,* and *haul* where something is moved with the hands or on the back. A load is *sacked* into camp; meaning it was *toted. Sack* does suggest a little more difficulty with the task. As Al Dunton said, "I contrived so he *sacked* all the canned goods, and all I had to *tote* was the bread and corn flakes."

❧ / SAILCLOTH   The canvas or other material from which sails are made, but also a piece of such cloth used for some other purpose. Sometimes no more than a synonym for tarpaulin. *Sprayhoods* (which see) are made with a piece of *sailcloth*. A piece of *sailcloth* may be tacked over a broken window until glass can be reset. A saltwater farmer will cover his tomato plants against the first frost with *sailcloth*. Elizabeth Coatsworth tells of the Monhegan grandmother who died, and as rough seas prevented a trip to the main for a casket, her frail little body was lovingly wrapped in *sailcloth*. (This amused a granddaughter who had a comical vision of "Grannie scuddin' through Hell in a close-reefed mains'l.") As coastal Maine people use the term *sailcloth*, it means about any useful fragment of fabric of sail-making nature. A piece of canvas.

❦ / SALMON Maine is the only state in the nation where the Atlantic sea-run *salmon (Salmo salar)* may be taken in fresh water. And the landlocked variety of this fish was first identified in Sebago Lake and given the scientific name of *Salmo sebago.* So the Mainer has something special in his beloved *salmon.* The dramatic, even spectacular, action of a *salmon* when hooked makes him the angler's favorite. (But see *racer;* racers aren't much fun.) *Salmon,* at least Maine *salmon,* are called sam-m'n.

❦ / SALTED DOWN A people who went to sea and spent long months in lumber camps with great logistic problems well knew about salted meats. No wonder money in the bank is compared to corned menus in the barrel: "He's got his little pile *salted down.*"

❦ / SALT HAY Marsh hay cut on tidal meadows, now wholly a bygone business. While the very poor quality hay might be fed to young stock, it was mainly sold to crockery makers for packing. *Salt hay* was cocked on *staddles,* a circle of stakes which held the hay from floating off when extra high tides covered the marshes. Pronounced as if one word: saltay.

❦ / SALTS THROUGH A GOOSE A metaphor to delineate extreme speed: "He lit out like *salts through a goose!*" Reference is to the medicinal salts used as a purgative, and to the fact that geese rarely need to take any. A Maine expression of like import is "like diarrhea through a duck."

❦ / SAME AS A SINGED CAT A cat that gets singed, such as one asleep under a stove and unaware that somebody has touched off a fire, never forgets the great astonishment that came upon him when he found he was a-smoke. He lives always in a wary state. Thus somebody who is smarter for having learned a good lesson is *same as a singed cat.*

❦ / SAMSON POLE  A lumbering device using leverage to give the strength of Samson to *choppers*. When a tree being felled hangs up on the stump, binding the saw in the cut and "leaning toward *sawyers*" (which see), a pole is thrust under a limb, and a second pole is used to exert upward force against the first. By lifting, the choppers gain enough power to release the saw and tip the tree in the intended line of fall. The *Samson pole* suggests that Archimedes is still a competent authority. (Also see Judges: 13–16.)

❦ / SANCTIMONIOUS  A word used in Maine as anywhere, but in Maine always followed by *old bahstid*. All *bahstids*, of course, are not *sanctimonious*, but in Maine everybody who is *sanctimonious* seems to be elderly and of dubious ancestry. A *sanctimonious old bahstid* is a smiling sort of affable appearance who passes the plate in church and then forecloses on poor widows all day Monday.

❦ / SANDPAPER THE ANCHOR  A job that doesn't need doing, can't be done, and isn't attempted. Heard almost entirely as a command to get the children out from under foot: "Why don't you two go and *sandpaper the anchor*," i.e., get lost.

❦ / SANNUP  From Abnaki Indian, loosely used throughout Maine for a boy-child and usually a mischievous one: "You *sannup*, you! Stop *plaguing* that poor cat!" The real *sannup* was an unfledged warrior, perhaps a junior sachem. A young lady showing *sannup* tendencies will be called a minx.

❦ / SAUCE  Almost unknown in Maine as the word for gravy, *sauce* is rather the term for dessert. Preserved pears, peaches, and berries will be served in a *sauce* dish. Apple*sauce* and rhubarb *sauce;* and also sody fountain garnishes. Lemon (soft) and rum (hard) *sauces* are served to lubricate and adorn steamed puddings and mince pie. In Maine a *sauce* boat is a gravy boat, more often a gravy dish. "*Sauce* for the goose and *sauce* for the gander" is quoted in Maine in the tit-for-tat adage, but most Mainers will not automatically think of gravy in this connection. As used for upstart impertinence, *sauce* is pronounced sass and sarss in Maine, and is not generally thought of as a related word: "Kenny sarssed teacher and she *larruped* him good!" When a Maine man is offered a snort and he says, "My, that's good *sauce*," he isn't thinking about gravy either.

❦ / Sawdust sorter   One competent to *sort sawdust* is in the same professional category as one who does a good job "*pounding sand* in a rathole" (see *pound sand*). *Sorting sawdust* is excellent training for a budding idiot.

❦ / Sawyers   Anything in Maine which is aslant and askew, visibly out of plumb and *weewaw*, is said to "lean toward *Sawyer's*." Many have presumed a person or a family named Sawyer fathered the adage. It comes, instead, from lumbering, and the *sawyers* are the men felling a tree with a two-man crosscut saw. When things go as planned, the tree will fall away from them, but if for any reason it fails to respond as expected and tips backward, it is said to lean toward (the) *sawyers*. This binds the saw (which gives us the expression "to be in a bind"), and things come to a screeching halt. *Sawyers* who by miscalculation or infernal luck find themselves in such a bind are the butt of the crew's rude jests, and feel just terrible about it. Their remedy is to rig a *Samson pole*, which see, and force the tree off the saw. Such *sawyers* were paid by board feet scaled, so the delay costs them money as well as ridicule. When Adelard Gilbert (see *entrepreneur de bois*) retired and took his wife on a tour of Europe, he sent a postcard home to Henri Marcoux showing the Tower of Pisa, which he described as leaning toward *Sawyer's*.

❦ / SCAFFLINGS  From scaffoldings; an extra barn mow over the big front doors and inside the gable. Often the *scafflings* was a pole mow and unless needed for an unusually big crop of hay, it remained a catch-all for odds and ends. "Up on the *scafflings*" means out of sight, out of mind, and, considering the location of the *scafflings*, often out of reach. To go up on the *scafflings* is to go into retirement. Family treasures, laid away as heirlooms, can be said to be on the *scafflings*.

❦ / SCALE  Sea fog which lifts is said to *scale* off. When Tudor Gardiner was campaigning for governor, he rowed out to Beal Island in a dense fog and found everybody downcast, all sitting in their bait houses to wait out a fogmull. Tudor asked one lobsterman, "Are you interested in politics?" He answered, "I ain't int'risted in a gahdam thing till this fog *scales* off!" *Scale* is also the word for the measurement of board feet and cords in the forestry lingo, and also another word for the *log rule*. (See *scaler*.)

❦ / SCALE BOARD  A counting board with holes and movable pegs hanging by the *scaler's* elbow in a sawmill, on which he keeps running track of board feet turned out. Since the best woods *scale* is never more than a competent estimate, the first real measurement of actual production is done by the mill *scaler*. His *scale board* amounts to a Supreme Court decision—that's it. Accordingly, the test of a competent woods *scaler* is how well, day after day, his computations jibe with those of the *scale board* after the logs are sawn. Thus a just and upright man will not be found wanting when he's *scale-boarded*.

❦ / SCALER  One who estimates, computes, and measures cords and board feet at any stage of a lumbering operation. The first *scale* will be an estimate of standing timber; next a *scale* of logs piled, and finally the mill *scale*. Since *choppers* are often paid by wood turned out, the *scaler*, as agent of the employer, is responsible for payroll amounts, and there has persisted a timberland generalization that all *scalers* are *bahstids*. On the other hand, if a *scaler* is respected by his *choppers*, forestry can convey no higher praise and no greater reward. The *scaler* uses the *log rule*, but there are other devices available to him to arrive at his figures.

❧ / SCARF   The Maine *chopper's* preferred word for *kerf*, which see.

❧ / SCHOOL LOT   See *church lot*.

❧ / SCHOOLMARM   A forest tree which has suffered some damage to its top and as a consequence has developed into two tops. It will make pulpwood, but is good for long logs only up to the crotch. The suggestion of a lady with both legs in the air must have occurred to the first Maine woodsman who likened such a tree to a *schoolmarm*.

❧ / SCOFF   To gulp; to eat and drink with a guzzling effect: "Now sit up like a little man and stop *scoffin'* your food!"

❧ / SCOOCH   Acknowledged by the dictionary authorities as a Maine oddity for what other regions pronounce scrooch, the joke is on them: *scooch* is right. Derivation is from an Old French word, *escoutchier*. It means to hunker down, to sit on your heels. Maine children play *scooch*–tag, a schoolyard game in which a child saves himself from being "it" if he *scooches* before being tagged.

❧ / SCOON   To ride along merrily without cark and care, everything smooth and pleasant. From the same root as schooner.

❧ / SCOOT   A farm and timberland vehicle without wheels which slides on bare ground much as a toboggan or sled would. A *stone boat* (stone drag) is a kind of *scoot* and is often called a stone *scoot*. In the *twitching* of logs, a single log would usually be pulled from the woods to the brow by a team. The *scoot* would have several logs loaded on it to be drawn forth by the same horse-power. There was a considerable coefficient of friction to a *scoot*, but its advantage was in its closeness to the ground; logs could be rolled on and off easily with a *canthook*, and no rollway was needed. To *scoot* something is to move it along, usually implying a sliding effort rather than a lift. The movement of a scoot is recognized in the expression, "Now, *scoot* down to the store and get me a yeast cake!" The same movement is noticed in the interjection: *Scoot!* meaning "Beat it!"

❦ / SCOOTS   Reject lumber (it was tossed on a *scoot* to be hauled away from the mill carriage). Either given away or sold cheaply, *scoots* were a speculation cargo for Maine vessels. With good lumber in the hold, and a load of *scoots* on deck, the captain might turn a penny on the *scoots* and keep it for himself.

❦ / SCREECHER   A howling wind.

❦ / SCREWED HAY   Most hay balers turn out the rectangular product. Some bale hay in coils; that's *screwed hay*.

❦ / SCRIBE, SCRIVE (SCRIEVE?)   To *scribe*, as in carpentry, is to mark a board to make it fit, using dividers, compassses or *scribers*. Somehow the "b" became a "v," and Maine boatbuilders talk of *scriving* rather than *scribing*, and in turn the generally used term *scrieving* or screeving. The platform on which shapes are laid down is the screevin'-board. Hence, to screeve a thing is to shape and mold it, as a pithy editorial might screeve public opinion.

❦ / SCROD   The smallest marketable size of groundfish. In the beginning it was no particular variety, but in recent years public misinformation has determined it to be *cod*. It can be haddock, hake, *pollock*, as well. Until its late and lamentable disappearance in Bangor's renewal program, the Penobscot Exchange Hotel always meticulously stated on its restaurant menu just which fish was being offered each day as *scrod*.

❦ / SCROG   A wind-stunted bush, shrub, and tree that *hangs tough* on a Maine headland. Today, it also means anything wrongly done, hanging together bravely, and sort of fouled up. Have you ever seen a shed that was *scrogged* up by a two-foot overhang on one side and a flush eave on the other?

❦ / SCUPPERS   Drains along a boat's side, level with the deck. Loaded or *soused* to the *scuppers*, loaded to the highline, loaded to the gills, loaded to the *gunn'ls* are seaside equivalents to carryin' a *jag*: the *joker's* been drinkin'. See *kneehigh to a scupper*.)

❦ / SCURRYFUNGE   A hasty tidying of the house between the time you see a neighbor coming and the time she knocks on the door. This tends to be coastal. The upland version would be to *teakittle* up: "You *scurryfunge* your house and I'll *teakittle* up mine!"

❦ / SEA   As with *ocean* (which see), Mainers are careful with this word. To go to *sea* means to make a career of seafaring. A *sea* is a wave that breaks over the side of a boat or against a shore. *Sea* water means salt water, as used for cooking lobsters, or for pumping through a *sea* cock to keep live lobsters happy in a barrel on the way home from *haulin'*. A full *sea* is a high tide; a heavy or rough *sea* keeps the lobstermen in port. *Sea* fog is distinguished from land fog. In short, while *sea* has its uses, it is not heard as Eugene O'Neill used it in "dat ol' Debbil *Sea!*" Irish moss is called *sea* moss, but Mainers prefer rockweed to seaweed. Seaward is used for the opposite of landward. But "to be all at *sea*," from confusion and lack of coordination, will probably come out as the Mainer's "all afloat" or "all adrift."

❧ / SEA DUCK   The eider duck, numerous off shore and nesting on many Maine islands.

❧ / SEA SMOKE   See *Arctic smoke.*

❧ / SEASON   For the most part this means summertime, and the period of the pilgrim, *rusticator, dogfish,* out-of-stater, tourist, and *summer complaint.* The most pregnant use of *season* is in the Mainer's greeting to the visitor: "Are you down for the *season?*" It signifies that non-membership is recognized, and no matter how sincerely the fellow *from away* tries to infiltrate, he comes for the *season* only. However, *season* also means the wintertime, or off-season, in the signs that say, "Closed for the *season*— Open again in May." With the new enthusiasm for winter sports, the Maine publicity experts have been advertising the state as a four-season vacationland, which disposes of *mud season* (which see).

❧ / SEEDER   A female lobster the law requires be returned to the water when caught so she may replenish the Gulf of Maine. In the woods, a *seeder* is a mature forest tree left during a cutting to start a new generation.

❧ / SEED STOCK   In Aroostook County lingo, potatoes grown for seed instead of table stock. Certified seed potatoes are grown under rigid state supervision, and Maine supplies great quantities to other potato-growing areas as well as to retail seedsmen.

❧ / SEELECTMAN   Mainers always give a hearty "see" sound to the first syllable. Usually three in number, the *seelectmen* are elected annually in town meeting, and are the municipal officers. The term originated before the ladies had the vote, so today we do have female *seelectmen*.

❧ / SEEN   Not necessarily in error, but a solecism arrived at after long years, *seen* is a favorite Maine word for saw: "You never seen nothin' like it!" Except, however, that *seen* is not always used for saw: "I *seen* something today I never see before!" (See *tense*, where the Mainer's gift of vivid conversational interchange is discussed.) High-paid English teachers employed to refine Maine speech have been known to say, after a few terms' exposure, "I *seen* it with my own eyes!" Mainers do use *seen* correctly in the expression "*seen* dead": "I'd rather be *seen* dead than have to step into that house!"

❧ / SERENADE   The favored Maine word for a little party to honor newlyweds; shivaree (*charivari!*).

❧ / SERVE   The term for winding a cord on a rope's end in the *parceling* of a line. (See *parcel.*) Also the special word for the fulling of the tide: "What time does the tide *serve* today?" And on the farm, to breed, as in the good-natured colloquy:

> Teacher: You're late, Thomas, do you have an excuse?
> Thomas: Yes, ma'am; I had to get the cow *served*.
> Teacher: Can't your father do that?
> Thomas: No, ma'am; he ain't registered.

❧ / SET   As much as anything, a *chance* (which see). A *set* for smelts is an aperture in a rock dam where the net may be placed; upon filling his pail a man will turn the *set* over to someone else. A place for a trap: a mink *set*. To change position in fishing in any way is to find a new *set*. The *set* of a vessel's sails is transferred to clothing: "I don't like the *set* of the new dress," or, "This suit isn't right in the *set* of the shoulders." In Maine speech the difference between sit and *set* is more auditory than ungrammatical, but probably the mistake is more common than elsewhere, although in "sittin' *pretty*" it seldom comes out as *settin' pretty*: "With that new job at the bank, Hank's sittin' *pretty*." Henrietta Purington used to invite guests to *set* down until her booby boy Vincent came home after one term at Or'no and informed her "sit" was correct. Pleased to know this, she was ready the next time guests came to supper, and with distinct diction she announced, "All right, now ever'-body SIT theirselves!" (A Bowdoin professor used to have a dog named Beowulf; you could yell "Lay down!" and "Set!" all day at him and he wouldn't move, but if you said *lie down* and *sit* he'd obey instantly. Isn't that a good thing for a dog to know?)

❧ / SET FIRE YOU   An admonitory exhortation of obscure origin: "Now, *set fire you*; pay attention to what you're doin'!"

❧ / SETTIN' UP SHROUDS AND BACKSTAYS   From place to place along the coast of Maine various ways of saying much the same thing will be heard. It refers to the appearance of the afternoon sky when the sun is "drawing water." Diffused in atmospheric moisture, rays of the sun streak the sky. However the manifestation is described, it is a sure sign of rain.

❧ / SEVENTH WAVE   Many have always maintained that every seventh ocean wave is larger than the preceding six. Maybe and maybe not, but the idea gives Mainers their variant for the straw that broke the camel's back; a last misfortune which caps the climax is a *seventh wave*.

❧ / SHAG   Not a Maine exclusive, but because of the ubiquitous cormorant or *shag* that infests the Maine coast a very common word, in numerous allusions. It is inedible because of its exclusive diet of fish. Its worst offense is to clean out a pocket of herring awaiting transport.

❧ / SHAGIMAW   A well-authenticated Maine mythical animal that cruises town and lot lines, *tote roads*, and *log hauls*. Often called the *Toteroad Shagimaw*. A *deacon-seater* or *stretcher*, the *shagimaw* moved west with Maine *choppers* who went to the Great Lakes region and beyond. It has two feet like a moose and two feet like a bear and can make tracks that confound the *sport*. Conditioned by watching surveyors, it goes 80 rods like a moose, shifts, and goes 80 rods like a bear. The *shagimaw* always makes reverential gestures at *witness trees* (which see).

❧ / SHANDYGAFF   No reason to include this as a Maine-ism, except that in this vote-dry-drink-wet state the beer and ginger concoction was deemed harmless enough so children were permitted to join their elders in a glass.

❧ / SHARP   Quick and alert, and not always with the nuance of shrewd. A *sharp* boy in school is nimble with his lessons, although Mainers do use the term *sharp* trader for a tricky *cow jockey*.

❧ / SHAVING MILL   The origin is lost; this was a term for a small pirate vessel or privateer in colonial days. When heard today, a *shaving mill* is any small, fast, rakish sailing boat.

❧ / SHEARING A PIG   Unprofitable and absurd activity. *Shearing a pig* is "great cry and little wool."

❧ / SHEDDER   A lobster just after the biological shedding of the old shell. Marine biologists call this moulting. Lobsters grow only during the shedding period, and each moult is called a *stage*. During the shedding season, lobster-men find both hardshell and softshell lobsters in their traps. The *shedders* are softshell, as the new covering hasn't yet calcified. Not always, but in some shedding seasons the hardshells fetch a few cents more a pound; perhaps a paradox since most lobstermen think the softshells are sweeter.

**❧ / SHEEP CORNER**  Sheep are devilishly hard to catch, and a prudent farmer always made a special pen in his pasture corner into which the sheep could be driven for close handling. Anybody "caught in a *sheep corner*" will be without an answer, perhaps caught in a lie.

**❧ / SHEEP ROCK**  Of Scottish Highland origin, this term suited early Maine farmers and they used it as if 'twere their own. Gray granite field rocks in the dusk or in a fog can be mistaken for sheep, so a man totting up his flock can count in a few rocks and get confused. Anybody over-assessing himself is counting *sheep rocks*.

**❧ / SHELDRAKE**  The quite proper inland Maine word for the American merganser, and for the most part the only duck the Maine wilderness regularly sees. Downstate and coastwide the variety of waterfowl is great, but up in the woods the American and the less common hooded merganser predominate. One time a federal biologist came to Maine to lecture to a game-warden school, and when he held up what he called an American merganser the game wardens from northern Maine all hooted at him. He might have a degree and hold down a cozy government job, but he didn't know a *sheldrake* when he saw one.

**❧ / SHELLHEAP**  Maine preference for the kitchen midden. The Paint People, inhabiting Maine some 5000 years ago, left many *shellheaps* along the Maine coast, but Mainers didn't know they were middens until professors came and dug in them.

**❧ / SHILOHITE**  Communicants who migrated to Maine to join the communal religious colony instituted by evangelist Frank W. Sandford, in the town of Durham, were called

*Shilohites* by their unsympathetic neighbors. Around the turn of the century the community was much in the news, and the sizeable village on Beulah Hill had its own U. S. Post Office, which was named *Shiloh*. Descendants of the original members and some new converts still live in the vicinity and still hold services in the temple, the only building now standing of the once extensive Sandford complex. Some of the bitterness originally conveyed by *Shilohite* has evaporated with the passing of years until it is by no means as offensive as it was seventy-five years ago, and no longer intended to be. When the word is heard today it is used to explain the origins of various families now assimilated into the area. The full title of Sandford's venture was The Society of the Holy Ghost and Us.

❦ / SHIP'S WIFE   When a prosperous old-time Maine sea captain set a ne'er-do-well son up in business, the lad would own his vessel, but having no sea experience would require a professional navigator in his crew to sail it for him. Such a navigator was the *ship's wife*. The term is still used for an obsequious assistant, or a man who does all the work without any credit.

❦ / SHITEPOKE   Maine people make two errors with this word—they pronounce it wrong and they apply it to the wrong bird. They ignore the middle "e," and they use the word for the blue heron. The green heron is the *shitepoke*. Fishermen often use the same word for seagulls that bother them, usually as *damshitpokes*, but this can be taken as opinion, and not as accurate ornithological field usage.

❦ / SHIV   Maine way to pronounce sheeve, the rolling part of a pulley. In everyday usage, *shiv* pretty much means the whole pulley.

❦ / SHOCK   Shuck; to remove the shells or husks from about anything. Also, to *shock* off a jacket or boots. One exception seems to be crabmeat; clams are *shocked* but crabmeat is *picked*. An attentive ear will observe that Mainers sometimes *shock* one thing and *shuck* another. Clams almost always get *shocked*, but green peas may get *shucked*.

❧ / SHOO-ER    Sure. Mainers like to use *shoo-er* where others might reasonably say certainly: Sure will! Sure does! Sure can! A sure thing, such as an unbeatable wager, is heard in Maine, but more often it is an enthusiastic affirmative reply: Ask a man to come in for a drink, and he'll say, "*Shoo-er* thing!

❧ / SHOOK    The original meaning of *shook* was ready-cut material for making casks, but in Maine usage it has come to mean almost any pre-cut lumber, both hard and soft, for specific purposes, but not boards and dimension stock. The term is also applied to strips and square-bars that will later be turned into *shook*. A *shook* mill saws *shook*. While *shook* is used for materials to go into barrels, boxes, and even pallets, the one exception in Maine speech is the pre-cut material for lobster traps. The word *shook* is not used here; the material is called *trap-stock*.

❧ / SHORE    A general word much favored by Maine coastal people for the vicinity of the water, almost a synonym for waterfront. Setting foot on the actual *shore* is not necessary in going to the *shore*. It means the wharf, buildings on and near the wharf, and it is inclusive for business there: a lobsterman will say he is going to the *shore* when he has in mind a full day's work *haulin'* traps outside.

❧ / SHORE DINNER    *Shore dinner* and *clam bake* (which see) are not synonyms, although many tourists use one term for the other. The *shore dinner* originated before the turn of the century at New Meadows Inn at West Bath, where it was a seafood meal prepared on a range and served at a table in the dining room. Shortly, many other eating places followed suit, and the price at the time was "all you can eat for fifty cents." The meal began with fried and steamed clams, followed by a lobster stew or bisque. Then came a boiled lobster. Dessert was traditionally a thin sugar cookie (several Maine cookbooks include a recipe for New Meadows Inn cookies) with vanilla ice cream. The immediate great popularity of the *shore dinner* as an outing treat gained impetus from the electric trolley lines, since several of the early restaurants that specialized in it were reached by these conveyances. New Meadows Inn had its own platform so passengers could step right off at the door.

❧ / SHORE HUGGER   A timid sailor; thus any cautious person. (See *appletree-er* and *wharfside sailor*.)

❧ / SHOUT   To treat; to stand for the drinks. "I'm *shoutin'!*" means "I'm buying": "After the game, Coach Nelson *shouted* the team to ice cream."

❧ / SHOWIN' A FETCH-UP   Indicating by word or actions the way a child was raised, but the way the term is used it almost always alludes to bad manners and lack of breeding. To a noisy and ill-mannered child one says, "Stop *showin'* your *fetch-up!*" If one is rightly fetched up, he behaves.

❧ / SHOW YOUR HELM   To indicate your course at sea; the equivalent of blinking your directional lights on an automobile. A polite helmsman will move his rudder momentarily to reveal his intention whether to pass to port or starboard.

❧ / SHRUB   A temperance drink much esteemed in early Maine, and still made by many housewives, usually from raspberries. Laid down with sugar and vinegar, the liquid was strong in the bottle and was diluted with cold spring water when served. Absolutely non-alcoholic. A genteel refreshment during an afternoon chat, with cookies. *Shrub* seldom stood by itself as a word; usually in full: *rawzbreeshrub.*

❧ / SHUTTER "To close the *shutter*" is to *hang* the last plank on a vessel's hull in the boatyard; this closes the gap as when one closes the *shutter* on a window.

❧ / SICKY-SWEET That kind of sweetness which lacks flavor; thus, a mellifluous or even *sanctimonious* approach which is objectionable: "He might-a convinced me if he hadn't been so *sicky-sweet* about it!"

❧ / SIDDOUT To set out, in the sense of plan to and intend to: "I *siddout* to go to the store, but changed my mind."

❧ / SIDEHILL WINDER Or, sidehill gouger. A native Maine animal living on mountain slopes and having shorter legs on one side than on the other (except on Mt. Blue, where it's the other way around). *Sidehill winders* do odd things around camp, mostly when out-of-state *sports* are in the crowd.

❧ / SIDE-WHEELER A pacing racehorse, as different from a trotter. Mainers noticed the gait does remind of a side-paddle steamer.

❧ / SING Not limited to Maine in this meaning, but always used by Mainers when the sea term *sing out* applies; to call, shout, announce, etc. Lookouts on vessels, sighting something, always *sang out*: as in, "Thar she blows!" "I didn't know anybody was around, and then this *jeezer sings out* and scares me half to death!" The term never includes musical vocalizing.

❦ / Sing small   To change your tune; one who has been boasting and runs into a comeuppance will *sing small* after that. Usually the term suggests the aftermath of an embarrassment.

❦ / Sink spout weather   The first indoor plumbing was the gooseneck to drain kitchen sinks. Suspended in midair outside the house wall, the pipe made a kind of flute on which the wind would play. The whooo-whooo could be heard in the house, and, since weather changes with the wind, the tone of the sink spout could be a portent. *Sink spout weather* wasn't any particular kind of weather, because not all homes faced the same way, but each householder got his own kind of tootle-tootle and made what he wanted to of it.

❦ / Six weeks   The month of March, with thirty-one days following short February, usually disposes itself to take up four full weeks and a part of two others. The full phrase is *"six weeks* sledding in March." Snow was important to teaming, and an early spring thaw was bad news; if the farmers and loggers could have *six weeks* sledding in March they were content. Hence, numerous fortuitous situations are likened to *six weeks* of sledding.

❦ / Size up   To measure, and particularly to estimate, but transferred from lineal dimensions to abstractions: "He's *sizin' up* his chances, and may run for selectman."

❦ / Sizzler   Another term for a woods cook. (See *boiler.*) As the *boiler* knew how to boil food, the *sizzler* knew how to fry it. (Neither term should be spoken directly to a cook at any time.)

❦ / Skedaddler   A draft dodger in the war of 1861–1865. Many disappeared into the Maine woods to become early citizens of wilderness communities and in after times wholly respectable. Kennebago Lake has a *Skedaddle* Cove which keeps the term alive. It is also heard today for an eager exit and one who makes it: a *skedaddler* is one who skedaddles.

❧ / SKID ROAD    This original Maine term has been much abused by the world at large. It is not, was not, and never can be a "skid row." The *skid road* was an iced logging road over which oxen and horses pulled the sleds. On downgrades a snubline was used to keep the loads from running ahead on the animals. If this snubline parted, the team, driver, and load were said to be "sluiced," and the driver, if he survived, well knew what it was like to go to hell-and-gone down a *skid road*. Cities that have "skid rows" have borrowed a Maine lumbering term without knowing what it means.

❧ / SKITE    No doubt derived from skit and skitter, *skite* is given the long "i" by Mainers and means about the same; to sail fast or to move right along: "Well, I'll *skite* along now, I've got things to do."

❧ / SKUNK    In the popular Maine game of cribbage, to defeat an opponent by thirty-one holes or more is to *skunk* him. The victory is usually accompanied by the winner's loud "Phew!" To win by sixty-one holes is a *double-skunk*. In many places the Maine *skunk* is called a "tin hat." This cribbage *skunk* is adapted to other situations where one has come off badly; an angler who catches nothing is *skunked*.

❧ / SKUNK-OIL    An ointment for aches and pains, and stiff joints, rendered from the lard of skunks. It has no odor. When warm it becomes liquid, but in a jar in the medicine cabinet it will look like any animal fat. It was supposed to have a penetrating quality by those who used it, so it could reach an aching ligament. Today it is in the category of *blister plasters, Balm o' Gilead,* camphor bags, and *nanny-plum tea* as interesting old home-remedy lore.

❧ / Slab city    Term for the poorer section of town, and arising from the *slab*-sided houses that sprang up around new sawmills in the early days. The first cut off a log, with one rounded bark side, is a slab; and if a person is careful in selecting good slabs and takes the time to nail them properly, a comfortable rough dwelling can be turned out. Where actual *slab cities* existed in Maine towns, such rough homes were temporary, and today some of Maine's one-time *slab cities* are pretentious residential sections. The term is used more or less as "the other side of the tracks" for a less desirable section of town, without reference now to any sawmills.

❧ / Slab-sided    Used to describe a house boarded with slabs; accordingly, any rough construction not too pleasing to the eye. As applied to a person, let it be understood that a *slab-sided* woman will never become Miss America.

❧ / Slack    That period of the tide when there is no movement of the water; the high water *slack* and the low water *slack.* In another sense, Mainers use *slack* as derived from the nautical meaning of not taut; the *slack* in a rope. This gives us *slack* for untidy and slipshod: "She's the *slack-est* housekeeper in town." *Slack*-jawed means loose-jawed or over-talkative, particularly with nothing much to say, and very often foul-mouthed. Looseness in general is conveyed by *slack*: Skip Toothaker came to Grange supper one evening and said, "Boy, am I ready for a good feed! I'm so empty I can pick up the *slack* of my *poke* and wipe my eyes on it!"

❧ / Slash    Limbs, tops, and unusable parts of trees left on the ground after logging off. It creates a fire hazard, and tourists will see State Forestry signs that read, "Slash Area—No Campfires Beyond This Point." A *slash* fire is a brush fire in a *slash* area. The state has laws requiring lumbering operations to reduce *slash* danger.

❦ / SLAT   A sail that flaps, flops, and shakes violently is said to *slat;* the term conveys not only the motion but the little noise it makes, and from this Mainers have learned to use *slat* in numerous transferrals. A *slat* is a quick motion of the hand, as when one *slats* at a mosquito, or *slats* a mackerel off a hook into a tub. Mother will give a fractious child a *slat* behind the ear. Wind will *slat* the laundry on the line, and a strong wind will *slat* it right off the line. A barn door will *slat* all night in the wind. And a person who tears around in slapdash fashion is said to *slat* about.

❦ / SLED LENGTH   Random length; said of firewood which is brought out of the woods lengthwise of the sled instead of across it in four-foot cordwood. Gray birch and small growth are usually handled in *sled lengths* to save time in the woods, since a stick anywhere from 8 to 12 feet long is not too heavy to lift. When used to describe anything other than firewood *sled length* means random and unmeasured: "They got a whole bunch of *sled-length* kids."

❦ / SLED STAKE   The *bunks* of logging sleds were fitted with heavy hardwood stakes to keep the logs from rolling off during hauling. These sat in iron sockets and could be removed and replaced as desired. The term is used for any similar stake for the same purpose, so it is heard for stakes on carts and tractor trailers. The original *sled stakes* were handy, could easily be grabbed from a socket, and may have been used as weapons at one time or another, so in Maine speech today the *sled stake* is a hypothetical club: "He went down as if he'd been hit with a *sled stake!*" (*Pole-ax*, which see, is similarly used for a definitive clout.)

❧ / SLEEPER   See *tie*.

❧ / SLICER   Maine shipwright's term for a long-handled and wide-bladed chisel. *Slicing* is thus chiseling, and Mainers use *slicing* for chiseling, both in the sense of haggling a price down, and in that of working or worming your way in: "He sliced him down to four dollars," and "She sliced herself into the club," i.e., chiseled the price and chiseled a membership.

❧ / SLICK   Never heard in Maine for slippery. Slick means just dandy: "*Slicker'n* a whistle!" Crafty: "He's a *slick* one!" What lawyers call sharp practice is a *slick* trick. While in some Maine expressions that use *slick*, the sense of slippery may seem present, it is more correct to construe it as smooth. For instance, the expression "smooth as a schoolmarm's leg" is often rendered as "*slick* as a schoolmarm's leg." Smoothness is also conveyed when *slick* is used to qualify food: "That's a *slick* pie!" And when a boy is told to *slick* down his hair, it means to neaten it, not to make it slippery! *Slick* also means a large chisel of the *slicer* kind. (See *slicer*.)

❧ / SLOOP (1)   Except for the *Down Easter* (which see) the *sloop* will be the one type of sailing craft best associated with Maine. The word comes from the German through the Dutch, and *sloops* were sailed before Maine people took them up, but over the years the little *sloop* has been the work boat of the Maine coast and the favorite of yachtsmen. For fishing and short-haul cargoes the *sloop* was ideal for Maine waters, and Governor Winslow of Plymouth speaks in his journal of the *sloops* he saw plying the Maine coast in 1622. Adapted from time to time by Maine builders, the basic boat with single mast, gaffed, reached its ultimate fame when Wilbur Morse designed and built the world-renowned Friendship *sloop*, which he once modestly defined as ". . . . a *sloop* built at Friendship by Wilbur

Morse." To the hundreds he turned out, other boat builders added hundreds more, and the Friendship *sloop* seined and lobstered Maine waters up to and beyond the introduction of inboard motors. Today the Friendship *sloop* is a prized collector's item, and replicas in fiberglass are being turned out year after year for summer pleasures. Interestingly, Maine lobstermen, whose fathers and grandfathers used *sloops*, refer to the revived Friendship *sloops* as "them *sloop* bo'ts."

❧ / SLOOP (2)  A slope, an incline; as on a roof. A carpenter might say, "The *sloop* will be seven inches to the foot."

❧ / SLOP CHEST  A chest of clothing, bedding, and sometimes a wider variety of articles carried by vessels to supply crewmen. A Maine woodsman might consider it a kind of sea-going *wangan*. Hence, odds-and-ends storage, usually with the idea that if you keep something long enough you'll find a use for it. (See *rag out*.)

❧ / SLUICE  The chute built into a lumbering country dam for spillage, but more particularly to float logs through. To *sluice* logs is to stand with a picaroon and guide them so they won't jam, and the term applies to the entire operation of moving a drive out of a lake into the stream below the dam. Many times the *sluice* is called a *sluice*-way. Thus when a woodsman says he gave somebody a *sluicin'*, he means he gave him a kind of conducted tour, no doubt to his improvement. And, if a Mainer asks you for a splash of "*sluice* juice" in his highball, give him plain water and leave out the ice. For a special meaning of *sluice*, derived from the tumult of a spillway, see *skid road*.

❧ / SLUMGULLION  In whaling and sometimes in other fishing, *slumgullion* is the oil, blood, salt water, and general crud that occurs in the flensing (Mainers and Massachusettsers liked to call that flenchin' or flinchin'). Known, too, as lipperin's or dreenin's, *slumgullion* is considerable more than *gurry* (see *gurry*). *Slumgullion* is now used for anything that is an unpleasant mess, and particularly poor food.

❦ / SLUNG SHOT   The Maine law about carrying concealed weapons uses this term instead of sling shot. Reference is to the David type and not to the kind made with a forked stick and rubber bands, which is neither a *slung shot* nor a sling shot.

❦ / SLUSH   Mainers use *slush* as others do for wet snow, but some of the expressions in the lingo derive from *slush* for the grease used on masts so the mast rings would slide well. This was sometimes *boughten*, but often was waste galley grease. That's why a *slush* fund makes politics go smoothly, and *slush* is fine for greasing palms.

❦ / SLUT'S WOOL   Those kitties of dust under beds and in neglected corners associated with indifferent housewives. Mainers go back a long way for this, to the days when slut meant no more than a dirty, unkempt woman.

❦ / SMASHED   Used for mashed, as in *smashed* potatoes.

❦ / SMEAR   To cloud in, but reserved mostly for the increasing evidence of the high cirrus clouds that make *mares' tails* and *mackerel sky*: "Been *smearin'* in so I doubt if I'll haul tomorrow."

❦ / SMILE   If an occasional Mainer asks you, "Do you *smile*?" he is inviting you to have a drink with him. Sometimes the same question is asked when your would-be host isn't sure if you take a drop or not, and is cautiously sounding you out. Maine men who come home late for supper may explain to their wives that, "I was *smilin'* with the boys."

🌿 / SMOOTH AS A SMELT    A simile to describe any pleasant situation; a batch of cider may be *smooth as a smelt*. During spring spawning runs smelts are not really *smooth*, but have a sandpapery feel. So this smoothness may stem from an effort at alliteration, or from the smooth way smelts go down when brought to table.

🌿 / SMOKERS    In May, after alewives come, little signs appear along the Maine coast offering *smokers*. These are freshly netted alewives subjected to an immediate smoking, usually by an individual in small batches, and available to the public while the run is still on. They are tasty, and to some Mainers are an essential springtime feast, comparable to the first rhubarb, smelts, dandelion greens and *fiddleheads*.

🌿 / SMUDGE    A smouldering fire kindled at a woods camp to deter black flies and mosquitoes. To windward, it wafts acrid smoke across the clearing. When a person is said to be in a *smudge*, it means he is enveloped in the pungency of his own foolish thinking. Often the smoke is worse than the black flies.

🌿 / SNACK    Originally, this meant share. In cooperative ventures like fishing, men "went *snacks*," or share-and-share-alike. To go *snacks* is what two children do when they share an apple; thus, a bite to eat.

🌿 / SNAPPER    The magic ingredient in baked beans which causes flatulency. Maine hostesses have been known to assure timid guests that, " . . . the *snappers* have been removed."

❦ / SNARES   *Snares* were used to take wild animals long before Maine was settled, but they were much used by early Mainers when gunpowder was hard to come by. A sapling was bent down and triggered so it caught passing rabbits in a noose, and *snares* strong enough to take full-grown deer are possible. In many places the significance of "a *snare* and delusion" has been lost, but Maine people retain knowledge of snares. They are illegal in Maine today, but sometimes the game wardens find one—and sometimes they don't. With the *snare* and *deadfall* (which see) many Maine pioneers fed their families well.

❦ / SNATCHBLOCK   A kind of pulley, but Mainers use the term for two different devices. At sea, it is a pulley with an open side, so the line may be inserted at any point; lobstermen use *snatchblocks* on their hauling gear. On the farm, it is a pulley that snatches into a barn rafter with a grab like an ice tongs, so the dumping point of the hay unloader may be changed from mow to mow. The farmer's *snatchblock* doesn't have the open side, and the rope must be rove through the sheeve from the end. When used in metaphorical Maine speech ("They *snatchblocked* him to a fare-thee-well!"), it's hard to decide which of the two kinds of snatchblocks contributed to the imagery.

❦ / SNEDRICKS   For snide tricks, which is exactly what it means. However, in Maine usage there is an element of craftiness or cuteness, rather than malevolence, and *snedricks* doesn't always mean downright cheating. Captain Leander of Thomaston once had his vessel frozen in harbor ice, and he signaled to the water boat that he wanted to take on water. The water boat broke a way through the ice, and Captain Leander bought a dollar's worth of water. His tanks already full, he pumped the dollar's worth over the side. Since the tugboat would have charged him $20 to break the ship out of the ice, Captain Leander observed that ". . . a man's got to play a few *snedricks* now and then to get by."

❦ / Snood  The basic meaning of a hair net is understood in Maine, where that kind of *snood* is worn to cover the hair in food-packing plants, etc., but Maine coastal people have extended it to the twine from which a net is made, usually as the noun *snoodin'*. *Snoodin'*, like *ganging* (which see), comes in hanks and balls.

❦ / Snort  A quickie, usually from the jug, but if taken in a glass, always neat. It's sort of a social on-the-fly, when there isn't time or reason to linger longer.

❦ / Snowball's chance  No *chance* whatever. The full expression is, "He hasn't a *snowball's chance* in hell." (See *chance*.)

❦ / Snow fleas  Mainers call them *fleas;* others prefer the term lice. In March when warming sunlight strikes the bark on maples, tiny fleas or lice hatch under the bark and congregate on snowbanks near by until the snow will have a sooty appearance. Some say the insects live on food in the snow water. The first sighting of *snow fleas* proves the season is advancing.

❦ / Snow in the woodbox  Used to describe somebody down to the depths of poverty. If you've got *snow in your woodbox*, the Ladies' Aid will bring you a Christmas basket.

❦ / Snowshoe  In Maine the variable hare is called the *snowshoe* and *snowshoe* rabbit. The *snowshoe* is brown in summer and white in winter, and has long hind legs that permit him to travel over snow at incredible speed.

❧ / Snubbed up   In the sense of treating anybody with contempt and disdain, *snub* is a little foreign to Maine usage. Mostly, "cut" will be heard for those occasions when somebody walks right by without speaking: "She cut him dead!" To snub a thing is to bring it to a halt, as when an incoming vessel heaves a line to the wharf and a turn is made around a spile to check the craft's way. To be *"snubbed up with a round turn,* all standing" is to be jerked to a screeching halt, as when somebody is advancing an argument and has his logic ruined by an opponent. See *snubline,* below. Also, see *round turn* and *hold turn.*

❧ / Snubline   The heaving line described above under *snubbed up.* But for a special and dramatic application of the *snubline* in Maine affairs, see *skid road.*

❧ / Soakin' wet   From falling overboard, this expression is used to describe somebody of small size: "She wouldn't weigh a hundred pounds, *soakin' wet!"* Also heard as wringin' wet.

❧ / Sockdollager   This is a whopper in any category; better than a *baister* or a *lunker,* and even an old *rauncher.*

❧ / Sody   Soda. Either bicarbonate of or for a *tonic.*

❧ / So fashion   In this manner: a man to a boy, "No, Sonny, not like that; hold it this way and swing it *so fashion."* Also heard as like so: "See? Do it like so."

❧ / Soften   Said of the weather after a spell of cold and storm. Weather is said to *moderate* and to *soften,* and the two words are akin, but usually *soften* means a lesser change.

❧ / Soft soap   To *soft soap* anybody means to butter him up, make him amenable through cajolery. How it came to mean this is a good question: Maine pioneers made their own *soft soap;* the process stank to high heaven, and *soft soap* often took the skin away with the dirt.

❧ / SOME One of the most useful and overworked words in the Maine lingo. As an adverb, it is about equal to very: *some* hot, *some* mad, *some* used up. Often heard with old: "I was *some* old mad at him!" As a qualifying adjective, it depends on context for clarity: "That was *some* party!" can mean it was a dandy party or it was a dud. "Harold sure had *some* haul today!" can mean he set a new high for poundage, or he didn't get a thing. The Mainer's use of *some* in sentences where he could properly insert somewhat ("I was somewhat wet!") does not mean that *some* and somewhat convey the same thing. Somewhat wet could never convey the thought in, "We were *some* wet by the time we got home." The nuance of "very" is clear in *some* pretty for a young lady or *some* foggy for low vision.

❧ / SOT Correct Maine preterit of *set:* "I *sot* out my tomato plants this morning." Heard also in the reflexive past for sit: "I *sot* myself down." Consider, too, the stick-in-the-mud nature of one who is "*sot* in his ways."

❧ / SOUR APPLES Used as a measure of infinite time: "I haven't had a good piece of corned hake since God made *sour apples.*" Also green apples, and frequently little green apples: " . . . since Christ made little green apples." Since the Year One.

❧ / SOUSED A word heard in Maine in all the usual dictionary nuances, but with special local uses in some of them. *Soused,* as to alcoholic content, will probably be embroidered to *soused* to the gills or *soused* to the scuppers. *Souse* is interchangeable with *douse* and *rense* for the action of washing clams in a clam *hod,* but *soused* clams are a special treat: steamed clams shucked and pickled lightly with spices. After standing a few days in glass jar they "go good" with crackers.

❧ / SPAR   Besides nautical, the Maine clip for feldspar, a great deal of which is quarried in the state: *spar* quarry, *spar* mill, *spar* worker.

❧ / SPARE ROOM   The Maine home's bedchamber for company. It was the *spare room* that was offered to transients along the tourist routes before the motel was invented.

❧ / SPAWL   To *spawl* is to make a crude job of something, and more than one folklorist has assumed it is the Mainer's way of pronouncing spoil. Wrong! A poor workman, caulking seams in a vessel, would chip and splinter the wood, "*spawlin*' things all to flinders." Granite cutters spelled the word "spall" and it meant to chip stone. There is imagery, not the meaning of spoil, in a Maine remark like this, "Don't let her stitch up your dress, she'll *spawl* it the way she did mine."

❧ / SPEAK   To *speak*, but in Maine the word enjoys overtones. "Lem and Hod don't *speak*" means the brothers had a falling out, and although they live in the same house they have had no conversations for thirty-five years. Neither is mute. "They don't *speak* about Charley" means that once upon a time Charley disgraced himself and has been erased from memory. To *speak* highly of somebody is to give him an unqualified recommendation. To *speak* up means to assert your opinion, but to *speak* out implies some perturbation behind your remarks. One may *speak* up in town meeting only to second a motion, but if he *speaks* out he will make considerable harangue. To *speak* your mind is the same as to give somebody a piece of your mind, to inform him in no uncertain terms. To *speak* your piece has the same meaning, and derives from the popularity in old

268 / S

Maine of the declamation contest (see *speaker*). *Speak* is also a synonym for the nautical *hail*: "We *spoke* the yawl, and she came about."

❧ / SPEAKER An anthology of recitations suitable for declaiming *(speaking)* in public. Declamation contests have always been called *speaking* contests in Maine. To "learn something from a *speaker*" is to memorize a poem, oration, etc. *Speaking* was not just a schoolhouse matter. When the Grange was important in Maine life, each member was expected to be ready always with "something to *speak*" at that portion of the meeting known as literary program. Hence, *speaking* a piece is to stand before those present and recite, but today it means an offhand discourse rather than a memorized gem.

❧ / SPELL The use of *spell* for a period of time (a *spell* of weather) is common in Maine as elsewhere, but as a verb, *spell* means to replace somebody or relieve him: "The minister was sick, so one of the deacons *spelled* him in the pulpit." In shrimp dragging, one man sleeps while the other is at the wheel, and after two hours the rested man *spells* the other.

❧ / SPIDER *Spider* is the Maine word for any cast iron frying pan or skillet. In pre-cookstove days *spiders* had short legs to support them over hot embers on a hearth, and the legs suggested the insect; but the term remains for any fry pan. *Spider*-cake is a hot bread cooked in a *spider*.

❧ / SPIKE To old-time seamen, any kind of a nail from a carpet tack to a 60-penny was a *spike*. Mackerel one size smaller than *tinkers* are called *spike* mackerel.

❧ / SPILE A pile for piers (and as the British sergeant-major said to his troops, "H'I don't mean 'emorrhoids for the haristocracy!"). Green red oak suits best. Philologists

S / 269

suggest *spile* comes from *spike* or spire. Interestingly, the same derivation gives us *spile* for the little spout put in a maple tree to run off the sap.

❦ / Spittin' image   Various explanations of this have been offered, and sometimes the term is given as *spit-and-image*. The expression is used when a child resembles a parent closely: "He's the *spittin' image* of his father." Some say the original term was "spirit and image," but nobody ever says spit lamp, spit level, spit world, and Spit of '76.

❦ / Spleeny   Supposedly derived from some disorder of the spleen, the word is now used in Maine for somebody unnecessarily timid about bodily pain. If a child whimpers at having a splinter removed from his finger, Mother will say, "Now, don't be so *spleeny*, this isn't going to hurt!" Sometimes *spleeny* is used for a hypochondriac and one who "enjoys poor health," but mostly it means lack of physical bravery.

❦ / Splice   The joining of two ropes by interweaving the strands gives us *splice* for a marriage: "They're getting *spliced* tomorrow." Also surviving in Maine speech is the phrase "to *splice* the main brace," which means to take a drink in company, or even the cocktail hour. A minor ceremonial is implied, as when a men's club *splices* the main brace before going down to supper. A custom sometimes more honored in the breach.

❦ / Split   Used to indicate a marital agreement to disagree: "They've *split* up."

❦ / Spool bush   The term applies to several dooryard shrubs and small trees with botanical names Maine housewives never knew. The *spool bush* is a pith-wood, and when the pith was pushed from the center of a branch, the hollow piece left made a useful spool or bobbin that could sit over a peg. Almost all early Maine homes had *spool bushes* as well as lilacs, *Balm o' Gileads*, and other traditional flora; and while about everything had its own name, the *spool bush* remained the *spool bush*. Anybody of timid nature, unwilling to assert himself, may be called a *spool bush*—no backbone, no guts, a spineless jellyfish.

❦ / SPOOL WOOD   This connotes extra-good quality. Many of Maine's turning mills were subsidiaries of the cotton thread industry, turning out spools made from white birch. These mills paid extra for clear *bolts* with six inches or more diameter, and often demanded 52– to 54-inch lengths so a full 48-inch *square bar* could be had after sawing away the end-checks. When the bronze beetle decimated the Maine white birch growth, many of these thread companies turned to other regions and other woods for their spool supplies, and the Maine mills began making products other than spools as a major effort. Today, *spool wood* means top quality hardwood *bolts* not only for the turning mills, but for flatware products such as toothpicks, swizzle sticks, and tongue depressors. Anything of *spool wood* quality is the *finest kind*.

❦ / SPORT   The Maine term for a paying guest at a hunting or fishing camp, and usually one who has hired a registered guide. The word is now something of an inland synonym for the coastal *summer complaint*, when seasonal visitors are discussed in the aggregate: "We've seen more *sports* this year than ever before."

❦ / SPOTTED TREE   See *blaze*.

❦ / SPRAYHOOD   A canvas awning over the forward part of a lobster boat, and any similar protection on another boat. It substitutes for a *house*. (See *house*.)

❧ / Spud  Without reference to a potato, it means a Maine hand tool for removing bark from pulpwood. *Spudding* is done when the sap is fluid, and the *spud* is a lightly curved steel bar that rips the bark away. Interestingly, when automobiles came along, the tool used to take tires off a rim was so like a *spud* that Maine mechanics called a tire-iron a *spud*.

❧ / Squamish  Squeamish, and pronounced halfway between squammish and squawmish. As used, the word suggests *spleeny* (which see) but also carries the sense of stomach uneasiness. It is reserved mostly for that god-awful moment that precedes *mal de mer*: "Never been seasick in my life, but I was *squamish* once in a Fundy cross-chop."

❧ / Square bar  Most of the nation's wood turning industry is located in the Northeast, and almost all its pertinent lingo originated in Maine. A hardwood *bolt* starting through a turning mill is first reduced to *square bars;* sticks 48 inches long and squared to one inch, two inches, etc., depending on the product in mind. These, in time, proceed to the lathes to be made into spools, handles, toys, and what-all.

❧ / Squaretail  Mainers like this term for their beloved eastern brook trout, *Salvelinus fontinalis*, sometimes the brookie and sometimes the speckled trout. The *togue* (which see) is related, but has a forked tail. Many people think the *squaretail*, from his beautiful colored markings, is the rainbow, but all Mainers know better.

❧ / Squeakin' neat  See *nasty-neat*. The terms are about the same in meaning, except that while *nasty-neat* is an adjective, the other is most often heard in the sentence, "She's so neat she squeaks." She's neat to the point of bothering those about her.

❧ / STADDLES   The arrangement of short stakes driven in the mud to support a cock of *salt hay* (which see) and hence any small platform on poles. A man may rig a *staddle* as an aid to getting in and out of a canoe.

❧ / STAGE   Besides being the word for the moulting period of lobsters (see *shedder*), *stage* is a holdover term in Maine for a public conveyance. It goes back to the days when horse-drawn vehicles met the railroad trains and *packet* boats. Particularly in the resort areas, Maine had so many *stages* listed in the timetables that it took more space for them than it did for the train schedule. Places like Oquossoc at Rangeley and Sebago Lake Station had dozens of *stages* from resort hotels and surrounding towns. The word *stage* continued to be used for such accommodations after motor vehicles supplanted horses, and today a good many older Maine people will speak of "taking the *stage*" when they refer to an autobus.

❧ / STAKE DRIVER   The American bittern, a wading bird common in Maine whose call is a whooping, thumping noise that suggests the sound of driving a fence stake into the ground with a heavy maul.

❧ / STALLION   A sawhorse, but one with the crossed legs on one end only. A long pole extends in the other direction, so the *stallion* is an elongated tripod. It is meant for *sled-length* firewood, which runs too long to balance on the ordinary four-legged sawhorse. Usually called a sawstallion.

❧ / STANCHION   The dictionaries give this as a post or support in a stall, but in Maine *stanchion* has come to mean the entire *tie-up* (which see). The *stanchion* is the iron rod or pipe on which the cow's *tie-up* chain slides up and down, and this gives us the verb, to *stanchion*: "I'll be with you as soon as I *stanchion* the cattle." Accordingly, a farmer will be in the *stanchion*, meaning the stable. In the instance of a bull who breaks his *stanchion*, "breaks" has about the same meaning as to break jail, to get loose. *Stanchion* and its related word *tie-up* are reserved mostly for dairy cattle. A horse is stabled, sheep are penned.

❦ / STARCH   The *starch* mill has always been a leveling agent in the Aroostook potato industry, taking up surplus potatoes to stabilize prices. *Starch* is also important to the paper industry to stiffen certain papers. Accordingly, Maine housewives who speak of cooking *starch* made from corn will usually say in full cornstarch; otherwise *starch* is an agricultural and industrial term in Maine. The word is, of course, heard in many common expressions; to take the *starch* out of somebody, etc.

❦ / START   Another term for *hauling* or *yarding* wood.

❦ / STARVIN' DAYS   The first few days of any project before things get running smoothly. The expression comes from the lumber camps, where it took two-three days for the *barm* to work, and the cook couldn't turn out good bread until it did. It's a *sourdough* expression.

❦ / STATE   Used as to the *state* of one's health, or a *state* of mind, Mainers like to omit whatever is in context, and simply say *state* for a condition of excitement, anger, frustration, and sometimes even a mood. "When she found the neighbors' kids tromping around on her sweet peas, I tell you she was in some *state!*" (See *some* for added enlightenment.)

❦ / STATE OF MAINE (1)   Sometimes out-of-staters smile at the Maine insistence on the full title. People come from Nevada, Illinois, etc., but Mainers always come from *The State of Maine*. This is correct; the state constitution is explicit: ". . . do hereby agree to form ourselves into a free and independent State, by the style and title of The STATE OF MAINE . . . " There was much pondering at the time of separation from Massachusetts as to the appropriate style and title, and most Mainers agreed they had no desire to be another damn commonwealth.

❧ / STATE OF MAINE (2)   In deep trolling for salmon and togue on Maine lakes, an angler frequently finds his lure caught on a rocky bottom. He is then congratulated for "hooking *The State of Maine*."

❧ / STATE OF MAINE BANKROLL   Nobody seems to know how this term originated, but it means a wad of newspaper cut to size and sandwiched between two $1 bills.

❧ / STATE ROAD   Although the importance of distinctions is long gone, Maine people continue to refer to *state roads*. In the beginning, all highways were laid out and maintained by individual settlements and townships. Then came county roads, and Maine's first highway of more than local importance was the Post Road laid out by Postmaster General Benjamin Franklin soon after the American Revolution. Older people in York County still refer to portions of old Route One as the Post Road. Establishment of a state highway department came late in Maine's road program, so it was natural to distinguish town, county, and state routes. In World War I days and through the 20s, the *state road* would be the one that was paved. Tourists asking directions are still told to ". . . go down the *state ro'd* 'sfar's the schoolhouse, turn right on the town ro'd, etc. . . ."

❧ / STATE WORKER   Now saddled with a top-heavy state government, citizens not at the public udder have this wry term for those who are. In assessing somebody, the explanation "he works for the state" calls for a nod of understanding.

❧ / STEAM CAR   Railway passenger service, in the sense that one took the *steam cars* rather than the electric cars, or a *packet* boat. The only remaining passenger service in Maine is on the Canadian Pacific line across the wilderness from Lac Mégantic, Québec, to McAdam Junction, New Brunswick, and the trains have long since been converted to diesel power, but a man riding that line may well say he went by *steam car*.

❧ / STEAMER   In this instance, a simply delicious long-neck Maine clam not too small and not too large, just perfect for steaming.

❧ / STEEL   The word for the patent (see *patent*) tin ceilings that had a vogue in the early part of the century. Salesmen came around and were followed by traveling installation crews. To have at least one room *steeled* was evidence of gentility. A church in Union was *steeled* as a memorial, and a plaque on the wall says so, evidence that *steeling* was as good as a stained-glass window.

❧ / STEERS   Oxen. Although singly the beasts were the nigh-ox and the off-ox, Mainers always coupled them as a yoke of *steers*. (Give yoke its right Maine sound of, almost, youk.) "Lookit them *steers!*" was the rallying cry of Solon Chase in 1878 as he toured the state for the Greenbackers, and he would point with his *gad* at his oxen. Maine fairs use the term "neat cattle" in their premium lists, and the draft contests are known as ox-pulls, but the farmers who attend bring their *steers*. *Steers* do go for beef, but in Maine the term doesn't have the beef-cattle meaning of the West.

❧ / STEM TO STERN   In full, stem to sternpost; from the very front of the boat to the very rear. Hence, completely and overall. The nautical derivation by no means limits the phrase to seafaring. Farm wives in Aroostook will say they cleaned the house from *stem to stern*. (Unless they say, from attic to *sulla*.)

❦ / STERN SHEETS   The seat at the stern of a rowboat, and accordingly almost anything in Maine that is rearward; the back seat of an automobile or somebody's backside: "All he needs is a good boot in the *stern sheets!*"

❦ / STICKINGS   Boards fresh off a sawmill carriage are tiered to season or dry, and the tiers are separated by *edgings* or *stickings* to allow air to pass through the pile. Such a pile is "stuck lumber." The same edgings are sometimes used for firewood, so a man will buy a load of *stickings* or his wife will burn *stickings*. In another sense, *sticking* is an unlucky or unhappy outcome, deriving from the fate of a hog who is stuck in the slaughter house: "The garage gave me an awful *sticking* on that valve job."

❦ / STIDDY   Steady. A *stiddyin'* *hand*, and "*stiddy* as you go!" Use of *stiddy* in Maine speech runs to almost any situation from a supporting hand to a compliant wind: "You *stiddy* that joist until I get a *spike* in her!" means to hold it in position. A *stiddy* man is reliable. A *stiddy* job gives security. One time, Greenville's famous Dr. Pritham was operating, and he noticed the nurse assisting him was nervous. To reassure her he repeatedly said in a whisper, "*Stiddy it! Stiddy it!*" The poor girl thought he kept saying, "Idiot! Idiot!"

❦ / STIFF AS A CHURCH   It is not the edifice which gives this expression, but the primness and starchy appearance of those who attend services. One sits in fine clothes, stiffly well-mannered in a stiff-backed pew. Observe that a starched shirt is a *stiff* shirt. A *stiff* ship is a *stiddy* ship. To otherwise relaxed Mainers, going to church was a *stiff* matter.

❧ / Stifle   Heard in sections of Maine with certain mid-European folks mixed into the population, *stifle* is a meat and gravy dish not unlike a ragout. The word has the sense of smother, as in smothered beef: "We're having a *stifle* for supper." Women at the meat counter will ask for "meat for a *stifle*."

❧ / Stile   Maine farmer's word for the sod, as turned by a plow.

❧ / Stinkin' Benjamin   The purple trillium. If brought into the house as an early spring bouquet, it fills the room with a fetid stench. A perennial amusement with Maine young fry has been to bring a "green" schoolteacher a bunch of *stinkin' Benjamins* for her desk, and if she leaves them in a vase overnight it takes at least a week to air out the place.

❧ / Stinkpot   Any steamboat as viewed by a sailing *hand*, and today anything with a motor, particularly a diesel. There was a time steamboat *hands* would start punching if labeled *stinkpot* sailors; today the term doesn't have that lowly nuance, but, amongst the yachting set, high-flying sailboaters use it for fellow boaters who run on motors. If a becalmed *sloop* turns on its auxiliary power, it is said to come home on its *stinkpot*.

❧ / Stivver   A maximum; all that one can accept, stand for, put up with, endure: "That's about all I can *stivver* up to."

❧ / Stone boat   See *drogher*. Also, the farmer's stone drag for removing rocks from a plowed field is a *stone boat*. It has the highest coefficient of friction of all vehicles, but seldom tips over on a curve.

❧ / Stone boil   A measure of infinite time. Prehistoric man brought liquids up to temperature by dropping in hot stones. It took forever to come to a boil. Hence: "Migod! I can bring up a *stone boil* faster'n you're laying shingles!"

❦ / STORE   Markets, malls, shopping centers, and such modern emporia will be with us a long time before they wean the Mainer from his "goin' to the *sto-er*." This is the generic term for the business section and all that goes on there. It includes the socializing at post office, barber shop, *liberry*, and trading. In some communities the same sense is conveyed by going to the village, to the corner, over-street, and sometimes to town. If you wait long enough, you'll hear some Mainer refer to the splendid new Maine Mall at South Portland as the *sto-er*.

❦ / STORE CHOPPERS   False teeth. (Incidentally, anything *boughten*, which see, may be qualified in Maine as *store-boughten*.)

❦ / STORE PAY   In the old days of general stores, farmers and fishermen sold their products to the storekeeper with the understanding that the money would be "taken in trade." This kept credit ahead for family groceries, but didn't make a jingle in pockets. The system gave the storekeeper the advantage of his retail mark-up, so *store pay* wasn't wholly on the customer's side. It was never considered as good as cash. The term will be heard in some such sentence as this: "He'll take all I bring in, but it's *store pay*."

❦ / STOREHOUSE   Maine woods term for a company depot, and including the complex of buildings with its resident crew and all the business of directing woodlands operations in a region. See *farm*, as a company management base. The words are not interchangeable, but the purpose is much the same. Cupsuptic Storehouse is a Brown Company base near Rangeley.

❦ / STOVE   Past participle of stave. A barrel which has had its staves smashed is *stove*. Inland, Maine speech often uses *staved*, as when a cart rolled ahead and staved in a barn door, but coastal people always use the *stove;* and usually with up or in; "he *stove* up his truck," or "his dory was *stove* in."

❦ / STRAIGHT LINE   Just and upright action calls for walking a *straight line*, The Maine expression is usually construed in the negative: "He couldn't walk a *straight line* if his life depended on it." That is, he is a known swindler. Although sometimes used as a measure of intoxication, the *straight line* is more often applied to probity than sobriety.

❦ / STRAP OIL   A spanking, as done by a kindly father to his wayward son with a razor strop or a bit of harness. Sometimes called "harness oil." But in addition to that, a fool's errand. Just as people have been sent to get a left-handed monkey wrench and a pail of steam, boys underfoot have been sent to the blacksmith shop for some *strap oil*. Once in a while a cooperative blacksmith would box the boy's ears just to keep the so-called joke alive.

❦ / STREAKED   Used like peaked (peak-id) and probably a variant thereof. Anybody looking poorly and washed-out is *streak-id*. Sometimes streaky.

❦ / STRENTH   Proper sound for strength: "He don't know his own *strenth*."

❦ / STRETCHERS   Deacon-seaters, or any tale that stretches the normal Maine admiration for veracity beyond normal need. People who tell *stretchers* are said to be frugal with the truth.

❦ / STRIDDLES   Tatters or ribbons, rags, small pieces of fabric. You sew enough *striddles* together and you've got a patchwork quilt.

❧ / STRIKE Fresh-water fish do not nibble or bite; they *strike*. The word is used universally thus, but is inserted in this Maine manual in order to tell about a *sport* George Lund was guiding down in Washington County. At one point the *sport* said, "There, I think I almost had a *strike!*" The "almost" was what amused George.

❧ / STRONG Muscularity as applied to fresh country butter. One time Ed Grant asked the storekeeper for five pounds of butter. Wrapping it, the storekeeper said, "There you are, Ed, five pounds *strong!*" Ed said afterwards, "I got almost to Beaver Pond before the sun hit my *kennebecker*, and I realized just how *strong* that damn' stuff was!"

❧ / STRUCK WITH THE SPANISH MILDEW Anybody feigning or imagining some kind of illness, when his perfect health is evident to the world, is said to be *struck with the Spanish mildew;* an ailment not otherwise diagnosed by competent authority. Gold-bricking.

❧ / STRUGGLE-STRING First used by the veteran Rangeley guide and author, Bill Riviere, for the starting cord on an outboard motor, this term is now a favorite with all Maine guides who wish the *jeezly* manufacturers would make a motor that will commence.

❧ / STUCK ON THE WAYS A bad start for any project. A vessel that didn't slide smoothly down her launching ways was destined for ill-chance, so the old-timers thought. The shipyard phrase is now used for any situation or project that begins badly or hesitates in the take-off.

❧ / STUMPAGE A man who buys standing timber by the lot for logging off is said to buy *stumpage*. The word was borrowed by Maine's wild blueberry growers, and they use it for unpicked berries bought by the acre or lot. Some people own blueberry land and instead of harvesting it themselves will sell the *stumpage*.

S / 281

❧ / SUCCOTASH  Said to derive from the Indian, *succotash* is a widely known corn and beans mixture by no means unique to Maine. The important thing here is that true Maine *succotash* always uses what Mainers call shell beans, and not the limas liked elsewhere. Limas are slimas. In addition, Mainers prefer the cream style corn (see *corn shop*).

❧ / SUGAR PIE  Inland Mainers are not likely to call a sweetheart *sugar pie*. Québec *choppers* working in the Maine woods eat their *tartes de sucre* by the acre on the grounds that the rich brown-sugar filling imparts quick energy. They are far too sweet for Yankee palates, and English-spoken allusions to a *sugar pie* are seldom complimentary.

❧ / SUMMER  To pass the summer, as a cottager who *summers* at Old Orchard Beach; but also to spoil from summer heat and humidity: "This candy has *summered*, but it tastes all right."

❧ / SUMMERCATER  This improvement on *rusticator* gives Mainers another word for the seasonal visitor. An individual may be dubbed a *summercater*, but there is a tendency to use the word in the aggregate: "Saw the first *summercaters* today!"

❧ / SUMMER COMPLAINT  There actually is a warm-weather distemper Mainers call the *summer complaint;* it usually means loose bowels and an accompanying lethargy. Transferring the term to the tourist and recreation clientele undoubtedly involves editorial comment. (See *dogfish, summercater, ritchbitch.*) Actually, amongst well oriented summer people, the term is no longer wholly objectionable, because a lady *summercating* on Loud's Island said, "You'll have to ask somebody else for directions. I'm just a *summer complaint* and I don't know."

❧ / SUMMER MAHOGANY   The yachting set as seen by non-yachting boaters. It means the fancy boats and also the people in them; a man shopping at the village store in pink shorts will be *summer mahogany.*

❧ / SUNDAY DINNER   An excellent meal, regardless of the day it is enjoyed. The term arose in old-time Maine grocery stores when complete *Sunday dinners* were put up on Fridays and Saturdays and delivered to homes. Very often the meat was roasting poultry. Accordingly, Fridays and Saturdays were the busiest days for the clerks and delivery wagons, and a *Sunday dinner* was the finest meal of the week. The term will be heard today in this context: "We went to such-and-such a restaurant, and they put on a reg'lar *Sunday dinner.* Everything was great!" As applied to a meal, the expression *hot supper* (which see) conveys a similar sense of excellence.

❧ / SUNRISE-SUNSET   The east and west residential sides of a hill. *Sunrise* siders are supposed to arise earlier than *sunset* siders, and go to bed earlier.

❧ / SURPRISEDLY   Surprisingly: "For an old rooster full of experience, he roasted *surprisedly* tender."

❧ / SUSPICION   Used as a verb for suspect or mistrust: "I *suspicioned* there was chicanery afoot!"

❧ / SWALLOW THE ANCHOR   To retire from a career at sea: "He *swallowed the anchor* in 1888." Now applied to anybody who retires from a life's work; even bankers can *swallow an anchor.* (Banking bankers, that is.)

❧ / SWAMP   "Letting daylight into the *swamp*" was the old *choppers'* term for logging off an area. Maine lumbermen went to Michigan to let daylight into the *swamps.* In the old days of total harvest the saying was literally true.

*Swamp* has a special Maine meaning in the phrase "to *swamp* out," meaning to clear away trees and brush preliminary to building a camp or a road. Transferred, this term means to clean house: "She heard company was coming, so the *swamped* out the living room." *Brushing* out (see *brush*) suggests a lesser task than *swamping* out, as does *scurryfunge*. Also, see *teakittle*.

❧ / SWIFT   With reference to mental agility, *swift* is usually heard in the negative: "When it comes to thinking things out, he ain't too *swift*." See *lackin'*.

❧ / SWILL   Still properly used in Maine rural speech; *swill* and garbage are not synonyms in all respects. Food from the house for the pigs and hens is *swill*. Like garbage, *swill* is used for poor food, nonsensical talk, and unlike garbage it is used as a verb: "Don't *swill* down your food!"

❧ / SWIPE   As a verb meaning to strike or hit, *swipe* accordingly becomes a noun. To *swipe* somebody across the face with a wet paint brush is an overt act of hostility; the person thus affronted would receive a *swipe*. Mainers also use *swipe* as a gentler form of steal.

❧ / SWITCHEL   A haymakers' beverage compounded of molasses, ginger, and spring water. It was supposed to induce a cooling sweat on a hot day. Like *shrub* (which see) it is still occasionally mixed and taken in Maine, but mostly both drinks belong to the lore of the past. Sometimes *switchel* is used in general for a refreshing draft, and often with an implication of alcoholic content, but true *switchel* had no wallop.

# T

/\\/.\\/\\

❦ / Tackle and falls   The pulley arrangement with
blocks and line. In Maine, *tackle* in this combination is always pronounced take-'l.

❦ / Tail goes with the hide   In this expression the
uselessness of a deceased tail and its lack of value on the market suggests that one must take the bitter with the sweet,
and into each life some rain must fall. The expression comes
from the slaughter house, where the hide was the butcher's
fee. In short, it doesn't matter much one way or the other.
The expression is used today in almost any situation where
gain and profit are dubious, and the consequences not likely
to make or break.

❦ / Tail over bandbox   Politer phrasing of the common Maine expressions which mean "head over heels." Arse
over bandbox; arse over tail; arse over teapot; arse over head.
These phrases can mean a physical upset like falling down
stairs, or a mental jolt such as a simple *comeuppance*.

❦ / Take it ashore or tow it around   A delightful
expression encompassing a predicament, arising from the old
dory days when a man would make fast to a halibut or
other big fish he couldn't boat. He could *take it ashore, or
tow it around* until the fish gave up the fight. Accordingly,
in town meeting a motion may be made to take a subject

ashore or tow it around; to postpone action until people have had time to think about it. At Windsor Fair one evening, a race-horse driver was having trouble restraining his animal, and the horse made several complete turns like a pinwheel in front of the stands. Somebody in the crowd suggested in a loud voice that he *take it ashore or tow it around*.

❧ / TAKE OFF  Long before aviation, Mainers used this term for a quick start, equivalent to *light out*: "He *lit out* and *took off* down the trail." To *take off like a train of cars* means to start fast and keep *hyperin'*.

❧ / TAKE STOCK  Preferred by Maine merchants to take inventory. Usually to take count of stock. Around the first of the year the country stores would stay closed for a day, and a sign would say, "Closed Today to *Take Stock*." Use of stock for commodities explains why a Maine housewife stocks up on groceries for the weekend.

❧ / TAKE THE WIND OUT OF HIS SAILS  It now means any maneuver that deflates an opponent, ruins his argument, and leaves him with nothing to say. Any racing sailor knows the derivation; a boat to windward will blanket leeward sails, and before the blanketed boat can recover it is often out of the race. Accordingly: "Joe was bragging about his new car, and just then Charley showed up with a Caddie convertible. Boy, did that ever *take the wind out of his sails!*"

❧ / TAP THE ADMIRAL  To take a drink of whatever is at hand, no matter how inferior the quality. As used day to day in this sense, it is fortunate that the derivation has been forgotten, and *squamish* stomachs may not be happy to have the explanation now. The allusion comes from "the admiral," John Paul Jones, whose body was embalmed in alcohol and moved about considerably before it was permanently laid to rest at Annapolis. Similarly, Maine captains and seamen who died in distant ports of call were often headed up in casks of rum and brought home for burial.

❧ / TEAKITTLE   As used in Maine for a quick tidying this word is in the category of *brush out*, *swamp out*, *scurryfunge*, and *righten up*. In usage, it will appear this way: "While you're doing the chores, I'll *teakittle* up the kitchen."

❧ / TEAPOT   An anatomical member mentioned most often in the expression "*head over teapot.*" (For variations, see *tail over bandbox*.)

❧ / TEETER   A see-saw, as a plank and fulcrum for two children. Sometimes *teeter*-board. To ride a *teeter* is to *teeter*, and one who can't make up his mind is said to *teeter* his alternatives. Gentlemen who take too much to drink go home *a-teeterin'*. Teeter-totter is often heard for *teeter* in all meanings. Mainers have always called sandpipers and similar small wading birds, from their bobbing movement, *teeter* birds.

❧ / TELOS WAR   A lumbering and river-driving dispute of the 1800s, developing around water rights in the Allagash and East Branch areas. There were skirmishes with fists, *pickpoles*, *peaveys*, and similar available weapons. Today the term has a teapot-tempest suggestion, as in: "Joe and Pete, feelin' no pain, squared off 'sif they was reopening the *Telos War!*"

❧ / TENSE   An ear attuned to Maine's everyday conversations will notice a great deal is spoken in the historical present. Thus: "I knocks on the door, and she comes out, and I says . . ." All of which took place ten years ago. Occasional blendings of past and present are delightful: "I came down and found this party in my skiff, and I says . . ."

There is no loss of narrative clarity, and the effect is brightened by bringing things up close to hand where they may be contemporaneously examined and enjoyed. This tendency to move the low-vaulted past into the living now also causes Mainers to favor the past progressive (action continuing in the past) wherever it suits: "I was sayin'" is preferable to "I said." Thus, if a grammar of Maine speech were to be attempted, the principal parts of to sing might well be: I'm singing away, I was singing away, and there I am, singing away! Certainly there is never the humdrum syntax of the approved sing-sang-sung. Attention to tense is an academic obligation for all students of the Maine vernacular and must never be neglected. The Mainer's manipulation of past, present, and future is an important embellishment to his already rich language.

❧ / Tensed up    Filled with tension: "She all *tensed up* and forgot what to say."

❧ / Tent    In a state whose wilderness lingo employs *camp* for any residence, permanent or temporary, the canvas tent of the recreationalist often gets clarification by some such remark as, "No, they're not in a *camp*, they're *tenting*." One can make *camp* by setting up a tent, etc. One may also *camp* out by *wickie-upping* without a *tent*. The introduction and present prevalence of the tin camper which comes ready-made and fits in a pick-up truck causes no great difficulty with semantics, because most Maine woodsmen refer to them plainly as "them goddam campers."

❧ / Terrill Terror    D. D. Terrill, a Bangor manufacturer of lumbering equipment, is credited with inventing the raker-tooth bucksaw, a refinement of the old *Polack fiddle* (which see). His new bucksaw became popular and he had a good item, but the invention of the chainsaw broke his heart. Knowing the bucksaw was outmoded, he turned to make the first (and perhaps only) power chainsaw made in the state. It was heavy and unwieldy and it, too, was soon outmoded, but for a time it sold well and served well. Known as the *Terrill Terror*, it lamed many a back, and today has only museum value.

❦ / THACK   A curious and unexplained manipulation of "that" by a good many old Mainers: "*Thack's* just the way he said it."

❦ / THANK-YOU-MARM   See *yes-marm*.

❦ / THICK AS MARSH MUD   A variant of *pea soup* for describing a heavy fog; and also the coastal Mainer's requisite for a good cup of coffee.

❦ / THICKER'N SPATTERS   Thick, here, means frequency and not dimension. Freckles, blueberries, children, mosquitoes, *summer complaints*; anything in good supply is *thicker'n spatters*. Did you ever *slat* a loaded paint brush and see what it does to a floor?

❦ / THICK O' FOG   See *mull*.

❦ / THOLEPIN   Taking the strain of the oars, the *tholepins* creak and groan, and Mainers derived their expression "to suffer like a *tholepin*." This is an interesting reverse-play, because the old English meaning of "thole" is to suffer and endure, which is why they were called *tholepins* in the first place.

❦ / THRASH   Thresh. The crews who came to thresh grain were *thrashers*. To *thrash* around means to flail about (the flail is a hand tool for threshing) and flail about is similarly used for irrational movements of limbs and body.

A man who can't sleep may *thrash* around in bed all night. To give somebody a *thrashin'* is to beat him up, and the *thrashin'* of one's life is the superlative.

❧ / THREAD  A surveyor's term important in early land divisions where a stream was the boundary. The *thread* of a stream is the center of the visible current. The line between Brunswick and Topsham is the *thread* of the Androscoggin. There have been times when streams have so changed that land in one town has moved over to another without changing position! *Thread* is found in some deeds, and has puzzled non-Mainers who have bought a bit of land.

❧ / THREE DOLLAR BILL  A favorite Maine expression applied to anything irregular. The expression uses "queer" in the older meaning: "He's as queer (odd) as a *three dollar bill*."

❧ / THROURT  Throat. Listen for this, it comes warmly on the Maine tongue: "Little Teenie has a saw *throurt*." Here is a good place to include a similar word: *throurn*: "He's *throurn* three balls without a strike," or, "The king is on his *throurn*."

❧ / THUMPING  Variant for whipping, *larruping*, beating, *thrashin'*. But more important in Maine speech as an emphasis word when describing something big, good, wonderful: a *thumping* big piece of shortcake or a *thumping* good time.

❧ / TICKLED AS A CAT WITH TWO TAILS  This is the polite version of a very common coastal saying. Since a cat shows delight in owning a tail, two tails double the pleasure. The impolite version, the one we can't include here, is based on the utter irresponsibility of a dog, and assumes one may be doubly happy if he is doubly equipped.

❦ / TIDE WALKERS   Unsalvaged logs, or any river debris, that in the *boom* days were a navigational hazard in any tidal bay and harbor. The word is still used for a floating, half-submerged timber big enough to stave a boat.

❦ / TIES   Railroad ties or sleepers; half-squared logs laid on a right-of-way to carry the iron. There was always a good market for them, and they could be sawn from logs that were not top grade. In sawmill practice, the *sawyer* watched his logs, and when one came along that wouldn't cut profitably into other lumber, he'd take out a *tie*. A mill that turned out too many *ties* was accordingly handling some inferior logs.

❦ / TIE-UP   Random House gives definitions for this, but not the one common throughout Maine: a stable for dairy cattle. (See *stanchion*.) The stanchion chain is a *tie-up* chain; a chain used to tether a cow on grass is a *tie-out* chain. Although *tie* is not a favorite nautical word for hitching and the like, it is proper to say a boat *ties up* in reference to her home port: "She *ties up* at Bath."

❦ / TIGHT   This word has some meanings much favored in Maine and perhaps unique to the state. Since the word taut is well-known to coastal people, *tight* is rarely used in that sense. But a boat that doesn't leak is "*tight's* a cup," and a parsimonious man slow to haul out his wallet is "*tight's* the bark to a tree." Sometimes, "close as the bark to a tree," and for another variant see *near*. To *tighten up* means to make secure, but also to *righten up*, which see. Mainers use the expression "*tight* as he can jump or run" for full speed ahead, but philologists suggest this is another word and should properly be spelled *tite*.

❦ / TILL THE COWS COME HOME   Forever and ever: "I could eat Hannah's pie *till the cows come home*." Plausibly, if not possibly, there is the thought that bringing the cows from pasture to the *tie-up* is the end of the day.

❦ / TIMBER! ! ! The traditional warning cry in the forest when a *chopper* fells a tree. It is so ingrained in Maine lore as a safety requirement that men working all alone will shout it in full voice when a tree begins to fall. Thus *Timber! ! !* is heard as a warning or mock warning in any context. If Mother drops a batch of pans in the kitchen, making a clatter, somebody in the living room will yell, "TIMBER! ! !" *Timber! ! !* is also used as an exclamation of success, meaning that any job at hand is completed.

❦ / TIMER A time-keeper, except that in the lumber camps of the old days they didn't exactly have one. The day started before sun-up and didn't end until the last *chopper* had honed his ax on the *deacon-seat*, and pay was by the day or season. So, if a man fancied he had a grievance, he would be told to take it up with the *timer*, as in "tell it to the Marines."

❦ / TINKER In Maine usage, as elsewhere, the precise pot-and-pan duties of a tinker have been expanded to include any odd job and puttering in general. But to Mainers the *tinker* is a size of mackerel. In commercial handling, mackerel start with the *tinker*, the smallest, and then go to ones, twos, threes, and extries. The extras will go better than a pound. Mackerel smaller than *tinkers* and caught in the harbors are called spikes, but they are not offered to the market.

❦ / TIZZIC Included here because somebody who didn't know how to spell it suggested it was a "good Maine word." Phthisic is in any good dictionary. Its peculiar orthography made it a favorite in old-time spelling bees, and until spelling bees went out of style almost all Mainers could spell *phthisic*. Familiarity with the word, if not with the ailment, caused Mainers to apply it much as they use *Spanish mildew* (see *struck with the Spanish mildew*).

❦ / To    A preposition interchanged with "at" in the expressions "*to* home" and "at home," but with a difference, namely:

> "Is John *to* home?"
> "We have a piano at home."

❦ / TOE INJECTION    A remedy for inefficiency, waywardness, sauciness, etc., used long before modern wonder drugs and (some think) not used often enough today. Interestingly, the *toe injection* was applied about where some of the modern wonder drugs are most effective, i.e., a *toe injection* is a boot in the arse. (see *stern sheets*).

❦ / TOGGLE    Most Maine farmers would prefer *fid* to *toggle* for the pin used to shorten chain (see *fid*). In lobstering, another kind of *toggle* is the secondary buoy on the line. A few fathoms below the gayly painted pot buoy whose colors identify ownership, the fisherman attaches a smaller floating device, often a spent whiskey bottle but otherwise made of wood or Styrofoam. Its purpose is to catch up slack line at low tide so the *warp* won't foul on the ocean bottom, and to keep strain off the colored buoy so it will float freely and be easily spotted. At high tide the *toggle* will be submerged. These *toggles* rarely have identifying colors or marks. And, these *toggles* are never called *fids*.

❦ / TOGUE    The only word a true Mainer will ever use for the lake trout, *Cristivomer n. namay cush.* See *squaretail*.

❦ / TOILET    Considering the average reluctance of Maine people to come right out with this word (see *appleknocker*), it is not surprising they give it a special sound when they do. It is not "tawl't" and it is not "toll't" as in toll-road, but it hovers between the two and is definitely not tigh-l't. It is used for a *convenience* in the barn or out back, rather than one in the house, which is a bathroom. The word is never heard in Maine with any serious attempt to have it mean dressing, bathing, doing the hair, etc.

❦ / TOLL  Without reference to general meanings, this word remains a coastal call or enticement. Children are *tolled* home to supper when Mother yells from the doorway; garbage will *toll* rats; chumming (see *chum*) *tolls* fish. While inland sportsmen set decoys to attract ducks and geese, coastal gunners set out tollers. In certain usages toller is interchangeable with *toll*; mothers will "toller" their young ones home. *Toll* in this sense is archaic in the general language, but is also used in Appalachia as still heard in Maine.

❦ / TOMALLEY  Originated by Mainers for the liver portion of a lobster, there seems to be no other word for it and it is now found in most cookbooks. It has no relationship whatever to the Mexican *tamale*. Most people enamored of the Maine lobster are familiar with the word, but seldom do visitors and inland Mainers give it the particular pronunciation preferred by the tidewater people who thought it up. That is, it is usually pronounced as if it were the Mexican word *tamale*; listen next time you have a chance and your favorite lobster fisherman will probably say *tom-alley*.

❦ / TOMMYCOD  The tomcod.

❦ / TONIC  Proper Maine word for a soft drink from a bottle; a *sody* such as Coke, ginger ale, root beer. No medicinal properties are attached in this usage, even though Mainers are well aware that physicians prescribe *tonics* for run-down conditions.

❦ / TON TIMBER  A squared log laid by after slabbing and meant to be sawn into boards at another time. The term originated in colonial times when England, to protect domestic workmen, forbade sawmills in Maine. This meant that Maine's logs had to be shipped to England for sawing, and to save space aboard vessels they were hewn square with broadaxes. These squared sawlogs became known as *ton timbers* because they were paid for by weight instead of board feet.

❦ / TOO CLOSE APART  When summer visitors first hear this expression from a Maine fisherman, it sounds as if Reason had at last toppled from her *throurn*. Actually, it is an excellent rendition of just what is being considered. *Too close apart* means too near together, except that in fish nets and lobster traps togetherness is not the crux; apartness is. The lobsterman is spacing the slats of his trap according to the way he views apertures, and how near together the slats may be is of no importance; he wants them "close enough apart."

❦ / TOOTH CARPENTER  Upstate Maine-ism for a dentist.

❦ / TOP OFF  *Off* is used with *top* in all Maine expressions except to *top* "out" a chimney. A cup of tea filled to the brim is *topped off*. A load of hay is *topped off*; made neat so it will ride to the barn. Apple pie is *topped off* with a scoop of ice cream. A social evening is *topped off* with one more beer. Clooney Morrison was enthusiastic about a new minister and said, "He *topped off* the services with the best goddam prayer I ever clapped an ear to!"

❦ / TORCHING  Not exactly with the meaning of poaching, *torching* approaches it in the sense of playing the game with an unfair advantage, of pulling, maybe, a few *snedricks*. *Torching* is fishing at night with flares that attract herring. Accordingly, a boy may make a play for the young lady by squandering on a flashy automobile that will *torch* her.

❧ / TOTE    The Maine word for carrying anything, a ready substitute for *lug*, bear, *haul*, *sack*, and transportation in general: "I've got to *tote* the women to the store" means they will be driven in an automobile. Originally, the Maine usage was limited to carrying a packsack of supplies over a trail into *camp*. This is consistent with the dictionary meaning of a gift of food by southern planters to their slaves. But in time the element of food was eliminated from Maine usage, until boys *toted* wood to the woodbox, *cultch* was *toted* down from the attic, and a woman with child was *totin'*. When wagons took over wilderness logistics, the *tote* trails became *tote* roads. *Tote* in its broader Maine usage moved west with the loggers, and a Maine influence is the only explanation for the Wild West term, "gun-toter."

❧ / TOUCHIN' UP    A strange Maine euphemism for stealing, perhaps deriving from *touchin' up* somebody in the sense of borrowing. Specifically, it means taking fish or lobsters from another man's nets or traps. "Somebody's *touchin' up* my traps, and he just better not let me find out who!"

❧ / TOUGH AS A PITCH KNOT    Sometimes a spruce knot. An ax will bounce off one. Used to describe a wiry person who can *hang tough*, and sometimes somebody hard-hearted.

❧ / TOURTIÈRE    A pork pie associated with a Québec New Year's party. Pronounced almost as if spelled toot-shay. This is a word Maine's *Frenchmen* have introduced and, in the sense that it has become a good Maine word, the French Academy would be amused. Larousse (the authority on French cookery) says a *tourte* is a kind of pie, and the *tourtière* is the dish in which it is cooked. In Québecois the *tourtière* has become the pie itself; a round, covered pasty that looks like a mince pie before it is cut. Served hot, the *tourtière* is symbolic of French-Canadian festivity and frivolity, good fun and good food. It is not a confection too many non-French Mainers bake, but all Mainers with French-Canadian friends will take a toot-shay when offered.

❧ / Tow   In Maine the word has special meaning in lumbering for the hauling of great booms of logs across lakes during river drives. The Maine tow-boat is a specially constructed tugboat for this work, and before such heavy boats the *towing* was done by *alligators* and headworks (see *alligator*). Mainers use *tow* in related situations: "He had some tourists in *tow*, showing them through the mill," or, "She's had Archie in *tow* for some time. We'll hear wedding bells before long."

❧ / Town house   Preferred in most smaller Maine communities for the town hall. It is not only the seat of municipal government, but is the social center where dances, basketball games, art shows, and many another attraction is held; hence, *town house* encompasses the general activities of a community. Bob Ringrose took his wife to New York and they went to a night club, but Bob said he couldn't dance too well there because, ". . . they didn't have no lines painted on the floor same's the *town house*."

❧ / Town landing   Access to the waterfront is a public privilege, so when private landowners became possessive, communities along the coast provided *town landings* so nobody needed to cross another's lawn or back yard. Supported by a town meeting appropriation, the *town landing* is merely the public wharf.

❧ / Township   The precise Maine word for the minor civil division. Portland, while a city by charter, is nevertheless merely a *township*; so is uninhabited T4R8WELS.

❧ / Town team   Nowadays, as anywhere, the local athletic aggregation. But in former times the assembled oxen of every farmer in town, yoked together to form one big hook-up for a major job. The *town team* moved houses and *baulked* timbers. Thus, a "*town team* job" is one calling for a maximum community effort.

❧ / Trap   Although *pot* is used for the slatted cage for taking lobsters, most Maine lobstermen seem easier with the word *trap*; there is no difference in meaning. *Trap* is also the word for the flag-waving device used for freshwater fishing through the ice.

❧ / Trap nail   A special small galvanized nail used to fasten *trap stock* together to make the completed lobster *trap*.

❧ / Trap stock   The sawn bows, frames, and slats, generally red oak, that come in bundles and are nailed into *traps* by lobstermen.

❧ / Travelers   Low-flying dark clouds moving in from the south and promising rain. *Travelers* are prominent because they appear at a low altitude while the upper sky is carrying another kind of cloud.

❧ / Treat   Used in the sense of offering or buying (see *shout*) an ice cream, drink, etc., as a friendly gesture; but applied by Mainers specifically to the small gift a storekeeper makes when a customer pays his bill. Father gets a cigar, and if the children are along there will be a small paper bag with three-four chocolate creams. The cash-and-carry grocery has rather eliminated this pleasant custom from Maine life, but thanks-be there are still a few stores in Maine that *treat*. *Treating* by no means excluded a *jug* in the back room where customers so inclined could find a *snort* as their *treat*.

❧ / TREE-SQUEAK   Another mythical Maine animal of the deep woods, often confused with tree limbs that rub in the night wind and make noises.

❧ / TREE-TOPPY   Conceited; putting on airs. A top-lofty and heavily limbed tree might give the *choppers* some trouble and often seemed unreasonable in the way it wanted to fall. Hence: "She got real *tree-toppy* after one year at college."

❧ / TRICK   A turn at the wheel or on look-out; one's specified duty in a routine situation: "It's your *trick* to mow the lawn this week."

❧ / TRIG   A wedge or block to keep a wheel or bar-rel from rolling, and accordingly anything suggesting such a device: "Town meetin' got *trigged up* on some foolish parliamentary question." A *trig* is also a pronged device hinged at the rear of a sled runner; when turned down it bites into the roadway and holds the load from sliding back-wards while the team rests. When not needed, it is carried in a fold-back position.

❧ / TRI-WEEKLY   Franklin County pleasantry for pas-senger service on the old Maine Central line from Farming-ton down to Lewiston. You'd go down on the train one week, and try to get back the next.

❧ / TROLLEY PARK   Present-day references to *trolley parks* are wholly reminiscent, although Maine's famous Lakewood Theatre at Madison is, indeed, a *trolley park*. Until about 1930 Maine was crisscrossed with short-line electric railways, so by connecting interminably one could travel from Kittery as far as Old Town. Most of these lines had a park to which people thronged on the trolleys on Sundays and holidays for picnics, ball games, and very wonderful times. Some had zoos. Casco Castle at South Freeport is a remnant of such a resort. Others were at Riverton, Lake Grove, and Merrymeeting. Lakewood Park was operated by the Somerset Traction Company at Wesserunsett Lake midway between Madison and Skowhegan. In its proud enumeration of years continuously operated, today's Lakewood Theatre includes the years of trolley-line amusements when a merry-go-round and dance hall were featured.

❧ / TROUBLE  Decorous term for unhusbanded prenatal condition: "He got her in *trouble*."

❧ / TROUT CHOWDER  More than a few discerning palates have discovered that a Maine *trout chowder* exceeds the more publicized lobster stew in delicacy and delight, and more than a few tongues have said so. Put together much as a coastal fish chowder, it is a specialty of guides who prepare it at noontime for angling *sports*. It is thus made over an open fire and enjoys this advantage, but it also uses tinned milk, because of wilderness distances and lack of refrigeration, and when properly brought off will have a resultant "body" that coastal chowders do not always attain. The *trout* in reference is the eastern brook trout of Maine, and the chowder is usually made from fish that are but minutes out of the water. Inlanders who consider a *trout chowder* the masterwork of Maine cookery always pity coastal folks and out-of-staters who say, "A *trout chowder?* Why, I never heard of one!" They live short.

❧ / TRUTH  "If the *truth* be known . . ." is a favorite Maine preface to keeping the record straight: "He goes to church on Sunday all right, but if the *truth* be known . . ." It has a disclaimer tone, and can be substituted for *as the feller says.* Scholars will appreciate the subjunctive construction, which is good Maine.

❧ / Tᴜʙ    A varying measure of distance. The trawl line was baited on shore and carefully coiled inside a trawl *tub* with the hooks toward the center. The man who payed it out as the dory was rowed along over the fishing grounds used a payin'-stick to keep his hands clear of the flying hooks. The length of the trawl was thus equivalent to the capacity of the *tub*, and fishermen will say something or other is a "*tub* o'gear away."

❧ / Tᴜᴍʙʟᴇ ʜᴏᴍᴇ    The inward slant of a ship's side at or above the upper deck, inside the rail. A person who comes in over the rail from a small boat may, because of the way weight is shifted, *tumble home.* Any entrance that lacks grace.

❧ / Tᴜɴᴋᴇᴛ    A genteel term for hell: "Where in *tunket* did you put my *overhauls?*"

❧ / Tᴜɴɴᴇʟ    Given in dictionaries as dialect for funnel; both are used in Maine, both will be equally understood. Maine lobstermen prefer to call the *tunnel* openings in their traps funnels, and in this connection see *funny-eye.*

❧ / Tᴜɴɴʏ    When a Maine fisherman, *sot* in his ways, calls a *horse mackerel* a tuna, he'll probably pronounce it *tunny.*

❧ / Tᴜʀᴋᴇʏ    Mostly in the Penobscot watershed, this was a bag or bundle for the woodsman's personal *plunder* (which see). A more sophisticated *turkey* would be called a *kennebecker*, particularly if meant for carrying on the trail. Usually *turkey* referred to something tied up in a grain bag and thrust under a bunk.

✿ / TURKEY-TURD BEER   Of all known beverages, this one is least liked by true Mainers; the expression is: "meaner than *turkey-turd beer.*" It is not quite so bad, however, as "sour owl urine," which is an interchangeable comparison.

✿ / TURK'S HEAD   An ornamental knot most often used on a ship's wheel to mark the king, or midship, spoke. Amongst the umpty-odd Maine explanations of the origin of the doughnut is that a sea cook made a round cookie with a hole so a helmsman could mark his king spoke after the *Turk's head* was lost.

✿ / TURN   For a turn-off or a bend in a road; others may make a turn, or take a turn, but in Maine the *turn* is itself a place: "The bus picks up the children at the *turn.*" A *turn* is also one wind of a rope around a winch or spile: "Take a *turn* there to *stiddy* us!" For added security, one takes a couple of *turns*, and thus an adage was born: "One good *turn* deserves another." "Hold a *turn*, now" is advice to keep your courage up. (See *hold turn* and *round turn.*)

✿ / TWENTY MILE   Many places in the Maine wilderness were designated by their distances from other places. *Twenty Mile* is accordingly a Great Northern check point twenty miles beyond Rockwood. Helen Hamlin's excellent account of her experiences as a schoolteacher in a lumber camp are recounted in her book, *Nine Mile Bridge.*

✿ / TWICE AS COLD AS ZERO   An old Maine reference point now superseded by the meteorologist's discovery of the chill factor. The mathematical impossibility of computing zero gives the term its charm. Some old-timers who have seen it *twice as cold as zero* explain that it is zero with a high wind.

**❧** / TWICE-LAID   Old ropes used a second time to make do; accordingly, leftovers at table or hand-me-down clothing. Lay is the proper word for twisting strands to make rope.

**❧** / TWINE   A word of extremely general meaning in Maine fisheries; to some extent it is a synonym for cordage. *Twine* means fishing nets in the aggregate, so a man will tell how much *twine* he has out. However, specific words for various *twines* are meticulously used, such as *warp, ganging, snoodin'*, and so on. *Mash* (which see) is *twine*, but when a fisherman speaks of his *twine mash* he means the size of the opening in his netting.

**❧** / TWISTER   A loop of small rope on the end of a short stick to engage the attention of a fractious horse while being shod. The loop is put over the horse's soft nose and when the stick is *twisted* it has a high rate of efficiency. It brings the animal's snout to a pear-shaped point at which he can gaze, and this distracts him from kicking the blacksmith shop apart. The gentleman who assists the blacksmith by applying the *twister* was often referred to by the farrier as "my secretary." Figuratively, today, to apply the *twister* to somebody is to calm him down, and by persuasion and conviction get him to change his foolish mind.

**❧** / TWIST HER TAIL   Cows unwilling to step forward, being perhaps *notional* (which see), could be persuaded by a sharp twist on their tails close to the body. Indeed, a good twist would make one leap over a bridge. Accordingly, any reluctant situation where forthright remedy is needed may elicit the helpful suggestion, *"Twist her tail!"*

**❧** / TWITCH   After a tree is felled and cut into sawlog lengths, the first movement of it from the forest is called *twitching*. With a team, and often a single horse, the log is pulled by a chain around the large end, and is dragged over the ground or snow to the *brow*. Sometimes *twitching* is done with a *scoot* (which see), and today it is done by machine skidders using cables. The manner in which a *twitched* log bounces around on its way gives the word *twitch* great vividness when used in transferred situations: "Johnny sarssed teacher, and she *twitched* him right out'n his seat over the desk," or, "The dentist *twitched* a tooth."

❦ / Twitchin' Horse    A carefully trained horse that *twitches* logs out of the woods by himself. Some regard this as the highest development of equine management, superior to circus capers. Since the log being twitched bounces around over rough terrain, and a driver couldn't possibly ride on it, and because running along beside to guide the horse is dangerous, early Maine teamsters taught their *twitchin' horses* to work without bridles. Such a horse lines himself up for a hitch, proceeds to the *brow*, and stands to await unhitching. He will then walk back into the woods by himself. *Twitchin' horses* have been known to snag a log on a stump, turn to look the situation over, and extricate the log by changing direction. To compare a man to a *twitchin' horse* is to pay him the highest compliment as to intelligence.

❦ / Two Lamps    The expression is: "*two lamps* lit *and no ship out*." It means the height of extravagance and has the connotation of money to burn. There has always been the sentimental allusion to leaving a lamp burning in the window, and when lighting home a boat alongshore it was a kindly thing to do. But one lamp is enough; and to have *two lamps* lit with no boat coming home was an imprudent waste of oil.

# U

---

❦ / UP A STUMP   Pregnant. The term can be used for a properly married lady's condition, but more often refers to the results of premarital dalliance: "I hear she's only sixteen and *up a stump*." The same round-about information is conveyed by the phrase, "eatin' dried apples." "One look at her, and you can see she's been eatin' dried apples!"

❦ / UP AND DOWN THE MAST   When there is a light, variable air, not enough to fill the sails, and things are at a standstill, the wind is said to be all *up and down the mast*. If Mother wants to go *plummin'* and Father wants to go to the fair and the children want to go to the beach, and nobody can quite agree, the wind is all *up and down the mast*.

❦ / UPSTAIR   Not so much in southern Maine, but in Aroostook *upstair* is heard for *upstairs*: "Now, you children get right *upstair* to bed!" The same is true of *downstair*. Back of this there seems to be a concept that *upstair* and *downstair* are places, rather than directions. Compare up attic and down cellar in this sense.

❦ / USUAL MANNER   A term fraught with great humor for those who appreciate it, originating in (of all places!) the Maine Fish & Game laws. When fly-fishing became recognized as a conservation practice, certain inland Maine waters were put in the category of "fly-fishing only." It

then became necessary for the often less-than-smart legis-
lators to define fly-fishing. The best they could do was
come up with the vaporish phrase that "fly-fishing means
fishing with flies in the *usual manner*." So, what does that
mean? Anglers began tossing it off wittily, and soon everybody was doing about everything in the *usual manner*:
"The roof leaked, so we plugged the hole in the *usual manner*."

# V

/\V.\V.\V.\

❧ / VALLEY, THE    This means the valley of the St.
John River from Allagash Plantation until it passes into
New Brunswick. This is the home of the transplanted Acadians from Nova Scotia, and while English-speaking
Aroostookians have lived in *The Valley* since the early
1800s, the Acadian influence dominates. Scenically, *The
Valley* is as pretty as any part of Maine, a nook of verdant
farmland we share equally with Canada. This is a good place
to explain that in Aroostook County the four directions are:

Over eastward—to the Maritime Provinces.
Down County—In the direction of Houlton.
Up to *The Valley*—Toward Madawaska, Fort Kent, etc.
Outside—Anywhere else.

❧ / VEER    Although throughout the language in general *veer* has come to mean a turn or change, to coastal
Mainers it retains its original meaning of following the
sun: a clockwise movement. A *veering* wind moves from
east to west through the south and is said to *haul around*;
the opposite is to *back in*, that is, to move from east to west
through the north. In Maine, a *backing* wind after a storm
promises more foul weather in a day or so, but if the wind
*veers* there should be a period of bright weather.

❧ / VELVET    The *sody*-fountain delight otherwise
called a frap (*frappé*) was always called a *velvet* in Maine,

at least until summer people began asking for fraps. Why not? It's the milk and ice cream mixture whipped until it's smooth as *velvet*.

❧ / VENEER  In the veneer and plywood parts of Maine's forest industry, this word has come to mean the hardwood trees and logs from which *veneer* is made.

❧ / VOMIT  Vergil used *vomo* in the sense that "everybody poured forth from the house." The exact same classical use is heard in Maine where a theatre or *town house* crowd may *vomit* after a picture show or a basketball game. The nicer equivalent would be "to let out."

❧ / Wᴀɪɴ   A bark edge on a board, usually caused by a *yank* (which see) in the sawlog. Modern dressing of lumber removes such edges, but in undressed boards the *scaler* is expected to make alowance for *wainy* edges. The word is transferred wherever it suits: a parson's not-so-good sermon may be said to be on the *wainy* side.

❧ / Wᴀɪᴛ ғᴏʀ   Maine people *wait for* one another; they don't wait on. (*Waiting on* is a waitress's job. "She's *waitin'* on this summer at Squaw Mountain Inn.")

❧ / Wᴀʟᴋ ᴀɴᴅ ʜɪᴅᴇ   See *pack and back.*

❧ / Wᴀʟᴋᴇʀ   A good man on a woods trail. A guide hates to walk a trail with a *sport* who dawdles along; he'd rather have a *walker*. A good *walker*, carrying a pack, should hike at about three miles an hour along a trail. And, *walker* is the Maine word for crawler, as applied to those fat angleworms picked up on the lawn after dark and used for fishing bait. Many out-of-staters are puzzled by the Maine roadside signs that say, "Nite *walkers* For Sale."

❧ / Wᴀʟᴋɪɴɢ ʙᴏss   A lumber camp boss who is in charge of two or more operations and walks from one camp to the other. Called so today if he rides his pick-up truck.

❦ / Wallet The ordinary billfold for men, but used in a number of Maine monetary expressions. To haul out one's *wallet* means a bet is being paid or a deal has been made. To slap one's *wallet* is to protest that sufficient funds are at hand to back up a bet or an offer. To hit somebody square in the *wallet* is to inflict fiscal pain.

❦ / Wangan Found by Fr. Sebastien Râle in the St. Francis Indian language, this word meant the effects a brave carried on a wilderness journey. It remains today as the term for the gear and duffle of a canoe trip, and in general all the food and supplies needed for wilderness travel. It has come to mean the company store in a lumber camp, and also the traveling kitchen that accompanied river drivers down a stream. Besides the company store, it also has come to mean the account there, usually charged against wages, until a man will say he has to "pay his *wangan*." Maine woods people, to whom the word has long been second nature, tend to prounounce it *wong-'n*, with perhaps a little carry-over of the *g*, thus: *wong-g'n*. Always remembering that Maine Indian terms came into our English through the French, we should perhaps note that French-Canadians, to whom the term is equally easy, give it a *whang-g'n* sound. The Minnesota embellishment of "*wannigan*" is sheer bosh; the word has only two syllables. The quickest definition of *wangan* is woods supplies; Maine canoeists have rope-handled wooden boxes for carrying their *wangan*, and these are *wangan* boxes.

❦ / War bags Dufflebags, *kennebeckers*, and the Maine woodsman's back-packed gear in general. The old lumbering expression was that after the season the "crew packed its *war bags* and went downriver."

❦ / Warp The seacoast meaning of *warp* (to *warp* a vessel up to a pier by a line) takes care of the general Maine use of *warp* for various kinds of cordage. A quite different meaning is found in the *warp* of a board or timber, and the Maine expressions deriving from it. A *warped* mind is perhaps not utterly deranged, but twisted somewhat. To be *warped* in your politics is to have some funny ideas. A person or thing which is *warped* is odd and irregular.

❧ / WARRANTEE    A Maine verb deriving from *warranty*. It means to guarantee title to land, and hence to stand behind any deal. Early Maine land ownership often involved the "bond for a deed," which led to many situations where a simple quit-claim deed wasn't a firm transfer. Mainers have accordingly always preferred the *warranty* deed in which the seller guarantees good title. In Maine speech, thus, to give a *warranty* deed is to *warrantee*. Transferred, it is heard as, "Do you *warrantee* these colors are fahst?"

❧ / WART BEAN    Among Maine's many home-cures for warts, the bean had preference. The dry bean was rubbed on the wart (sometimes with gibberish incantations) and the bean was planted. Watch to see when the bean sprouts, and you will find the wart gone! The absurdity of this cure was noted, and when anything has "about as much sense as a *wart bean*," you can consider it a foolish endeavor.

❧ / WASHBOARDS    The planking on a vessel inside the *gunwale*, and on lobster boats outside the coaming. The washboards and coaming prevent a breaking sea from coming inboard. A boat with *washboards* under is heeled over, suggesting heavy going, speed, and forthrightness; hence, a person going to town with his "*washboards* under" is bound on some purposeful errand with considerable on his mind. On a lobster boat the washboards are used as a work bench, and will be littered with starfish, kelp, etc., after *hauling*, so sweeping down the *washboards* signals the end of a day's work. A *washboard* broom, as distinguished from a house or barn broom, is bought for cleaning *washboards*.

❧ / WATCH AND WATCH   The term suggests heavy going, and perhaps an emergency. The *watches* aboard ship were of four hours (however, see *dog watch*), and the crew rotated. But in a storm all hands would be on alert around the clock and half the men would take one *watch*, half the next. The sea-going term is transferred ashore for any situation requiring constant attention; around-the-clock nursing of a patient is *watch and watch*.

❧ / WATER THE HORSE   See *pump ship*.

❧ / WAZZAT   See *billdad*.

❧ / WEASEL JUICE   An imaginary ingredient which imparts vim and vigor to human beings; probably from the quick movements of the weasel: "I never see nobody so plumb full of *weasel juice*. He's always on the go!"

❧ / WEDDING TREES   A term throughout New England for the pair of stately elms a newly-married couple planted by their front door. Mainers liked to call them "marriage elms." The Dutch elm disease has left them ghostly of late.

❧ / WEEWAW   Aslant and askew, not plumb or vertical. Also *eeyaw*. Used for quirks and oddities in the same sense as *warp*, which see.

❧ / WEIR   Pronounced ware. A maze-like fish trap built alongshore of sticks, brush, and poles, and sometimes nets. Never to be confused with a *pound*, although some tourists do.

❧ / WELL-DIGGER'S ELBOWS   The politer version of well-digger's arse. Used in Maine comparisons as a measure of coldness, and interchangeable with *clamdigger's hands*, which see. It's pretty cool down there in the hole.

❧ / WELS    The cryptic initials and symbols used in identifying Maine geography are numerous and always puzzling to out-of-staters. They derive from early surveys. *WELS* means West of the Easterly Line of the State. Thus, T14R5WELS refers to a wildland township in Aroostook County, adjacent to Perham, and in the parlance of timberland management will probably be dismissed as "fourteen-five." Its full name would be: "Township number fourteen in Range number five, west of the easterly line of the state" —and if you look on a map you'll find that's exactly where 14-5 is. There are many other such designations; WBKP means West of Bingham's Kennebec Purchase. The best authority on these initials (and on almost everything about Maine geography) is a book titled *The Length and Breadth of Maine*, compiled by the late Stanley B. Attwood, long city editor of the *Lewiston Daily Sun*. (It is out of print, but most Maine libraries have it, and the University of Maine at Orono has recently published a paperback edition.)

❧ / West Coast    See *Out East*.

❧ / Wet smack    In Maine, except as the term has been intruded by outside influences, this does not mean a juicy kiss or a party-pooper. It means a fishing smack with a well in which fish are kept alive until port is reached; sea water is circulated through the well. The *wet smack* is also called a well smack and a well bo't. Lobstermen rig a tub through which sea water is pumped to gain the same effect.

❧ / Whacks    The rations a sailor will receive during a voyage. To "get one's *whacks*" originally meant sugar, tea, coffee, beans, rice, etc. Not to get one's *whacks* meant the ship didn't live up to its agreement. Today, *whacks* are a fair share of whatever is going around.

❧ / Whale    *Whale*, horse, and bull have about the same meaning in Maine for brute strength and forthrightness in doing some physical chore. (See *plunder.*) To *whale* around comes from the frantic protestations of a harpooned whale. To *whale* into a matter is to approach it with no holds barred: "Joe *whaled* into Fred like a tornado!" A man lost in the woods and running wild in terror is described as *whaling* around all night in the *puckerbrush.* Another expression deriving from whaling is to "heave a *tub*" in the sense of making a distracting remark, or to change a subject to avoid a dispute. It comes from heaving a cask overboard when a harpooned whale threatens to attack the boat; it gives the beast something to go for instead.

❧ / WHALER   The word is waler and comes from the wales or planks on a ship's hull. (See *gunwales.*) But upland Maine carpenters spell it *whaler* and use it without reference to its coastal origin for a shore or brace used for temporary strength. A concrete form will have *whalers* attached horizontally, to which braces are fitted. A long partition, being framed flat, will be reinforced with *whalers* to keep it from buckling when lifted into position. The word is also used as a verb: "We'd best *whale* it now." A *whaler* is a sizeable timber, not less than 2 x 6, and usually 12- to 16-feet long. Such a timber, however, is not called a *whaler* until it is put in position and used as such.

❧ / WHALE MANURE   A marine product used to measure the lowest IQ. Anybody notoriously stupid is "dumb as a bucket of *whale manure.*" All Mainers will relish this definition because they don't really say manure. (Also, see *lower than whale dung.*)

❧ / WHARFSIDE SAILOR   A boat owner who, from lack of skill or timidity, does his sailing close by. Applied mostly to the let's-pretend summer yachtsman who has to have a boat because he has a cottage on the water, and who sits on it at the pier or on mooring. An unappreciated term for the *summer mahogany* set *appletree-er* (see *appletree-er*).

❧ / WHAT-DA-YA-THINK? A greeting, and not necessarily a question, this is one of the many conversational openers Mainers favor. It, and all the others, are to be answered in kind. *What-da-ya-think?* is often answered with, "I think damn, that's what I think!" "What's the word?" (see *word, the*) and "Do-ya think they'll have it?" are acceptable variants. "Do-ya think they'll have it?" is a favorite to pull on *summer complaints*, because they usually answer, "Have WHAT?"

❧ / WHAT SMELL? The standard reply of Maine papermakers who are asked by tourists what the smell is. *Rap full* pay envelopes seem to overcome the offensive kraft process amazingly. If pressed, the people in papermill towns will say, "You get used to it!"

❧ / WHIFFLETREE Folks from other places seem to prefer whippletree and are surprised to hear the Maine version. However, *whiffletree* is sanctioned, and Mainers never say whippletree. Sometimes, of course, they specify singletree or doubletree. Any dictionary will clear this up.

❧ / WHIMPER Pronounced whimp-puh. From the small crying of babies and puppies, Mainers use the word for protesting, wheedling, and even advanced profanity. A man caught *touchin'* *up* lobster traps will protest vigorously that everything is a mistake, and is said to *whimper.* An outraged taxpayer will approach the assessors, and they will say he "came in to *whimper.*" A gentleman shouting curses across his dooryard at boys stealing apples will be said to *whimper* a mite. The uses of *whimper* in Maine speech illustrate pleasantly the native ability to down-play for effect.

❧ / WHISKER A *doit.* Another of the many Maine synonyms for a small and indefinite quantity, such as *dollop, dab*, touch, *smidgin*, etc. A *whisker* is just a hair's breadth: "That board is just a *whisker* too wide."

❧ / WHIST AS MICE  Said of well-behaved children who do not interrupt their elders. Whist! is a command to be silent, and the children who obey are said to be *whist as mice*.

❧ / WHISTLE  Becalmed seamen resorted to *"whistlin'* up a wind." Nobody took it seriously enough so it became any kind of a superstition; a man did it in whimsy and his mates considered it comical. When one *whistles* up a wind, he simply whistles as if calling a dog. The old wheeze, with which down-Maine folklore buffs have had many a picnic, concerns the sailor who whistled too loudly and brought on a gale that dismasted the vessel. Anybody bemoaning present conditions may elicit the suggestion that he *whistle* up a wind.

❧ / WHITE WATER  The inland term for rapids in a river, as viewed by river drivers and canoeists. The examination for a Registered Maine Guide license asks the question: Can you handle a canoe in *white water?* Coastwise, the term is used for breakers on a shore or reef; but in navigation terms, those seen from a vessel.

❧ / WHORE'S EGG  A term all serious students of graphic language will admire. The creature thus identified by Maine fishermen is the sea urchin, a common marine echinoderm with a somewhat globular shell beset with tremendously sharp spines. Although sea urchins have a market and Maine does ship many to cities with Italian populations (the Italian people use the pinkish-yellow flesh as a spread for bread), the few that a lobsterman finds in his traps on a day's haul are not enough to make it worth his while to bring them in. The whimsy of the first Maine fisherman to dub this creature a *whore's egg* has been applauded ever since by all right-thinking linguists. It reminds one faintly of the parrot that laid square eggs and could say only "Ouch!"

❧ / WICKIE-UP   A temporary and usually one-night bedding down on a wilderness trail. It suggests a man overtaken by night, and a make-do shelter which, while primitive, becomes comfortable through his woods wisdom. It also suggests the experienced and competent woodsman, such as a timber cruiser or a game warden, rather than a recreationalist with sophisticated equipment. A man who makes such a camp *wickie-ups*, and is said to have *wickie-upped*. Maine use derives from Abnaki Indian.

❧ / WIDOW MAKER   A tree with a broken top or loose limbs that can drop when the tree is felled and kill a man. In chopping, the admonition is "Always look up!" The tendency to let your eyes follow the descending tree prevents your seeing the *widow maker* that can be coming down from directly overhead. Today all *choppers* are required to wear hard hats, a tribute to the constant threat of the *widow maker*. Persons who have tried the ski trail on Sugarloaf Mountain known as *The Widow Maker* may appreciate this derivation.

❧ / W. I. GOODS   This term is occasionally heard in Maine today as a good-natured nickname for booze in general: "Well, I think I'll go pick up some *W. I. Goods*." Originally the term included molasses as well as rum, and stores that handled the true West Indies products put out signs that said *W. I. Goods*. Nobody now living in Maine remembers those days, but once in a while the lingering holdover will be heard: "Well, I guess I'll go see Dr. Goods"; i.e., buy a *jug*:

❧ / WILD GEESE   Little sparks of burning soot that appear on the fireback of a fireplace, and seem to follow the wedge pattern of migrating geese. (See *marching soldiers*.) The manifestation depends on the right barometric pressure, and it foretells a storm: "*Wild geese* tonight; be snowing before daylight!"

❧ / WINDED   Quite apart from nautical meanings in general language, in Maine *winded* means pooped, tired, tuckered. "I mowed the lawn until I got *winded*." Heavier breathing from exercise is involved, and after getting his second wind a man will mow some more.

❧ / WIND UP   As to *wind up* a clock; anybody tense and jittery is all *wound up*. "Are you ready?" may be answered by, "All *wound up* and ready to go!" Another set of Maine expressions derives *wind up* from the coiling of ropes after a voyage or the tidying of fishing lines, signifying that a job is finished. "The Legislature *wound up* on Friday" means it adjourned. An executor will *wind up* an estate. Somebody who was born in Eastport may *wind up* running a banana plantation in Panama.

❧ / WING   The *wing* of a barnyard hen being readied for Sunday dinner was used by almost all Maine people as a small brush. Mother had one to brush flour off the breadboard back into the bar'l, and Father would have one to tidy his workbench. In the occasional uses heard today, *wing* means *brush*, as with a whisk broom. Since heavy snow equipment came into use, *wing* is the Maine word for pushing the plowed snow along the highways farther back so there will be room to plow the next storm. It is done with a supplementary blade or *wing*. In such usage the past tense is often *wung*; "They've got the roads all *wung* back." (See *wing and wing*, below, for nautical justification for this onshore oddity.)

❧ / WING AND WING   A sailing vessel running before the wind will have booms out on both sides and is said to

be *wung out* or sailing *wing and wing*. Hence, almost anything at full tilt, or bulging in both directions, is *wing and
wing*.

❧ / WINTER   To *winter* out; to come successfully
from fall into spring:

> "Did you *winter* well?"
> "Nicely, thank you."

Also, to keep cattle through the winter: "I'm *winterin'*
nine heifers and a bull." Early cabbage and late cabbage
are usually designated by Mainers as summer cabbage and
winter cabbage. And the term is applied to fruits and vegetables that keep well in cellar storage: the Northern Spy
is a *winter* apple; Greenings *winter* better than Alexanders.

❧ / WISHING BOOK   This name for the big mail-order
catalog originated in the Maritime Provinces for the T.
Eaton publication, but Mainers picked it up for Sears,
Monkey–Ward, etc. "Wish I had this, wish I had that!" It
is interesting that Sears, Roebuck now uses *Wish Book* on
their front cover.

❧ / WITCH   *Witch* remains the favored Maine word
for a water dowser, and it is applied to both men and wom-
en who divine underground water. Usually Mainers say in
full, *water-witch*, and the divining is called *water-witchin'*.
Although Mainers have about the same percentage of belief
and disbelief as other people, there has never been any
black-magic nuance in this use of *witch*.

❧ / WITHY   From the supple nature of a withe, the adjective means sinewy, wiry, and often supple in spite of age.
The dictionaries do not seem to hit upon exactly the Maine
shade of meaning in, "You tackle him, and you'll find he's
real *withy*!"

❧ / With-it   The other things served at dinner; the vegetables, pickles, dessert, etc. Hence, there will be a roast of beef and *with-its*. When asked what's for dinner, the woods cook gives the standard brush-off, "Victuals and *with-its!*" (Vittles, that is.)

❧ / Witness tree   A *witness* mark is a stake or post set by surveyors as a reference point. In surveying Maine, trees were plentiful enough so nobody had to drive stakes. When seen in the wilderness a *witness tree* is easily recognized by its blazes, spots, and daubs of paint. (See *shagimaw*.)

❧ / Wizzled   Maine substitute for wizened. Berries gone by on the vine are *wizzled* up, and older folks fading from age and ill health *wizzle* away.

❧ / Woodbox   The kitchen box for firewood which has additional duties in transferred usage. To be "sick a-bed in the *woodbox*" is to be laid up with a minor complaint which, although distressing, doesn't put you to bed. To be flabbergasted by sudden bad news is to be "knocked clearn into the *woodbox*" by surprise. To get "hit in the *woodbox*" is somewhat like taking a poke in the breadbasket. (See *snow in the woodbox*.)

❧ / Woodchuck   Mainer's term for a woodchuck. The only time a Mainer says groundhog is when he says, "Today is Groundhog Day. Wonder if any *woodchucks*'ll come out?" Even then, he's more likely to say Candlemas.

❧ / Woodpile cousin   About like a *buttonhole relation* (which see), but less likely to mean actual blood connections. Perhaps Maine usage is explained by the old German *Sprichwort*: "Two who steal wood together are friends for life."

❦ / Woods   In general, the preferred Maine word for the forest. Forest seems to be reserved mostly for the purposes of the Forestry Service, and in ecological references. One goes into the *woods* on business or pleasure. Although wildland owners employ foresters, they are used for woodlands management. The Tree Farm program encourages good forestry but the signs put up say "improved woodlot." A forest fire is called a *woods* fire, *brush* fire, and *slash* fire.

❦ / Woods line   A wilderness telephone line. Everything in a whole region would be on one line; sporting and lumber camps, company offices, game and forestry wardens, and strategic emergency stations along roads and trails. The *woods line* had one wire, the ground being the opposite side, and a lightning bolt would jingle every instrument in fifty miles. A few survive, but radio has made many obsolete. Talking over a *woods line* often required more energy than walking over a mountain to converse in person. There is much Maine lore about the *woods line*. One story involves the *chopper* who was called into the *cock shop* to take a 'phone call. It was his wife from St. Zacharie, Québec, to tell him he had a new son. Astonished when she spoke, he turned to the *bullcook* and said, "Migar! Dis tam t'ing talks French!"

❦ / Woodsman   Used in general for *choppers, cruisers*, etc., and thus an appropriate trade name for Maine's favorite insect repellent. It has a tang that lingers, so if a man who uses some in June goes out for Christmas dinner the cook will come in from the kitchen to sniff. All good Maine stores carry it, and if the spray-can kinds don't work for you, ask for *Woodsman*.

❦ / Word, the   Another Maine greeting, heard thus: "Well, what's *the word?*" (See *what-da-ya-know?*) Some say it derives from the Mainer's tendency to be a joiner and the general familiarity with lodge work where a password identifies members. In the Grange, for instance, each member is obliged to whisper *the word* to the stewards before the meeting commences; this delay in the program is known as "taking up the *word*."

❧ / Working    Timbers of elderly vessels, straining at sea, are said to be *working*, and this means trouble. *Working* is also the term for natural fermentation in a barrel of cider, but this occasions no great alarm.

❧ / Worming    The digging in coastal tide flats of clam worms, blood worms, and sand worms to be shipped as bait for sportsmen. It is now big business in Maine, and Wiscasset boasts modestly that she is "the worm capital of the world." Men digging worms (they can be seen at Cod Cove in Edgecomb) look like clam diggers, but they will have pails instead of *hods*. A worm digger is called a wormer. Maine's chief market is the New York and New Jersey surf-casting area.

❧ / Wormwood    More often spoken of in full as Roman *wormwood*, this is a common weed on Maine farms that became the scapegoat for hay fever under the name ragweed. Nobody in Maine knew it was ragweed until hay fever was invented, but everybody had been weedin' out Roman *wormwood* for years.

❧ / Wringin' wet    See *soakin' wet*.

# X

## ᴧᴠᴧᴠᴧᴧ

❧ / X    An axle. Probably all Mainers who say X would spell it ex, or maybe put down axle, but the single letter best suits the sound: "He *goosed* his truck and twisted the X right off."

# Y

❧ / YANK   The natural growth bend of a tree and of a log after felling. Hemlock always grows with a *yank*. *Sawyers* adjust *yanked* logs on the carriage so the slabbing straightens things up, but a *yank* always cuts down on board feet produced. *Scalers* make allowances when measuring logs with *yanks*. Hence, anybody who walks bent over, or anything lopsided or *weewaw*, has a *yank*.

❧ / YANKEE   It is improbable that this word originated anywhere except Maine. *Yankee* has long been said to be the Indian's approximation of English, i.e., *Englishmen*. However, we like to forget the French influence on Maine before any Englishmen came here. We should, rather, notice that the first Englishmen who did come to Maine were first identified to the Indians by the French as *les anglais*. It is far more logical to develop *Yankee* from *anglais* than from English. A *Yankee* was thus an early English visitor to Maine as pronounced by an Indian trying to say *anglais*. The most important thing to say about *Yankee* in this day and age is that it has retained a proud place amongst all similar terms now in disrepute. Everybody is careful to avoid popularisms for ethnic minorities, but New Englanders take no offense whatever in being called *Yankees*.

❧ / YARD   The place where any harvested wood is piled when brought from the cutting to await the next step in moving toward the mill. In addition to the place itself, the word applies to the job of doing it; logs are *yarded*. Sometimes *skid*, *scoot*, and *twitch* are synonymous, but not always; a log is *twitched*, but the total harvest is *yarded*. *Yard* is also the Maine word for the congregation of deer in winter, they *yard* up in a deer *yard*. This will be an area, usually in swampy country, where they can find food without roaming too far in deep snow. This usage in Maine lacks the dictionary requirement of an enclosure.

❦ / YELKS   About as written, a Maine pronunciation of yolks, as in eggs.

❦ / YELLER-HAMMER   Maine farmer's word for the flicker, a woodpecker.

❦ / YES-MARM   Heard more frequently in Maine than thank-you-marm for that unexpected dip or bump in the road that jolts the buggy seat. Let us assume a boy is dozing in school, and the teacher nudges him. He will awake with a start and say, "Yes, ma'am!" Thus *yes-marm* or thank-you-marm is a startle response, and suits very well when a bump in the road jerks you out of your socks. The hummock itself is called a *yes-marm*.

❦ / YESSIR   In spite of the Maine reluctance to use sir in social respect, *yessir* (one word) is used for emphasis. On viewing a deer somebody has shot, a man may say, "*Yessir*, he sure is a beauty!" It is also a confirming word: "*Yessir*, that's right!" When strangers hear this in Maine speech, it should never be taken as "Yes, sir."

# OBBLIGATO

❧ / THERE IS AN OLD STORY OF A DOWN-MAINER WHO WAS
traveling across country and put up at a hotel in Duluth.
In the evening, he was approached in the lobby by a confidence man who had noticed his country manners and
thought he might be an easy touch. Finding his intended
victim was from Maine, he thought to ingratiate himself,
and he said, "That's interesting; I was born in Maine myself!"

"Is that right?" asked the Mainer. "Whereabouts?"

The con man said, "Sayko."

The Mainer said, "You're a goddam liar!"

Now, if you were born in Saco, you don't say *say-ko*
and you don't say *sack-ko*. You say *saw-ko*. Such Maine
oddities are, as with the Ephraimites in the Bible and the
touchstone word, shibboleth, trifling distinctions that prove
who the enemy are. Accordingly, an effort has been made
here to present those Maine pronunciations of place names
which strangers wouldn't know about, in order that confidence men will not be caught like that again.

A few Indian names are included here, but mostly the
Indian names are pronounced rather much as written
by syllables, and are not much of a problem. It is unlikely
a confidence man in Duluth, or anywhere else, will profess to
being a native of some such place as Winnebuxalooksomoc.
With many place names, there has been considerable difficulty in finding phonetic equivalents which come anywhere

near the Maine sounds. The best that can be done in cold type can be only an approximation for *Calais, Houlton, Madrid*, and many another. It is suggested the serious and careful student use this list as a field guide in black and white, and seek out the true colors and the living songs of each *rara avis* in its native haunt.

❧ / ADDISON  *Add-s'n.*

❧ / ALNA  First syllable rhymes with *pal;* second is clipped to a y: *Al-ny.*

❧ / AMITY  As in *am;* not as in *aim.*

❧ / AMHERST  Again, as in am; *Am-'st.*

❧ / ARUNDEL  Kenneth Roberts, who used this Kennebunkport name as the title of his historical novel about Arnold's march on Québec, liked to give it the French sound of *Aar-r'n-DELL.* Perversely, most of his neighbors like *Uh-RUN-d'l.*

❧ / ATTEAN  In the Jackman region. Out-of-staters often try to make it *At-TEE-'n.* It's *ATT-ee-'n.*

❧ / AUGUSTA  As in Alna, clip the final syllable to a y, and if you omit the first syllable it won't be noticed: *'Gus-ty.* Mainers also say *Floridy,* and of course, *sody.*

❧ / AVON  As in "*Avon* Calling!"

❧ / AZISCOOS  There is a Coos County in New Hampshire and a Coos County in Oregon; it's *Ko-oss* in New Hampshire and *Cooze* in Oregon. Aziscoos follows the New Hampshire style: *Az-ziss-co-oss.* But folks in the Magalloway region of Maine clip it to *Esk-uh-hoss,* sort of.

❧ / BANGOR   As least two choices here, and some say three. We'll try two. *Ban-gor* and *Bang-g'r.*

❧ / BASS HARBOR   Usually *barss*, but often *bass* as in basket (not *bahskit!*). Harbor in all instances is *hah-b'r* or *hah-buh.*

❧ / BATTIE   On old maps the mountain near Camden was *Betty*, so there is reason why some older folks give *Battie* a sort of halfway 'twix *Battie* and *Betty.*

❧ / BELFAST   Take your choice; some Mainers say *Bel-fast* and some say *Bel-fahst.*

❧ / BERLIN   Maine's Berlin gets the *burl* accented: *Burl-l'n.*

❧ / BERNARD   *Barn-n'd, Burn-n'd,* and *B'n-NARD.* An attentive ear sent *clearn* to Mt. Desert Island to research this one reports that *Burn-n'd* seemed the homeland choice.

❧ / BETHEL   Clip the last syllable; never with the Hebrew *Beth-ELL.*

❧ / BIDDEFORD   Almost like *Biddy-f'd.* Conductors on the poor old Boston & Maine used to shout, "Biddy-FORD! Biddy-FORD!" and this created some amusement.

❧ / BOOTHBAY HARBOR   Use the customary Maine *hah-buh*, and clip and slur Boothbay until you get something like *Boobay-hahbuh.* Some, hearing this for the first time, think it's more like *Booby-hahbuh.*

❧ / BOWDOIN   The original Huguenot family name, important in Maine history, was Beaudoin, which had the proper sound of *Boo-dwarn.* But Mainers say it as if it were almost like *Boardin'*. In any event, clip the second syllable to *d'n*, and don't try to French it. The only exception is in the cheers used at Bowdoin College football games when they emphasize the last syllable for effect and the word is an elongated *Beau-dunn*. The approximation *Boardin'* goes for the town of Bowdoin, the college in Brunswick, and the town of Bowdoinham. In Bowdoinham keep the *ham* intact: *Boardin'-ham*.

❧ / BRASSUA   The stream and the lake in the Moosehead region. Give it the *sh* of *sugar* but run the word together nicely: *Brash-you-uh*.

❧ / BREMEN   Never as in Hanseatic League. It's *Bree-m'n*, although occasionally it comes out as *Bremm-'n*. *BRAY-men* is in Germany. In speaking of Bremen Long Island (or any other Long Island in Maine) never extend the *g* to make *long-guyland*. The only instances of such an extended *g* in Maine occur in *Bang-ger* and *Sang-gerville*, that part of Brunswick called *Bung-ganuck*, and *Songo*.

❧ / BRIDGEWATER   Except in Bridgewater, a not unimportant small Aroostook County town, this is often pronounced *Bilgewater*.

❧ / BROOKLIN   No problem with the pronunciation, but notice that the Maine town has an *i* instead of a *y*.

❧ / BRUNSWICK   The *n* is almost converted to an *m*, and the second syllable is clipped oddly. It comes out somewhat like *Brum-zick*. Frequently, more like *Bum-zick*.

❧ / CALAIS   Never as in France. The first syllable is pronounced as in Calvin or calisthenics, but pleasantly flattened just a wee bit. The second syllable requires practice. The finished word will be a sort of cross between *callous* and *careless*.

❧ / Caribou One of Maine's better shibboleths. Rightly spoken only in Caribou and Aroostook County. Almost *Care-boo*. They don't exactly ignore the central *i*, but take care of it with a slight, almost imperceptible, hesitation.

❧ / Carmel *Kar-m'l*.

❧ / Castine The hoity-toity *Car-steen* or *Cah-steen* seems to be an outlander's affectation. *Cass-steen*.

❧ / Caswell *Kaz-w'l*.

❧ / Cathance In the Topsham area. Two full syllables: *Kat-hanse*.

❧ / Caucomagomac Attwood gives five variants for the spelling of this lake and stream, but in Maine speech they all come out as *Cock-muh-gommick*. However, Mainers familiar with the region reduce this to Cauc; Cauc Lake, Cauc Stream, Cauc Landing, Cauc Dam.

❧ / Charlotte *Shar-l't*. (In Vermont it's *Sh'LOT*.)

❧ / Chebeague The Casco Bay islands. *Sh'beeg*.

❧ / Chesuncook Make the sun shine: *Ch'SUN-cook*.

❧ / Chisholm The Chisholm family has been prominent in Maine papermaking, and gave its name to a village in Jay. *Chizzum*.

❧ / Concord An unorganized plantation in Somerset County. Say it as in Massachusetts, not as in Carolina: *KONG-k'd*. Mainers are startled when somebody says *Kon-CHORD*.

C / 331

🌿 / COOPER'S MILLS   See *cooper* in the main vocabulary. *Koup-puh* is about as close as anybody can come. First syllable is closer to *cook* than *coop*.

🌿 / COPLIN   *Cope-l'n.*

🌿 / CORINTH   As with Charlotte, don't give this the Vermont twist. In Maine it's *Korr-r'nth;* in Vermont the same word is *K'RINTH.*

🌿 / CRIEHAVEN   With a *kree.*

🌿 / CYR   A plantation in Aroostook County, and a common surname among Acadians. *Seer.*

🌿 / DAMARISCOTTA   No harm in saying it carefully in full, but most folks get it down to *Dammiscotty.* Familiarly, Damariscotta becomes plain *Scotty.*

🌿 / DEBLOIS   Don't try the French *wah* for *oi: D'bloy.*

🌿 / DERBY   Always *Durby.*

🌿 / DETROIT   The word means a *strait* in French. Mainers give the first syllable more action than do Michiganders: *DEE-troyt.*

🌿 / DURHAM   Not like any other Durham. Rob Coffin once tried to reduce the Maine Durham to phonetics, and the closest he could come was *Deor-'m.* Perhaps *Derr-r'm* is closer. Anyway, never rhyme the first syllable to *cure*, and always clip the *ham.*

🌿 / FAYETTE   Accent the *yet*, but keep the *fay* active: *Fay-yet.*

🌿 / FORT FAIRFIELD   If you wish to sound like a true Aroostookian, just say *The Fort.*

❧ / GILEAD   Clip it to *Gill-y'd*.

❧ / GREAT WORKS   Maine has three places so named; villages in Old Town and South Berwick, and a location in New Portland. Give the *great* a mite more stress than the *works*: *GREAT-works*.

❧ / GUERETTE   Part of Madawaska: *G'rett*. With all the French-derived names in northern Maine, it is kindly to come as near the French sounds as you can when occasion calls. (However, see *St. Francis*.)

❧ / GUN POINT   In Harpswell; give both words equal stress, and if you favor one, let it be the *Gun*, but ever so slightly.

❧ / HALLOWELL   A long *haul*, and the final syllable is clipped: *Haul-uh-w'l*.

❧ / HARPSWELL   Older folks flatten this name considerably; the newer generation not so much. The *harp* becomes almost *hairp*, and in extreme Pott's Point instances, even *happ*. Let's say: *Ha'p-s'l*, but let the first syllable be aware that it has a slight *R* sound.

❧ / HEAD TIDE   The community at the head of tidewater on the Sheepscot River gets about the same emphasis as *Gun Point*, and somewhat that of *Great Works;* keep the stress fairly even, and if you lean on *head* a little, you're doing fine.

❧ / HOLEB   One might expect this to taper off a mite, but it doesn't: *Hole-leb*.

❧ / HOULTON   Mainers have a special sound they give to the o in *holt* (*take a-holt of*), *bolt*, and proper names

H / 333

like Houlton and Knowlton. The dictionaries give no key that approximates it. Something of that same sound is found in the Maine pronunciation of *Bowdoin*, and also in the rendition of *boat*, which is frequently shown as *bo't*. Accordingly, for Houlton, try *Ho'l-t'n*.

❦ / ISLE AU HAUT    Early French visitors to this island at the entrance to Penobscot Bay named it Ile au Haut, which makes it *Eel-au-haut*. Today's occasional *Aisle-au-haut* is not preferred by the islanders. Besides, there is a particular local tone to the *haut* which is difficult to catch in type. Try *Eel-a'-hut* with just a bit of *o* sound to the *hut*. The final *t* on *haut* gets sounded, but lightly.

❦ / KENNEBAGO, KENNEBEC, KENNEBUNK, KENNEBUNK-PORT    Mostly, Maine tongues avoid a "kenny" with these names, and prefer *Kenn-neh-bay-go*, *Kenn-neh-beck*, *Kenn-neh-bunk*, *Kenn-neh-bunk-port*. The "kenn-neh" part is Indian, and old papers and maps show so many variations of the spelling that sometimes one wonders how it came out as kenn-neh at all. Canabais, for instance. However, while in many spellings the first syllable has an i (Quinebequi, Kinnebequi, Kinebais), most of the variants retain the e in the second syllable. Notwithstanding, nobody will jump with alarm if somebody says *Kenny-bunk-port*. A kenny in York County is commonplace but, up state, Kennebago and Kennebec hold pretty well to the kenn-neh.

❦ / KITTERY    Ignore the middle syllable: *Kitt-ree*, with a slight push on the *kitt*. (Portsmouth, New Hampshire, just across the Piscataqua River from Kittery, is pronounced by Mainers in that area as *Po'ch-m'th*.)

❦ / KOKADJO    As spelled, but the place is known familiarly as Cock-Eyed-Joe. Kokadjo is a discontinued post office north of Lily Bay on the Ripogenus road.

❦ / Lewiston   Folks in that area give this an odd twist, as if *Loys-st'n.*

❦ / Linneus   En route to Houlton: *LINN-ee-'s.*

❦ / Machias   Boston radio announcers still give this the old *Mack-ee-yass* if the town gets in the news. *M'chigh-'s.*

❦ / MacMahon   In Georgetown; as if *McMann.*

❦ / Macwahoc   In Aroostook County: *Mack-WAW-hock.*

❦ / Madrid   Another excellent Maine shibboleth. Franklin County people dwell on the first syllable and clip the second. Something like *Ma-a-a-d--dr'd.*

❦ / Maquoit   The Freeport-Brunswick area of Casco Bay. The older spellings are the key to pronunciation: Mac-quait, Mcquaite, and the Indian Me-quaite. Try *M'quate.*

❦ / McFalls   A type-saving abbreviation seemingly invented by the Lewiston newspapers for Mechanic Falls, a suburb. As far as is known, it has never been attempted orally except by a green radio announcer on WLAM, and he did it only once.

❦ / Medomak   *Muh-DOM-m'k*, but if you turn the middle syllable a mite towards *DUM* there will be few complaints.

❦ / Mere Point   Always *Mare Point.* Part of *Bumzick.*

❦ / Mount Desert   *DESS-ert* or *Des-SERT*, as you please. Mainers do it both ways. At best, either attempt is merely to English the original French, which was *les monts deserts*. The Sieur de Monts didn't have a sandy desert in mind; he named the island hills that way because they were uninhabited, which is to say *deserted*.

❧ / MUSCONGUS    The middle syllable gets the common English *o* of constable, pommel, etc., so all three syllables of this word have the same value of u: *Musk-kung-gus*.

❧ / MONHEGAN    Only true Monhegan Islanders say this precisely in their own way, and all other Mainers can only attempt it. As much as anything: *M'n-higgin*.

❧ / MONMOUTH    Monmouth and Monson get the regular *on* sound and the second syllables are clipped: *MON-m'th* and *MON-s'n*. But Monroe is *Mun-ROE*.

❧ / MONTSWEAG    The Indian suffix *eag* regularly gets the *egg* sound in Passadumkeag, Mattawamkeag, Kenduskeag, and Wassookeag, but in Montsweag it gets an *eeg*. *Mons-sweeg*. (As in French place names like *Montréal* and *Puligny-Montrachet*, the *t* in *Montsweag* should be ignored in pronunciation, but there is a perversity that insists on leaving it in.)

❧ / MOSCOW    *Moss-cow*, not *Moss-koe*.

❧ / NEQUASSET    *Nek-kwaw-s't*.

❧ / NEWCASTLE    To be pronounced full out, not with the British *nooxle*.

❧ / NEWAGEN    Attempts to get cozy with the Indian often cause visitors to give this a *Knee-woggin*. Just say *New Wagon*.

❧ / NOBLEBORO    Here and also with *Waldoboro*, Mainers give a little more than the English *burr-ruh*. It will be well to listen a time in the area before attempting either.

🌿 / NORTH EAST CARRY   This famous carrying place at the peak of mighty Moosehead Lake is always pronounced in full with complete dignity. It never gets the coastal *no'theast*.

🌿 / OGUNQUIT   *Uh-gung-kwit.*

🌿 / OLAMON   Pretty much like *O, Lemon!*

🌿 / ONAWA   In Elliotsville Plantation: *On-uh-waw.*

🌿 / OQUOSSOC   Some visitors to the Rangeley region like to start this off as in *O'Connor.* Make it *Uh-kwoss-sic.*

🌿 / ORONO   The touchstone of touchstones for a Mainer. Visitors rarely approach the true tone. Almost *Or-no*: The University of Maine at *Or'no.*

🌿 / ORR ISLAND   Keep away from any *oar* sound; *Orr* is a family name: *Or-ryeland.* (Any tendency to make *Orr* plural or possessive is to be discouraged.)

🌿 / PALERMO   *Plerm-moe.*

🌿 / PALMYRA   *Pal-myra.*

🌿 / PEMAQUID   Just notice the middle syllable the slightest, and give what's left equal treatment: *Pem-kwid.*

🌿 / PEMBROKE   Always and forever *Pem-brook.*

🌿 / PEQUAWKET   *Pee-kwawk't.*

🌿 / PERHAM   *Purr'm.*

🌿 / PERU   *Prue.*

❦ / Piscataqua, and Piscataquis   Otherwise competent scholars, beguiled by the profusion of Indian names in
Maine geography, frequently offer erudite explanations that
*Piscataqua* means something like "place where the squaw
dipped water while deer jumped over blowdown." Such
academic effort merits its own reward. Look in your Latin
dictionaries under *piscatus* and *aqua*. *Piss-kat-uh-kwiss* and
*Piss-kat-uh-kwaw*.

❦ / Pownal   Maritimers like to say *Pawn-n'l*, but in
Maine it is *Pow-n'l*. The same for *Pownalborough*.

❦ / Pripet   One of the lovelier Maine place names:
*Prip-it*.

❦ / Range   For the chain of ponds in the town of
Poland, forget the final *e*: *Rang*.

❦ / Ripogenus   The dam and the lake at the Chesuncook outlet: *Ripper-jeenis*.

❦ / Royalls River   In its great and expensive wisdom,
the Maine Department of Transportation has erected signs
at Yarmouth which identify *Royal River*. In loving memory
of William Hutchinson Rowe, late apothecary of Yarmouth
and one of Maine's better historians, the correction to
*Royalls River* is here entered respectfully. Mr. Rowe spent
a good part of his life explaining and insisting that the river
winding from Sabbathday Pond to the sea had a significant
history and he deplored the Tory implication of Royal. The
original Royels or Royalls, whose family name deserves
recollection in this connection, are forgotten by our highway sign painters, but some people in Yarmouth still correctly follow Mr. Rowe's desire and say *Royalls River*.

❦ / Saco   See introductory remarks, above.

❧ / St. Agatha    In the Acadian country *Sant-taggat* will be appreciated.

❧ / St. Francis    But while you are practicing *Sant-ta-gatt* (above) you will want to watch this one. Some tourists, exercising their high-school French, think to please the locals by giving it a *San-franswaw*, and this leads to a small confusion. St. Francis is in Maine and is pronounced *Saint Fransis*; St. François is the Canadian town just across the river.

❧ / Sangerville    Carry the *g* over: *Sang-ger-vil.*

❧ / Scarborough    Notice the careful citizens of Scarborough insist on spelling things out; this is no longer done with Waldoboro, Nobleboro, and Vassalboro.

❧ / Sebago    The lake is so well-known few err in its pronunciation. Unlike *Saco, Newagen*, etc., Sebago retains the long English *a*: *S'bay-go.*

❧ / Sebasco    Rhymes with *tabasco.*

❧ / Seboeis    The Piscataquis County lake. Three syllables, but clip the first and last: *S'boe-'s.*

❧ / Skowhegan    Skowhegan continues to be a mirth town like Brooklyn and Sheboygan, and people who toss it off like to give it full treatment: *Skow-hee-g'n.* There is a Somerset County tendency, however, to do what the folks on the Island do with Monhegan: sort of *Skow-wiggin.* In many instances, Skoweganites seem to ignore the *h* when they give it a *Skow-eeg'n* slur. The original Indian name was probably something like *skoogun*, and Attwood gives thirteen variants which led progressively to the present Skowhegan, none of which justifies the spurious folklore that an Indian once said, "Skow, he gone!" (An Indian didn't know what a skow was.)

❧ / Somesville   Rhymes with *homesville*.

❧ / South West Bend   In Durham, so named from a bend in the Androscoggin River. Unlike North East Carry, this does get the coastal contraction to *sow-west*.

❧ / Squapan   Notice it is not *squaw*, although it is pronounced *squaw*: *Skwaw-pan*. When the Bangor & Aroostook Railway made a depot there, they gave it two words: *Squa Pan*.

❧ / Steuben   This town in Washington County was named for the Baron Friedrich Wilhelm Ludolf Gerhard Augustin von Steuben, who came to George Washington's aid before foreign entanglements went out of style. In the Baron's native Prussia he was called *Stoy-behn*. The English of it is *Stoo-b'n*. The Maine of it is definitely *Stoo-BEN*.

❧ / Sullivan   *Sull-v'n*.

❧ / Tenants Harbor   *Tents Hab-b'h*.

❧ / Thomaston   Carefully enunciated by all except those who give it a *Tumst-t'n*.

❧ / Topsham   Topsham people give adjacent Bow-doinham full emphasis on the *ham*, but they clip their own: *Tops-s'm*.

❧ / Tremont   *Tree-mont*.

❧ / Union   The exact sound that Unionites give the first syllable of their town cannot be rightly approximated here, but it is the same sound heard in Maine for union suit, as in underwear. They do not give it the *you* or *yew* but weewaw it a bit until it approaches the first sound of *onion*. The word approaches must be carefully noted. If you put a *y* on *onion* (yonion), you will not be even close but you will have something of the idea. The peculiar twist given *Union* never applies to the town of *Unity*, which is *Yoo-nitty*.

❧ / WELLINGTON    Forget the *g* and clip the *ton*: *Wellin-t'n*.

❧ / WINNECOOK    In Burnham, they tend to say *Winnercook*; whereas, down in Sagadahoc County, Winnegance gets *Winnie-gance*.

❧ / WOOLWICH    Across the bridge from Bath; forget the second *w*: *Wool-itch*.

❧ / WRECK ISLAND    The Nature Conservancy recently came into possession of the Wreck Island off Stonington, and seems to prefer to call it *reck*, but the Wreck Island in Muscongus Bay is properly called *rack*.

GRACE NOTE:

When the extremely successful (and very goo-ood!) phonograph record called *Bert and I* first appeared, a summer lady on Mt. Desert Island played it one day for the little Butler boy. Afterwards he went home and told his mother he had just heard *Bert and I.*

"Oh," she said, "I hear that's quite a record. What did you think of it?"

He said, "Wel-l-ll, if it's really about Maine, why don't they call it *Me and Bert?*"